CW00322148

ROLL OVER, CHE GUEVARA

THE HAYMARKET SERIES

Editors: Mike Davis and Michael Sprinker

The Haymarket Series offers original studies in politics, history and culture, with a focus on North America. Representing views from across the American left on a wide range of subjects, the series will be of interest to socialists both in the USA and throughout the world. A century after the first May Day, the American left remains in the shadow of those martyrs whom this Haymarket Series honours and commemorates. These studies testify to the living legacy of political activism and commitment for which they gave their lives.

ROLL OVER, CHE GUEVARA

Travels of a Radical Reporter

MARC COOPER

VERSO
London · New York

Photo credits are as follows. US adviser by Donna DeCesare;
Chilean soldiers by Steven Rubin; Malecon seawall by Hazel Hankin;
Russian street trader by David B. Reed; LAPD officer and LAPD officers
in training by Ted Soqui; Republican delegate by Thomas Dallal; Dan
Quayle by Brian Palmer; Comandante Marcos by Cuartoscuro, all used by
permission from Impact Visuals and copyright by the photographers.
Salvadoran guerrillas used by permission from Impact Visuals. 'Light of a
Thousand Fires' is copyright by Debra DiPaolo and is used by permission.

First published by Verso 1994
© Marc Cooper 1994
All rights reserved

Verso
UK: 6 Meard Street, London W1V 3HR
USA: 29 West 35th Street, New York, NY 10001-2291

Verso is the imprint of New Left Books

ISBN 1 85984 970 9

British Library Cataloguing in Publication Data
A catalogue record for this book is available from the British Library.

Library of Congress Cataloging-in-Publication Data
A catalog record for this book is available from the Library of Congress.

Typeset in Monotype Dante by NorthStar, San Francisco, California
Printed and bound in Great Britain by
Biddles Ltd, Guildford and King's Lynn

To Patricia Vargas and Natasha Vargas-Cooper
for the privilege of being the conduit that allowed
one to create the other.

CONTENTS

CONTENTS

ACKNOWLEDGEMENTS

As a writer I tend to view all editors as adversaries. But I have been blessed with working with some outstanding exceptions. Almost all of the reports in this book were underwritten by the *Village Voice* and were edited by Dan Bischoff, the former National Affairs Editor. No other single individual has had such a direct influence in shaping my work. His vision, his humor, his around-the-clock availability and his compassion have made the bulk of this book possible. Jonathan Z. Larsen, Editor-in-Chief of the *Voice* until April 1994, spoiled me with attention, assignments and that most precious of all journalistic commodities, space on the page. Former *Voice* Executive Editor Amy Virshup also took a share of my jumbled dispatches and made them legible. Washington Correspondent Jim Ridgeway is a continuing source of support and insight. Research Director Matt Yeomans always got my facts right, even if I didn't. Sara Jeweler made sure my reports got on the same page as the pictures that accompanied them. Tom McGovern made sure the pictures were even taken. Marilyn Savino and Keith Campbell saw to it that my paperwork never got lost. Thanks also to my new Editor-in-Chief, Kate Durbin, for her continuing support as well as to Publisher David Schneiderman, who brought me to the *Village Voice* in the first place. One piece in this collection originally appeared in *Mother Jones,* and at that publication I thank former editors Doug Foster and Sara Miles.

Then there's an interminable list of colleagues, friends, activists and contacts of the sort that I, and every other journalist for that matter, depend on to look competent and smart when reporting on some breaking news event around the corner or thousands of miles from home. Let me thank just a few: Tim Frasca and Roberto Naduris for assistance in Chile; Tony Cavin, who worked with me in Los Angeles, Managua and Washington; Mario Velazquez, 'Se-

ACKNOWLEDGEMENTS

bastian', 'Noe', Frank Smyth, Jeremy Bigwood, Chris Norton and Gene Palumbo for their help in El Salvador; Margarito Ortiz, Marco Gandasegui and John Dinges for helping me manage Panama; Paloma Saenz, Willie Neuman, Paco Ignacio Taibo II and all the *cuates* of Patito S.A. for giving me the keys to Mexico City; Justo Vasco, Daniel Chavarría, Angel Tomás Gonzalez and Pablo Armando Fernandez for holding my hand in Havana; Carl Boggs for those unforgettable dinner debates in Rio de Janeiro; Vince Cobb and Dennis Marker for getting me in, and out, of the Baghdad public hospital; Suzi Weissman and Jennifer Gould for unraveling the mysteries of modern Moscow; and Patrick Caddell for his always pungent and entertaining deconstructions of American politics. Eternal gratitude to my agent David 'The Big Vig' Vigliano for getting me out of Las Vegas alive, if not solvent. Thanks to George Moll, Rich O'Regan, Karen Burnes and David Gelber for their help and support. If it were not for Dr Larry Littwin, I'd have never gone to Chile and never would have become a journalist.

A special thanks to Greg Goldin, co-author of one of the reports in this book, for his absolute reliability as a reality check in a profession that too often melds fact with fiction. Mike Emery is my main safeguard against turning totally cynical about the future of journalism. And without Mike Davis this book would have never happened. Thanks also to Colin Robinson of Verso, and to Steven Hiatt and Megan Hiatt, who copyedited the manuscript and managed its production.

Someday I will find a way to repay my debt of gratitude to my high school literature and composition teacher, Richard Battaglia, who taught me how to read and write. For the moment, a heartfelt Thank You will have to suffice.

INTRODUCTION

Many things changed on Tuesday, 11 September 1973. In the eyes of the world, the most important event of that day was the rocketing of La Moneda, the Chilean presidential palace in downtown Santiago, by British-made Hawker Hunter jets. As US policy makers applauded the immolation of Chile's constitutionally elected president, Salvador Allende, those warplanes reduced Latin America's oldest functioning democracy to smoking rubble. Consumed in the Moneda blaze was the office I used as one of Allende's translators.

As troops of the new military dictatorship combed my central neighborhood, breaking down doors and carting away real and imagined Allende supporters, I took refuge in the home of a generous and courageous low-level foreign diplomat. By that afternoon, with the Moneda still burning, with Allende and Chilean democracy dead, I, at twenty-two years of age, had unwittingly taken up my new profession of full-time journalist.

My gradual immersion in journalism had always been accidental and, until that moment in 1973, always provisional. In fact, as I've usually described it, I never really *chose* to be a journalist at all. Instead, I was cornered into doing what I now do for a living only by the arrogance of established authority. My first nudge into writing came when I was a sophomore in high school in Los Angeles, back in 1966. That year a mild anti–Vietnam war satire I and a small group of friends had written was rejected by the official newspaper of the very middle-class and very progressive Fairfax High School. So I founded an 'underground' campus paper that was happy to print such things – and which wound up costing me several short-term suspensions.

By the time I was ready to enroll at the heretofore sleepy, suburban Southern California commuter college I'd applied to – ostensibly to study psychology – college campuses all around the country had exploded into hotbeds of antiwar student radicalism. By my second semester I was not only co-editing an anarchist bulletin but operating an A.B. Dick 350 offset press in my living room, noisily cranking out antiwar pamphlets on Vietnam and the Middle East as well as selections from Bakunin, Kropotkin and Emma Goldman. Still, I had no notion of becoming a journalist. To me the written page was nothing more than a draft script for the full dress production that was my political activism. Indeed, in my college days of the late sixties, reporters were the declared enemy, seen as mouthpieces for an establishment hell-bent on napalming Vietnam and snooping on domestic dissidents.

And yet events kept pushing me in the direction of journalism. In 1971, by executive order of the then-governor of California, Ronald Reagan, I was banished from the state university system for my antiwar activism (the actual charge was 'organizing demonstrations inside of classroom buildings'). By now a political science major, I had nowhere to go except Chile – a country I had studied, whose language I knew, and where the hemisphere's first freely elected Socialist head of state, Salvador Allende, had just assumed office. Within two months of arriving in Santiago I got a job in the state publishing house, but as a bottom-rung researcher/translator, I still saw my work as more political than editorial.

As my youthful career ascended and I became Allende's translator for publication, I also became a prolific letter-writer, regaling my friends back home with the breathless narrative of a 21-year-old who had a desk in the office of a president engaged in peaceful but real revolution. Without telling me, one university-era friend turned over some of the letters I'd sent him to the now-extinct *Los Angeles Free Press*, a stalwart of the original underground newspaper circuit and an early, gritty prototype of today's genteel yogurt-and-futon-fueled 'alternative' urban weeklies. I found out I was an author one day in 1971 when I opened my mailbox and discovered a couple of $25 checks and tear sheets from the *Free Press*.

In what today's J-school professors would call an appalling conflict of interest, I then began to write longer articles about Chile and the rest of the region for an expanding list of sixties-era publications while continuing to work for the Chilean government. Journalism was still the sideline, a secondary supplement to my real work, my political commitment.

That changed on 11 September 1973. The new military regime, intent on 'extirpating the cancer of communism' from Chile in an orgy of fire and blood, naturally clamped down a fearsome censorship on news going abroad. But the diplomat who offered me safe haven also gave me carte blanche to use his phone, to break the censor's blockade and report the horror we could see from his living-room balcony.

For one week, until given safe passage out of Chile by the UN High Commission on Refugees, I dispatched one anguished radio report after another over those phone lines, protected only by a thin wall of diplomatic immunity. I saw no conflict then in drawing upon my political passions to fashion and inform my reporting. Twenty-one years later, I hold to that position.

The outrage of Allende's death was deepened by my conviction, at that time, that his cause was not only just but inevitable, part of the great sweeping trend of history. But as the seventies and eighties progressed, the aborted Chilean Revolution began to look ever more like the political highwater mark of my generation. More than a setback, General Pinochet's coup was merely an overture to the devil's symphony that marked the massacres in Cambodia and East Timor, the disappearances in Argentina, the scorched-earth campaigns in Guatemala, the first and second Gulf Wars, CIA assassination manuals in Central America, the rise of Thatcherism in Europe, the Reagan-Bush counterrevolution here at home, the overall degrading spectacle of seeing human aspirations and hopes converted into crass calculations by a voracious global marketplace.

But during that week in September 1973, I *did* make a life-changing transition. Until then, communications – writing, editing and translating – were only the necessary tools of my political activism. But in reporting the Chilean coup I had found my voice, one which could be effectively employed if not any longer in the cause of expanding human freedom, then at least in resistance to its extinction. From that week forward, journalism *became* my politics.

In the ensuing two decades I have worked for just about every sort of journalistic outfit imaginable. My work has run the gamut, from those first radio reports dispatched to listener-sponsored WBAI in New York to NBC News, to the CBC, to producing and reporting TV documentaries for CBS, PBS and the august *Christian Science Monitor*. I graduated from $20 features for the Liberation News Service to regular columns in alternative weeklies, to *Playboy* interviews, to reporting for cautious metro dailies, to magazine pieces for *The Times* of London and *Los Angeles Times*, to the Sunday sections of *Washington Post*. In each case, I've had to alter my product to the tastes and sensibilities of the employer, trying not to compromise too much. But none of this varied experience matches the satisfaction, the sheer exhilaration, of writing the pieces included in this collection. For the twenty-one reports that make up this book – most of them written for the *Village Voice* – all have something in common. They are unabashedly partisan and passionate.

It's a sort of writing that journalism textbooks call, mistakenly, Advocacy Journalism, as opposed to Objective Journalism – as if the truth can always and only be found in the mythical middle, precariously perched at the fulcrum of a painstakingly balanced continuum of two conflicting extremes. But as I spent the last two decades travelling through the dark night of that Chilean winter, through the dirty war of Argentina, across the murderous Green Line in Beirut, over the killing fields of the Guatemalan highlands and the South African veld, into the haunts of the Moscow mafia and down the fire-scorched avenues of South Central Los Angeles, I have usually found the truth cowering in some remote and dank corner, unsure not only of the future, but even of the next ten minutes.

Objectivity for me, then, is not a symmetrical construct, a dispassionate equilibrium of pros and cons, of equally measured quotes, references and soundbites, a finished product that, like a child's Roly Poly, always bounces back and stands upright as promised. Objectivity is, rather, an ongoing process, a good faith investigation, an open-minded search that you are willing to sign on to, accepting that it more often than not takes you to some unexplored and unfinished edge. Is this what it means to be an 'alternative journalist' – the clumsy sign usually hung around my neck when I'm invited to sit on any panel of reporters? That's one possible definition, one I have used myself in the past. But I think the more telling demarcation to be made in my profession is no longer between 'alternative' and 'straight', but rather between 'corporate journalist' and 'independent journalist'. This distinction, by the way, is not strictly a function of employment. Some of the best reporters I have met have worked their entire lives for the grayest of journalism monopolies and were simply willing to take the risks. And, likewise, some of the most craven, obedient and unimaginative hacks are to be found among the ranks of nonaffiliated freelancers.

To be 'independent' requires approaching each story unburdened by the nostrums that hum like white noise in most American newsrooms and magazine offices. Again, in this collection, I hope to take the reader beyond the simplistic and conventional equations of standard American reporting, which usually derive much more from the policy needs of our own government than from any sincere reading of history. Caught in a Manichean maze, American reporters are quick to gnaw and rip at first sight of state-dominated economies, market regulation, any questioning of an expanding global market. Sometimes this criticism is on the mark. Often it isn't. The independent, as opposed to corporate, approach can be captured in a single anecdote. There's a scene midway through this book in which a Brazilian legislator emerges dumbfounded from a speech by then-Senator Al Gore. Extolling the breakdown of world Communism, Gore has just told his Brazilian audience that the fall of the Berlin wall has opened up unparalleled opportunity for worldwide environmental and social progress; beyond the superpower rivalry, Gore could see the first rosy streaks of a new dawn for all mankind. The incredulous Brazilian congressman, try as he might, can't see any such thing on the horizon. He sees the country where he was born submerged in debt, its rainforests afire, its air and rivers choked with contaminants, its derelict street children victimized by death squads, its teenagers forced into prostitution – and yet each succeeding government he has witnessed has been run only by *anti*-Communists. This, perhaps, is another demarcation. The corporate journalist dutifully and single-mindedly reports the words of the American senator. The independent writer matches those words with the real living conditions in Brazil's urban centers, and hears the baffled despair of someone who suffers from, rather than makes, global policy.

That's not to say that as an independent journalist I am free of bias. Not by any means. And in introducing this book allow me to fully disclose my personal prejudices: I tend to believe that all governments lie, all military and police institutions are repressive, that those who hold power in any system tend to put the retention of that privilege above all other interests, and that social problems, no matter how thorny, are always better solved with *more* democracy rather than less. I also believe that nations have a moral obligation to provide for the general welfare, and that the best indicator of any society's commitment to that notion is its treatment of the most vulnerable of its citizens. Any journalism that doesn't have these values at its core makes me nervous. It recalls those nightmare visions of journalism that I had in the sixties, indelible images of eager reporters, backlit by the phosphorescent glow of burning villages, flatly reciting the Pentagon's optimistic predictions of body counts and victory.

Woodland Hills, California
June 1994

THERE

1

HOUR OF THE WEREWOLVES

Like a voice in the desert, I call upon the foreign journalists
to earn their living honestly. If they must lie, let them
do so about their own countries, not about El Salvador.
Manuel Isidro Lopez Sarmeño, Minister of the Interior
[sign in the press office of the Salvadoran High Command]

SAN SALVADOR: MARCH 1983.   Jammed around the poolside bar of the Sheraton San Salvador are about fifteen US military advisers, out of uniform, but
many sporting aviator sunglasses. Along with 200 other Saturday lunchtime
guests they were there to watch the long-legged, green-eyed daughters of the
oligarchy participate in a swimsuit fashion show organized by Catalina Sports-
wear. Having paid a worker's daily wage to get into the balloon and streamer–
festooned pageant, El Salvador's elite cheered the strutting girls and waited for
the raffle, a chance to win suntan lotion from Diane of Paris. One Salvadoran
about twenty years old joked loudly with the advisers, his broad chest stretching a T-shirt emblazoned with 'El Salvador: Apocalypse for the Communists',
against a background of silk-screened Huey helicopter gunships.

A few hundred years from the Sheraton, another gathering was taking place
in the San José Chapel. Here the people were shorter, darker, many of them
barefoot. Under the gaze of plainclothes police, they came to pay their final
respects to the first woman ever to practice law in El Salvador. Forty-year-old
Marianela García, her legs broken, face bruised and body pierced by bullets, was
laid out under glass in an expensive coffin. Six days earlier she had been murdered by government troops. The Salvadoran High Command press office described her as a 'terrorist and a subversive'. She was known to most others in the
country as the president of the El Salvador Human Rights Commission.

Meanwhile, inside the fortresslike US Embassy compound, surrounded by high walls and around-the-clock guards, Public Affairs Officer Donald Hamilton kicked back in his chair, tugged on his suspenders, and listed Reagan administration priorities here: 'We want to stop the Marxist takeover. We want to encourage political and economic reforms. And we want to build the democratic center.'

This is El Salvador 1983. It was two years ago that Assistant Secretary of State Thomas Enders told Congress, 'The battle for the western hemisphere is now under way in El Salvador.' And so it is, at least in the view of the Reagan administration and its allies in the Salvadoran government. Secretary of State George Shultz, Salvadoran president Alvaro Magaña, and the US Embassy all agree that a new phase of the war is being initiated. And while the Embassy denies charges of a new Indochina in the making, the commander of the US Military Group, Vietnam veteran Colonel John Waghelstein, said, 'The only piece of territory we are interested in winning here is the four inches between the ears of the Salvadoran peasants.' With the local Embassy staff lobbying hard for increased military aid to El Salvador, US officials seem optimistic that the new, two-pronged approach – massive military sweeps against guerillas linked to economic redevelopment programs – will bring a turnaround in the war effort and save the US-backed government.

The dusty town of Berlín, forty-five miles to the east of San Salvador, is being used as the pilot case in this new 'hearts and minds' strategy. The city of about 30,000 people was seized by 250 guerrillas of the Farabundo Martí National Liberation Front (FMLN) in late January and held for four days, marking the most significant insurgent victory in two years. The Salvadoran army had to use more than 2,000 troops to retake the city, and this only after launching devastating artillery and aerial bombing attacks. Now, in the bombed-out center of town, two signs dominate the rubble. One proclaims that a joint US–Salvadoran government reconstruction project is under way. The other simply states, 'Military-Civic Action Program'.

Now that the guerillas have been chased out, the State Department Agency for International Development (AID) is moving into town; in the words of Salvador AID director Martin Degata, to 'facilitate things as we do all over the world'. In Berlín, the AID project, budgeted at somewhere over a million dollars, includes a program to rebuild the center of town, a three- or four-square-block area destroyed by US-built A-37 war planes, improve the city's sewage system, vaccinate the children and build a new school, already baptized the Clarencio Long School, in honor of the Maryland gentleman whose vote on the House Foreign Affairs Committee is so crucial to the Salvadoran government. The mayor of Berlín, Santiago Yazbek, seemed pleased to administer his newly ac-

US MILITARY ADVISER IN EL SALVADOR: HEARTS AND MINDS , AGAIN

quired pork barrel and claimed that the AID program has given work to about a thousand townspeople, who are being paid the equivalent of a dollar and a half a day. The Berlín AID project was kicked off last month by US Ambassador Deane Hinton, who helicoptered in for the event, and whose pep talk, according to local lore, was heard by a number of unarmed guerrillas who filtered in for the occasion.

If in fact the guerrillas did come to listen to Hinton's speech in Berlín, they would not have had to travel very far. The showcase of economic assistance in Berlín borders what is called a 'controlled zone', a 200-square-mile chunk of land where the FMLN guerrillas call the shots. Government troops can enter the zone only in large convoys and even then must stick to the main roads.

Just nine miles south of Berlín, guerrillas are firmly entrenched in the town of San Augustín, population about 2,000. Since driving the national guard out on 1 March, the guerrillas move freely through the main streets of the town and are indistinguishable from the local residents except for the guns they carry. The civilian residents, unlike those in towns under army control, spoke freely with reporters.

On the northern edge of town, twelve open-shirted, unshaven guerrillas, dark and roughed by farming, sat on horseback in a scene reminiscent of the Mexican Revolution. They explain that they are with the militia of the ERP, the People's Revolutionary Army. 'We are farmers in the hills about an hour's ride from here', said the oldest of the group, who packed a government-issue G-3 automatic rifle. 'We work our fields most of the time and participate in patrols when necessary', he said as he loaded his saddlebag with provisions.

In the dirt-floored central plaza of San Augustín two young guerrillas sat under a large tree to take refuge from the exhausting heat. As the townspeople carried out their daily business all around us, 25-year-old Rafael defined himself as a 'regular soldier' of the ERP. Dressed in blue jeans, a blue T-shirt, a straw hat, boots, and with a US Army equipment belt around his waist, he showed off his American-made M-16 rifle. 'You know, if Reagan sends more aid to the armies here, in a crazy way it's good for us. It's that many more guns we can get our hands on.'

His companion was a sullen, straight-haired, fourteen-year-old girl. She said she had been in the ERP for six months, but still had seen no combat. Asked if she was afraid of meeting with army troops she responded without blinking, 'We who are born poor are born to die.'

Some thirty miles to the east of San Augustín is the provincial capital of Usulután. Located in the middle of the country's important cotton-growing zone, the town of 50,000 people is accessible only by the coastal highway. It's along that road that the guerrillas frequently descend to collect what they call 'war taxes' from passing motorists or to burn supply vehicles. Over the past year, government control of that highway has progressively eroded. Where a dozen army posts lined the coast highway a year ago, there are now only two.

Inside the city of Usulután, however, one of the three gems of El Salvador's armed forces is housed, the elite immediate-reaction Atonal battalion. Along with the Atlactl and Belloso battalions, this unit was trained by US military advisers and paid for with American tax dollars. As a private led me to the Atonal headquarters, he spoke fondly of his US trainers: 'They felt so much affection for us that they wanted to fight alongside of us, but their captain said no.' US law prevents the trainers from engaging in combat, though three trainers were sent home for violating that rule after one was wounded in the recapture of Berlín.

As in a growing number of cases, the town of Usulután is 'secure' only to its immediate borders. Just to the south of Usulután, for the ten miles to the coast, a large swath of land has been under guerrilla control for a solid year. The presence of the crack Atonal battalion nearby has done nothing to change that.

In Puerto Parada, a muddy, ramshackle fishing village seven miles south of Usulután, the townspeople said they had not seen army troops in the last year. The area around the port is in such firm guerrilla control that even the insurgents no longer bother to patrol. Groups of curious fishermen gathered around our small knot of reporters and offered us fruit and warm Coke. 'We live peacefully here. We just work and try to make a living. But since we have no more army and no more mayors we do live better', gummed a septuagenarian resident as he arranged his fishing gear. Some US military advisers here grumble in disgust about the situation in Puerto Parada and the entire coast south of Usulután. They claim it is a 'major guerrilla resupply point' and blame the 'Monday through Friday, nine-to-five work ethic' of the Salvadoran army.

Reagan administration policy in El Salvador is aimed at completely revamping the local armed forces. One expert after another here confirmed the general sweep of US military policy in the months to come. The primary object is to increase the number of immediate reaction battalions, like the Atonal, to fourteen, so that each province has its own elite force. This would require an immediate increase of about 5,000 troops in El Salvador's army. The US has already helped build the army from 16,000 men two years ago to more than 23,000 today. The US military would also like to see, apart from the new combat units, an increase in the size of the Salvadoran navy, and an addition to the eighteen Huey helicopter gunships and eight A-37 Dragonfly bombers that the air force already possesses.

There's a consensus among the US personnel stationed in El Salvador that the administration's self-imposed limit of fifty-five US advisers isn't enough. Embassy officials say it would be easier to get their jobs done with more US military personnel here, but no one will say how much that increase should be.

Once the buildup of Salvadoran armed forces is under way, pending more US military aid dollars, the scenario is for the government to begin a major military counteroffensive. The first phase of the coming operation envisions the dispatch of thousands of freshly trained troops into the eastern provinces of Usulután, San Vicente and Morazán to crush the guerrillas. The second phase of the plan would be to go into the same areas with massive US-sponsored economic aid programs à la Berlín. Phase Three would be to 'saturate' the countryside with small, locally based military units to keep the lid on any insurgency. 'In other words, a re-creation of the CORDS (Community Operated Rural Development Support) program in Vietnam. Maybe even with strategic hamlets', is the way a Salvadoran history professor characterized the strategy. 'There's only one obstacle to this plan', he added. 'What makes Reagan and the generals here think they will ever get past stage one? This really isn't new. They've been trying to wipe out the guerrillas for three years now. But the FMLN is stronger than ever.'

Whatever the strength of the guerrillas, it's estimated that the part of the Salvadoran army truly able to fight is itself no greater than 5,000 men. And even using Waghelstein's low estimate of 5,000 guerrillas, at best the army is fighting the guerrillas at a one-to-one force ratio. That's a long way from the US–British formula applied in Malaysia fifteen years ago, which claims that guerrilla insurgencies can be beaten only by a ten-to-one ratio in favor of government forces. It's partially for this reason that even the Embassy military staff never tire of talking about a 'political solution' to the war. Ostensibly by 'building the democratic center', offering a credible amnesty to the guerrillas, instituting reforms, and improving human rights, the campesinos, or as Colonel Waghelstein calls them, 'the Salvos', will no longer be tempted to join 'the G's', as he calls the guerrillas.

Unfortunately, none of the preconditions for a political solution to the war of the sort envisioned by the US exists in El Salvador. The 'democratic center' was driven from the country two years ago by the political forces supported by the US. The political and social reforms promised remain just promises. Few serious observers believe that the guerrillas, with much higher morale than the government troops, would turn themselves in on an amnesty law. And as far as human rights are concerned, the crucial 'four inches between the peasant's ears' are more frequently used as targets by the government forces than as ideological battlegrounds.

In spite of Reagan administration certification to the contrary, hundreds of civilians continue to disappear and die every month in El Salvador. A variety of human rights monitoring organizations, from Amnesty International to the Salvadoran Catholic Church, to the Jesuit University in San Salvador, to the Salvador Human Rights Commission agree that between 4,500 and 6,000 people died in political violence here in the last year, bringing the total since October 1979 to over 42,000. And they agree that the overwhelming majority of deaths are those of civilians that disappear into the hands of the security forces and the paramilitary death squads or who are killed in government military operations. The US Embassy keeps its own account of the number of deaths, and its figures are usually half those of the human rights groups.

The director of the San Salvador Catholic Archdiocese Legal Assistance Office, María Julia Fernandez, agreed with the Reagan administration that the number of military killings has decreased over the last year. But she asked, 'What difference does it make? Those responsible for the killings still go unpunished. And we in the Salvadoran church still affirm that there is no real improvement. A change in numbers, yes, but the abuses still continue.'

The man who best embodies Salvadoran government policy and engenders the most fear in San Salvador is soft-spoken, US-educated Francisco Quiñonez. Interviewed in his sprawling farm equipment factory, a picture of his young daughter and a certificate from the Boy Scouts on the wall behind him, Quiñonez denied FMLN charges that he is the financier of El Salvador's right-wing death squads. Now sitting as the unofficial leader of the government's also newly created Peace Commission, the middle-aged businessman did what few will do in El Salvador; he denied the very existence of the death squads: 'It's all baloney. There's no problem here with what you call the extreme right.'

Quiñonez argued that many of El Salvador's problems could be cleared up with the amnesty law he had just written and which was about to be approved by the government. 'Even though the leftists and guerrillas have no place in our society, they are unfortunately Salvadorans, and they should be allowed to return to productive society. The left is just making excuses when it says it cannot participate in the political process because of fear of repression', argued Quiñonez. He saw the political future of El Salvador as a simple formula. Either the guerrillas accept government terms for participating in upcoming presidential elections, accept the amnesty, accept the statement that military death squads don't exist, or face a military solution. 'You know, war is not a picnic. It can be messy and none of us wants to continue the fighting', Quiñonez warned. 'But if these guerrillas, backed by Russia, Cuba and Nicaragua, don't give up, then all I can say is that I hope we Salvadorans have the courage to do what is necessary.'

One man gearing up for that all-out war is the 43-year-old military commander of the Salvadoran province of Morazán, Lieutenant-Colonel Jorge Alberto Cruz. Wearing a recruit uniform and toting an Israeli-made Galil automatic rifle, Cruz directs the battle from front-line positions. 'These guerrillas aren't ever going to give up. The amnesty means nothing', he told me while on patrol in territory recently recaptured by the government. Pointing to the half of Morazán province still under FMLN guerrilla control, he promised that he is 'ready to advance as soon as the orders come down'.

Called a 'hardass' by those who work with him, Cruz is the type of commander the US military would like to see more of in El Salvador. With a good head for PR, the colonel readily informs reporters that 'economic aid is just as important as military aid. We need investment and technology.' Riding through the miserable and nearly treeless hamlets of southern Morazán accompanied by an armored personnel carrier and twenty heavily armed troops, Cruz carried himself as a benevolent proconsul. While literally handing out suckers to the malnourished children of Gualococti, and making arrangements to treat the sick, he called on this reporter to 'tell the free world, the democratic countries, the truth. We are fighting for a better world, and need their help.'

The colonel showed off the latest AID project in Gualococti. With $25,000 in US grants, about seventy disheveled campesinos were laying rocks down on a dirt road in 100-degree heat for the normal dollar-and-a-half day's pay. 'This is a road improvement project', said the colonel as he embraced two of the older workers. 'When finished, this town will have 5,000 square meters of road with a hard surface.'

One had to wonder what the AID priorities were and which hearts and minds were going to be won by throwing rocks down on an untraveled road in a town with no transport, no water, no medicine and no schools, and where most people live by eating, drinking and clothing themselves in material derived from mescal plants. The colonel, however, was convinced that his troops, backed by the Atonal and Belloso battalions and bolstered by the AID programs, would win the war in Morazán. 'If we don't finish this off in seven or eight more months, we never will. But I am more than optimistic. We have faith in God and in our democratic allies like the United States.'

Dr Wayne Smith, who served as the top US diplomat in Cuba until he quit his post in disgust last year, told me recently, 'Central America now exercises the same influence on American foreign policy as the full moon does on werewolves.' The administration, believing its own propaganda, has effectively limited its own options in El Salvador to extended war and a military solution. The poor of this country fight for social justice and the administration calls them 'foreign-backed subversives'. A right-wing, essentially military government assassinates its political opponents by the dozen, and the administration says it is building the democratic center. A former army major who runs the Constituent Assembly and who is accused of murdering an archbishop, is a man who offers amnesty instead of pleading for one. Thousands of people come to pray with the pope and the church for peace, and Secretary of State Schultz promises more Huey helicopters and A-37 warplanes. The guerrillas offer an unconditional dialogue, an idea supported by broad sectors of the population including the church, but US officials say such a move would be a 'sellout of our allies'. At the Sheraton San Salvador death squad members sip their beers in the same patio restaurant where, in Janurary 1981, two US land reform advisers had their heads blown open by 'unidentified assassins'.

State Department officials talk of building 'American credibility in the region', while the two McDonald's outlets in San Salvador are obliged to be protected by armed guards merely because they are US identified. AID officials plan to 'win hearts and minds' when that was accomplished long ago by those calling for a just peace.

The administration promises a political solution while US advisers train fifteen-year-old soldiers at Ilopango air base on how to fire fifty-calibre machine guns. News on the shortwave tells of US-backed counterrevolutionaries in Nicaragua, an American radar base being set up in Honduras and more military aid for General Ríos Montt, the evangelical ayatollah in Guatemala. In the El Camino Real Hotel coffee shop, reporters who lived through Vietnam debate whether we are now at the equivalent point of 1962 or 1963. One nine-year veteran of that 'noble cause', as President Reagan defined it, looked out at the blue mountains in the lush countryside, shook his head, and concluded, 'We all know where this is going, we just don't know when.'

Village Voice
March 1983

2

SOWETO

SOUTH AFRICA: NOVEMBER 1985. The two-lane road that leads from Johannesburg to the black township of Soweto can only be called a sealed corridor. The ten-mile stretch is lined with walls of barbed wire. Travelling from Jo'burg, the heart of the White Man's world – created hauntingly in the image of Kansas City – toward the township in which the city's blacks are relegated, there are no turnoffs or side roads. It's a straight, fast run from one world to another. Fast, that is, if you are travelling by car as I am. It's maybe a fifteen-minute ride. But for the million-and-a-half blacks who are forced to live in Soweto but work in the 'white-designated' city, it's a gruelling one-hour ride in one of the thousands of pale blue buses that cart the Servants to the Served and then back home again. And all that for no more than 15 to 20 percent of the average black salary.

On the other side of the barbed wire are the gold mines of the Anglo-American Corporation and the diamond pits of DeBeers. In those mines a skilled, unionized black miner with five years' experience can earn up to 500 rand a month – about half of what a white receptionist fresh out of a segregated school will earn. The profits from the mine, controlled by the English-speaking monopoly capitalists, help finance South Africa's 'opposition' liberal political groupings. The surplus extracted from the sweat of the miners pays for the full-page ads run by the 'enlightened' industrialists now calling for a scrapping of apartheid. Quite a joke. Another joke: it is precisely this sprawl of mines that stands between Jo'burg and Soweto. As the road cuts a slash through this wealthy real estate, you take a turn, drive around one of Anglo's slag heaps, over another, and then before you rises Soweto.

Soweto. It had become almost legendary in my mind, especially after two weeks of kicking around the austere white streets of Pretoria and Jo'burg.

Soweto, a symbol of resistance to dictatorship. But when it finally appeared to me over the crest of the hill, Soweto loomed as anything but heroic.

Soweto. Dozens of square miles of rambling, ramshackle settlements creating a crazy quilt of poverty and decay. The sun reflecting off the corrugated tin roofs of the hovels and shacks that stretch along the unpaved roads of reddish-orange soil, so rich in minerals. A noxious cloud hangs overhead from the thousands of coal stoves used to warm the daily fare of mealy-meal.

At the junction where the Soweto Highway melts into the dirt roads of the township stands a huge green sign warning that 'Non-Bantu Persons (read: whites) May Enter With Permit Only' – this being about the only place in the republic where the notorious pass laws are applied *against* whites. As if whites had some reason to want to frolic or picnic inside the world's largest ghetto. Though until the current round of rebellion exploded last year, for about five dollars it was possible for white tourists to board an air-conditioned bus to take a guided excursion through the township.

Parked next to the warning sign is a mud-brown troop carrier of the South African Defense Force. Around it is a knot of ruddy-faced, beefy soldiers searching cars and their passengers as they descend into the demi-world of frustration and oppression that is Soweto. The troops have become a permanent fixture in this country's townships, which have languished under a declared state of emergency since last July. A draconian set of measures that, as Bishop Desmond Tutu said to me, 'makes *de jure* what has always been *de facto* for blacks'. As I near the checkpoint I get very anxious. I have no pass to enter. Journalists, in any case, have been banned from Soweto. And while I know that as a white I may be thrown out of the country for my transgression, I am concerned about my black South African colleague, Monti, who is driving our car. For simply escorting me, illegally, into Soweto, or for any other reason, or more likely, for no reason, he could be indefinitely 'detained' under martial law. I can see that he is nervous, too, for the first time.

As we roll slowly by the soldiers they stare at us eyeball to eyeball; they are discussing among themselves whether to stop us. But then, they wave us through. 'Dumb fuckers', says Monti. He explains that our rented purple Mazda is the same sort of car the omnipotent plainclothes Security Police use. 'They didn't want to take a chance and have us turn out to outrank them. And with you and me being black and white and travelling together in the same car meant it was even more likely we were from the cop shop.'

From the inside Soweto looks much like other Third World shanty towns. It could just as well be the seedy outskirts of Mexico City, or São Paulo, or Lagos. When I mention this to Monti, he smiles. 'I don't know because I haven't seen those others', he says. 'But this is worse. Because townships like this are actually planned and consciously created by the state. They don't mushroom up like they do in other countries. This is actually where the government intends for us to live – and to die.'

I am amazed by the way Monti dodges the prowling armored cars and troop carriers; the labyrinth of roads and alleys are all unmarked. There are no street lamps here, of course. But after protests from the community, the government was forced to install illumination. So now Soweto is staked out with grotesque 'mast lights' – towering seventy-foot steel poles with high-intensity yellowish mercury lamps on top. Exactly the sort of fixture used to light up a stockyard or a train depot, not a neighborhood. Garbage is strewn everywhere. The few playing fields have evolved into pock-marked rubbish dumps.

For the million-and-a-half people who live here there is one cinema, one hospital and two supermarkets. Some of the shacks have no running water, some no electricity. Until last year there were parts of Soweto that had no phone service at all. Barefoot children run through the roads with makeshift toys fashioned from hubcaps and clothes hangers. The women are gathered around communal concrete tubs where they do the wash. It is midday but the streets and yards are full of young and not-so-young men; unemployment in Soweto is estimated at more than 50 percent.

Beer. Beer. And more beer. Everywhere beer. Bottles empty and full. In people's hands and on the ground. Four thousand 'shebeens' – unauthorized drinking parlors – dispersed through the township. And although there are no clinics or markets or theaters, there are dozens of state-owned 'bottle shops' that dispense booze through a guarded window on the street. But today most of these government liquor stores are burned out and looted; they were among the first casualties in the now fifteen-month-old uprising.

Also gutted are the homes – true mansions amidst the hovels – of the members of Soweto Town Council, the dummy body created by the white regime to give the appearance of local self-rule. The Town Council headquarters itself is an oasis of modern, clean architecture and lush sod lawns. But it is cordoned off from the rest of the ghetto by row after row of barbed wire and by squads of heavily armed all-white police and troops.

On the Barclay's Bank next to the City Hall someone has spray-painted in bright red letters 'Violence is the answer to Apartheid – Communism is the answer to Poverty!' Across the way another wall reads: 'No to Conscription – Yes to Guerilla Warfare'. Soweto is, after all, one of the primary pressure-cookers of the youth insurrection. It is a place where no one claims to be in control. Where no one claims to be a leader. Where there is barely a program or a vision of the future. There is, for now, only the unbridled, burning determination to destroy The System. 'The young people have become determined to the point of recklessness', says Bishop Tutu. 'They believe they will die and they don't care. And the police and the army say to themselves, "Who cares? What's another black life?"'

'Not much' is the unavoidable answer. At least not here in the section of Soweto known as Orlando. 'You have an Orlando in the US too, don't you', Monti razzes me. 'Isn't that where you have Disney World?' We have parked our car and have begun to walk through the nastiest stretch I have seen anywhere. Orlando is a concentration of single-sex hostels. Barracks-like structures that house black workers who have been declared 'foreigners' by the Afrikaner regime. They are allowed into South Africa from their 'independent homelands' only after securing a job from a labor recruiter. They are then given a pass to reside in the hostel, having to leave their families hundreds of miles behind. Every eleven months they must return to the 'homeland' and reapply for their job and their pass.

As Monti takes me toward the hostel, I am, as the only white man around, an immediate attention-getter. I'd say there is about a fifty-fifty split. Half the locals raise their right hand in a salute to me and shout out 'Hello, Boss!' The other half stare at me, my clothes, my car and my camera with a cool resentment. They are silent. It is about the only time in my life where I am dying to announce, 'Hey, I'm an AMERICAN! I'm not one of "them".' But I keep quiet, sick and disgusted inside, realizing that here in South Africa there are no 'innocent bystanders' – there are no innocent whites. Everyone's ass is up for grabs. Monti, seeing my discomfort, paraphrases Malcolm X: 'If your child is bitten by a snake you go out in the forest to hunt it down. And when you come across the first snake you can – you kill it. You don't take time to ask it, "Excuse me. Are you the snake that bit my baby?"'

Monti takes me into a hostel where a miner sits with a few friends, the door open to the street. He has been working for Anglo-American for six years, separated from his family the whole time. 'I save up money so I can see my wife and children every three or four months', the miner explains. We stand in the doorway talking and I see his friends sitting on boxes around a bare table just a foot or so off the concrete floor. Against the left wall is a shelf with a few cans on it. Against the right a few crates of beer are stacked. Against the back wall is a folded-up bed. But wait. It hits me almost like a body-blow. This is it. The doorway we are in and three walls. My eyes strain to move on but quickly slam into the brick walls that enclose the miner and his friends. His entire home measures no more than eight feet by eight feet. His bed is folded because, unstrapped, it would fill his home. There is no bathroom. No stove. No heater. Just one bare light bulb. And again I remember what Monti said earlier. This is not casual. This is not 'the invisible hand' of the marketplace. This is where the mining

company planned to have its workers live. And this is where they live in exchange for 18 rand a month – as long as they are employed.

Before I leave Soweto, we go to the home of a long-time activist. A fortyish
editor, his face twisted from police beatings, one eye permanently damaged under torture. The activist speaks in a barely audible whisper – a sort of chilling,
quiet monotone that escapes from his tightly clenched jaw. 'What we see now is
the beginning of the end. But only the beginning. People are realizing they need
much more than what they have now to win their liberation', the activist says.
'They need guns. That means unrest may taper off in the next few months. But
then the calm will give way to war. It's going to get a lot worse before it gets any
better.'

It is now dusk and the scene in Soweto is unreal – surreal. The fumes from
the coal stoves make the air unbreathable. A rain is falling that is heavy enough
to turn the streets to mud, but too light to clear the air. An eerie glow is created
from the glare of the mast lights reflecting off the smoke. An interminable line
of blue buses is streaming in from Johannesburg. Monti and I drive in the other
direction, to where the highway leads out of Soweto. 'Can you find your way
back OK?' he asks. 'Yes', I answer and mumble some nonsense about wanting to
see him again in a Free South Africa. We embrace and say goodbye. On the
highway back through the gold and diamond mines, the skyscrapers of Jo'burg
in front of me, I am still shaking, even sobbing. It is night and Monti has disappeared into his own world. I have driven into mine. I am pleased that I am
leaving South Africa in the morning. Monti is staying.

This Magazine
December 1985

3

TEETERING TOWARD TET

Central America is Fantasy Isthmus, a region of the American mind,
peopled by our own political demons, where too often expediency rules
and rhetoric substitutes for reality. In this alone, the region resembles
Vietnam, a place of polarization of American opinion, a place for stereotypes
and for telling Presidents what they want to hear, and a place where the
middle of the road is a good place to get run over.
Frank McNeil, Former US Ambassador to Costa Rica

SAN SALVADOR: MARCH 1989. At 4:15 a.m. a scanner radio I share with a
friend locks on a narrowband FM channel used by the hundred or so US military advisers stationed here. A prolonged alarm signal screeches and wakes us.
Then a voice tinged with a Texas drawl and ratcheted up with apprehension:
'This is Commando Two Zero. We are getting probed! We are getting probed
again!' Once again the Salvadoran army's major engineering base, located
thirty miles southeast of the capital in Zacatecoluca, is under attack from dozens of guerrillas of the Farabundo Martí National Liberation Front (FMLN).

Machine gun fire, rocket-propelled grenades and *rampas* – homemade cata-
pult bombs – pound the installation and rake support units rushing to the scene.
'Listen!', an adviser codenamed Commando Two Zero radios the US military
command in San Salvador, 'the shit's hitting the fan pretty bad out here . . . I'm
. . . I'm bailing out of here, I'm getting out of here!'

The American military adviser eventually escapes the attack unharmed. But
eight Salvadoran soldiers including a major are killed, and thirteen others are
wounded, by government count. At the same hour, FMLN units ambush a government infantry company in the northeastern province of Morazán, causing at
least a dozen casualties. At dawn, so-called Urban Commandos level the town
hall of Apopa twelve miles north of the capital. And at 6:20 a.m. two powerful

car bombs explode on the perimeter of the First Infantry Brigade – the capital's major military garrison. The blast leaves the base intact but takes the lives of a septuagenarian couple whose house was blown away.

On this explosive February morning, after an eerie, disorienting period of relative calm produced by the debate over a guerrilla peace proposal, El Salvador returned to normal: the nine-year-old war came roaring back to center stage, and with a vengeance. The next day over a lunch of conch cocktails and filleted sole in an outdoor cafe, 'Rogelio' curses the bungled carbombing of the First Brigade that killed only the two civilians. 'That was a real *cagada* – a fuck up.' Pushing thirty-five, and dressed in a pale yellow guayaberra shirt, a plastic pen-holder in his breast pocket, horn-rimmed glasses riding high on his nose, his hair razor-parted and greased down, and a leather briefcase on the chair between us, 'Rogelio' looks like any one of a thousand other faceless government bureaucrats or accountants that might be upset over the unpredictable messiness of urban warfare.

But his reasons for objecting to the bombing are different. 'Rogelio', that is 'Comandante Rogelio', is the director of the Urban Commandos of one of the FMLN's five 'armies'. He explains: 'One of the other groups placed that bomb and should have realized that the enemy, no matter how inept, is starting to make that tactic unviable. The security around the base had been expanded far enough to not allow the explosive device to get in close.' Since last fall, guerrilla car bombs have taken the war to the doorsteps of the government's military installations inside the capital. Rogelio adds, 'But some people, our own people included, are slow to adjust to new situations.'

'Rogelio's' own personal history mirrors the 'adjustments' the FMLN has undertaken over the years to hone itself into what some US officials call the 'most tenacious guerrilla movement in the world' and has allowed it to survive the most sustained American military commitment since Vietnam: nine years and 3.5 billion in US tax dollars to support the Salvadoran military.

As an impoverished teenage peasant in the mid seventies Rogelio joined a US-financed campesino union 'to get the credit and land they promised us' only to quit a year later 'when I saw we were only being manipulated to support political candidates'. After reading pamphlets by Colombia's late guerrilla-priest Camilo Torres given to him by an uncle, Rogelio by 1975 had moved to the capital and joined one of Salvador's radical trade unions. 'Government repression came down hard and that's when I joined the guerrillas in the city. By 1978 I was in charge of twelve to fifteen fighters carrying out execution of police, expropriation of banks and the kidnapping of the rich. In 1981 I participated in the general offensive here in the city. ... Seeing we were still too weak to overthrow the regime we expanded our field of action and I helped build our new

TEENAGE SALVADORAN GUERRILLAS PREPARE THE FINAL
MILITARY CAMPAIGN AGAINST THE US-BACKED GOVERNMENT

front on the Guazapa volcano [twenty miles north of San Salvador]. By 1983 we changed strategy and built up large concentrations of regular forces, which I was in for two years in Morazán. I became an artillery specialist thanks to the 90mm US cannons we captured along with the 75mm and 80mm mortars. When the enemy was given a fleet of bombers and helicopters by the Reagan administration we moved to a dispersal strategy and by 1985 I was back in Guazapa. There we resisted and overcame the army's attempt to "dry us up" by bombing out the civilian population. Near the end of 1986 we began to concentrate new efforts here in the capital. Now I divide my time among three bases: the city, Guazapa and among our forces right there on the hill', he says, sipping a Suprema beer and nodding his head toward the 4,000-foot San Salvador volcano, whose slopes gently slide right down to the deck of the Sheraton swimming pool and whose peak is about as near the US Embassy as the 'Hollywood' sign is to the Los Angeles City Hall.

'What you saw yesterday', Rogelio says, referring to the FMLN's simultaneous attacks, 'is a test, a rehearsal. Next week or the week after there will be

another, bigger one. And then more escalation. The army has brought two battalions to the northern perimeter of the city, convinced that we are going to
come running down from the mountains. But they are wrong. We are *in* the city.
It is our commandos who stalk them. The explosion will come from right under
their feet.'

For months now the guerrillas have been promising everything from overrun-
ning army bases in the city to a major nationwide offensive to a general insurrection. In the hills of FMLN-dominated Chalatenego – a rocky, three-hour
drive north of the capital – some insurgents go so far as to claim they are
readying to take state power in the next few months. At the very least, the
guerrillas seem to be building up for a Central American repeat of the 1968
Vietnamese Tet Offensive – a coordinated, multifront strike that while militarily
inconclusive gave the lie to the US claim that the insurgency was containable.
While the Salvadoran government, the army and the US Embassy (three indistinguishable entities) counter that the guerrilla boasts are mere Marxist pipe-
dreaming, even they agree Salvador is simmering again. Better said, boiling.

As my lunch with Rogelio ended, a thousand unionists, their faces covered
with paper masks, outraged by the dynamiting of their office earlier in the day
(they say by the National Police, who they also blame for blowing up the country's largest union headquarters a week before), rampaged through downtown
San Salvador, burned state vehicles and buses, smashed and looted a number of
stores, and for the first time since 1981 erected two lines of barricades from
behind which, armed with machetes, molotov cocktails and home-brewed contact grenades, faced down troops, tanks and armored personnel carriers for a
dizzyingly tense half-hour. The whole affair didn't come close to adding up to an
insurrection. But it did fit Rogelio's description only an hour earlier of what a
'rehearsal' might look like. Only the presence of a dozen TV camera crews
quashed what appeared to be a certain bloodbath. Or, more likely, just post-
poned it.

It's a cruel irony – at least for Washington – that the 'electoral process' here,
cooked up in 1982 to provide democratic cover to a bloodsoaked de facto government (and therefore to open wide the spigots of congressional underwriting), has now turned into a factor of dangerous destablization, one more
catalyst for rebellion and revolution. There's a prevailing perception, and hardly
an unfounded one, that when the neofascist ARENA party wins the presidency,
as is expected in this month's elections, El Salvador will become so polarized
that it will become not the next Vietnam, but the next Lebanon.

Facing the certain electoral victory of ARENA – which is pledged to a war
of extermination against 'subversion' – is no doubt what motivated the January

other ten or twelve years of Constructive Engagement and Quiet Diplomacy. And so it seems this war will continue and escalate. Which leaves us all staring over the edge into a very deep black hole. In spite of Embassy assurances that the war is but a low-intensity struggle against 'terrorism', both contending armies are dolling up for what promises to be one helluva prolonged, bloody and uncertain *danse macabre*.

The capital itself has become a major theater of war. Since last November, the FMLN has attacked the headquarters of the National Police, the National Guard, the Treasury Police and the Army High Command, all located in San Salvador. The government has responded by militarizing the city. All army and police leaves have been indefinitely cancelled. Troop convoys, army foot patrols and battle-ready tank and armor units are commonplace sights on city streets and boulevards. By 9 p.m. most of the streets are deserted and by 11 p.m. roadblocks and police checkpoints sprout every few blocks like a bad case of German measles. In the working-class neighborhoods in the netherworld of the capital, house-to-house searches for weapons are a weekly occurrence. FMLN Urban Commandos and Army and Air Force Special Forces units play out an increasingly bloody war in the nighttime shadows.

The 55,000-man Salvadoran army is larger and better-equipped than ever before in its history. Its impressive fleet of US airplanes and helicopter gunships gives it extraordinary mobility and deters large concentrations of guerrilla forces. After years of US prodding, the Salvadoran command is finally, but slowly, fielding small-unit patrols that aggressively hunt down guerrilla forces. And these so-called Long Reconnaissance Patrols are taking their toll on insurgent forces.

Nevertheless, after nearly a decade of battle, the FMLN now operates in every one of the country's fourteen provinces. A guerrilla campaign targeting local mayors as the advance guard of the government counterinsurgency campaign has cost ten lives and forced the resignation of more than 100 other mayors, leaving nearly half of El Salvador's towns without local government. Recently, the guerrillas have taken to bombing the homes of army officers, and some observers speculate that it won't be long before the insurgents begin a concerted campaign of attack against ARENA congressional deputies.

The ongoing guerrilla sabotage campaign has permanently affected 60 percent of the nation's electrical grid. Every day different power pylons and transformers are dynamited, plunging whole cities and provinces into darkness. (For the second night in a row I write by candlelight, hoping that my computer batteries will hold up because the power hasn't been on long enough in the last forty-eight hours to give them a full charge). The insurgent sabotage is costing the government dollar for dollar what US aid is pumping into the country.

ROLL OVER, CHE GUEVARA

The FMLN has recently opened a major front in the once conflict-free western third of the country. The traditional guerrilla strongholds of Chalatenango and Morazán provinces remain as such despite years of on-going military sweeps. The Guazapa volcano, declared 'guerrilla-free' three years ago, is today one of the areas where the army is taking some of its heaviest losses. On the outskirts of Usulután, which houses two major garrisons, FMLN forces operate freely – as they have for years – on El Tigre mountain. And even the armed forces admit that the San Salvador volcano, the virtual backbone of the capital, is an area of major guerrilla persistence. A recent reporter's trip through the area revealed that the guerrillas on the volcano are among the best-trained and best-armed in the country and that they have built a network of impressive civilian support. All this in the very heart of the enemy rear guard, never more than a ten-minute walk from army lines and less than a morning's hike down to the gates of the US Embassy.

'The volcano is full of guerrillas', Colonel Gonzalez Brito, head of training for the army garrison in the capital tells me. 'They cut coffee by day. At night they put down their machetes and pick up their guns. Who knows who's who? This war could last forever.'

Sound familiar? Familiar enough to those in Washington who bother to follow events down here to start seriously worrying about the immediate future of US policy. One leftish Washington lobbyist on one of last month's dozen or so factfinders to San Salvador expresses hope that 'now that the Reagan cowboys are out and the Bush trilateralists are in, especially with Jim Baker at State, there's finally a chance that policy will move toward a negotiated settlement.'

But most other beltway insiders remain pessimistic. 'We know very well that after a decade of deep US involvement in El Salvador we are just about back to where we started from', a legislative aide to an East Coast liberal tells me over breakfast (at the same table where guerrilla defector Miguel Castellanos had his last meal the previous morning before ingesting the fifty-six bullets that ripped through his car). 'But it's just not an issue on the Hill. If we even got an up/down vote on military aid to El Salvador – which we haven't had in years – we'd get creamed right now. It's not just that most members agree with policy, it's that they don't even really know what's going on. Take a look over there.'

The aide points to a long table across the hotel breakfast room where ARENA's President-to-be Alfredo 'Freddy' Cristiani, is quietly meeting with a dozen or so young congressional staffers. 'Now half the people at the table are going to come away from that meeting thinking that Cristiani's our new white hope', the aide complains. 'He's smooth, says all the right things, he speaks perfect English, he went to Georgetown, he *looks* like a moderate. So half of them are going to go back and say, look, Cristiani is not Major D'Aubuisson. He's not the death squads. He's a centrist; we can work with him. Now the other half at the table are like me. They come down here and see right through the bullshit and the Embassy dog-and-pony shows. You see that the killings are a reality. That the injustice and suffering are real. You see that our policy is a total failure. All that's real credible and understandable when you are down here. But by the time you get on the plane and get to Miami it all begins to fade. And by the time you get back to D.C. and get up on the Hill and tell the people who count what our $3 billion has bought, you can hardly find anyone who knows or even cares what you are talking about.'

For most Salvadorans, day-to-day living conditions are worse than when the US aid program began in earnest in 1980. Unemployment hovers at 50 percent. Infant mortality is now the highest in Latin America. Real wages have fallen 40 percent in the last five years. More than half the population has no access to clean drinking water. There is a housing shortage of 700,000 homes in a country of 5 million people. Some 16,000 Salvadorans emigrated in just the last month. Late last year, the Salvadoran Foreign Ministry signed a deal that would send 5,000 Salvadoran campesinos to 'colonize' parts of the countryside of Bolivia, itself the poorest, most desperate nation in South America.

The Salvadoran army continues to fill its fodder quotas by press-ganging poor teenagers off of city streets and subsistence farms. But in the elegant Zona Rosa discos the lighter-skinned sons of the oligarchy and middle class dance and drink free of any worry that they may have to actually fight in a war being waged in their economic interests.

'You Americans have poured $3 billion into this country thinking that the roots of the conflict are in Communism', Father Ignacio Martín Baro, vice-rector of the Central American University, tells me (Baro has been the object of sixteen separate bomb attacks of which 'only six actually exploded', as he loves telling you). The American-educated cleric-psychologist continues: 'But the whole American diagnosis is wrong. The root of the conflict is poverty, maldistribution of wealth and injustice. If somehow the army could win today, if the guerrillas were just wiped out, conditions in El Salvador are such that within two or three years a new insurgency would be born, a new war would begin all over again.'

And the killing in this war goes on, unabated, unpunished. The nightmare spectre of the government-linked death squads, that at the beginning of the decade took a thousand lives a month, still lingers and over the past year has undergone a resurgence. In the first days of February Dan Quayle bumbled into town armed with a media script that was supposed to be a warning that the US would not tolerate human rights abuses by government forces. But the Salvadoran army seems to take Mr Quayle even less seriously than do the American people. On the very eve of his speech, according to an investigation by the Catholic

Archdiocese Human Rights Office, five uniformed, heavily armed troops of the Salvadoran army broke into the homes of university students Mario Flores and José Gerardo Gomez and drove them away in a red Datsun pickup. The next day, as Quayle was yukking it up with reporters at the Embassy, the students' bodies were found dumped in a ditch. Both had been shot in the head at close range after having their hands and ankles tied together. Gomez's body showed signs of 'foreign objects' having been driven under his fingernails. His 'hands, legs, arms, face, chest, back and the area between his pubis and stomach showed signs of bruises', according to the Church's forensic report. Flores's body showed signs of 'fractures to his facial bones, lacerations by a sharp object in his legs, fractures of lower vertebrae; and his penis and scrotum showed signs of bruises and swelling as a result of severe pressure or compression.' No army investigation of the murders has been initiated as a result of Quayle's 'stern admonition'.

Eleven days later, again according to an onsite inspection by the Church Human Rights Office, the US-trained Atlacatl Battalion operating in Chalatenango overran an FMLN field hospital and shot to death ten noncombatants: a Mexican doctor, four paramedics (two of whom were raped), three wounded and convalescing unarmed guerrillas and two seriously disabled unarmed guerrillas. This latest massacre 'flagrantly violated' the 7th, 9th and 11th articles of the Geneva Protocols, according to Catholic Church Legal Aid Director María Julia Hernandez.

Another university student, picked up by the National Police three days after the field hospital massacre, was later found dead with his hands tied behind his back inside a wooden box thrown from a speeding car. Five days later, two mutilated bodies showed up in San Jacinto Park, at the foot of one of San Salvador's only tourist attractions – a hill-scaling cable car from the summit of which, on a clear day, you can see the A-37 Dragonfly bombers dropping their loads on the Guazapa volcano across the valley.

But no better barometer of Salvador's anguished plight exists than the El Camino Real Hotel. One of the last great 'press hotels' left in the Third World, after the recent closure of the Commodore in Beirut, the Camino's second floor houses a beauty shop, a couple of conference rooms, the meeting room of the El Salvador Chess Club and an ever-changing jumble of European, Latin American and mostly American journalists' and network offices. It's along this hundred yard stretch of worn red carpet that a dozen rumors a day are born and die, and then sifted through and reconstructed and patched and sewn together with facts, factoides and raw hunches in an attempt to make some sense out of what is going on outside and, often enough, inside the walls of the hotel.

And here, along the second-floor row of press offices, as in the rest of El

Salvador, a rigid class system prevails. The Ivy League graduates rep for the first-string papers and agencies, draw comfortable salaries and perks, do at times some very good reporting but rarely good enough to compromise their access to Power and the Embassy; and they mark time, waiting to be promoted out in a year or two to the more comfortable Paris or London bureaus.

A cut below are the reporters with only state college degrees who move in and out of the country and on and off the second floor on assignment for some fading midwest daily, or stick it out here 'stringing' – reporting on a payment per article or broadcast basis – for as many stateside clients who care enough to cede eight or ten column inches or a minute/ten seconds of airtime to the Salvador story. And free from large corporate office politics, really with no chance or hope of ascending an institutional career ladder, they often do the better reporting out of here.

Then there is the subclass of strictly Salvadoran hangers-on, helpers, freelance camera and sound operators, drivers, 'fixers', messengers; the guys known usually only by a first name, or a nickname, but the people without whom the networks and wire agencies, at least, would sink. Their livelihood, their economic well-being rises in direct proportion to the level of *bergazeo* – violence and disorder in the streets. The more bang-bang and blood the more the thirst back on the news desks for vivid copy, hot pix, reliable tips, fearless driving and 'good video'. Footage of a burning car is worth twice that of one whose flames have just been extinguished. Photographing or filming a dumped, mutilated body before human rights workers arrive on the scene is more valuable than afterward, when the frame gets crowded with onlookers.

This, my last afternoon in El Salvador, is topping off a slow news day. No marches, no shootings, no bodies. As I stroll the second-floor hallway of the Camino a knot of these Salvadoran dependents of the networks hunch down and noisily slap five-colon bills on little piles of cards in a simple game known as *banquillo*. The bets come fast and furious, the game played feverishly as if under a pressing time restraint, as if precious time is running out. And, in a sense, it is. All know that it can't be long before a phone will ring or a beeper will burp or a tip will be whispered and once again it will be time to fan out into the streets and hustle up the gore that is life – and death – in El Salvador.

L.A. Weekly
4 May 1989

NOTE: Eight months after my lunch with Comandante 'Rogelio', in November 1989, the FMLN did indeed launch its threatened general offensive and brought the Salvadoran government to the edge of collapse. In the government's counterattack, Father Ignacio Martín Baro, interviewed in the story above, was murdered along with five other Jesuits in a dawn massacre by army troops. The intense fighting eventually led to a peace agreement that embodied a range of democratic reforms and demilitarization. The FMLN became a legal political force and in the April 1994 presidential elections won 27 percent of the vote. El Salvador's new president is Armando Calderon Sol, another politician tied to the country's death squads.

4

PUPPET SHOW

PANAMA CITY: DECEMBER 1989. Into the second week of the US invasion and occupation of Panama, life here in the capital is taking on a routine 'normalcy'. The gunfire has stopped, the miles of looted out stores on Avenidas Central and España are beginning to restock, the notorious Ancon Inn brothel across from the US military's hemispheric Southern Command (SOUTHCOM) is open again (along with the scores of foreign-owned banks), the networks are gangbanging the Manuel Noriega story in front of the Vatican Embassy (where the deposed leader is holed up) and, most notably, US soldiers are *everywhere*.

American MPs who can't read Spanish are manning dozens of traffic posts and roadblocks, going through the motions of 'checking' the papers of bottled-up motorists. Though there's been no shooting for days, heavily armed combat troops, daily touching-up their camouflage facepaint, hold their positions on tanks and APC 'tracks' or behind sandbag emplacements on every major inter-section and thoroughfare. Armored units continue the blockade of the Cuban and Vatican diplomatic missions. Ranger foot patrols stalk the financial district. Marines help clean up the garbage and debris downtown. And elite detachments are finishing up house-to-house searches for Noriega collaborators – real or al-leged – or have begun acting as uniformed Repo Men, searching private homes for looted goods.

Then there's that *other* American corps. For the first ten days of the inva-sion as many as sixty or seventy US reporters – nearly all of the TV persuasion – were able to live the ultimate Banana Republic fantasy thanks to US SOUTH-COM. Inside its permanent hilltop command facility at Quarry Heights, the Pentagon gave volunteers from the press bunk space on the floor of the Officer's Club (a structure replete with a red-tile patio overhung by six regulation tropical ceiling fans), and spoon-fed them three cafeteria meals a day along with the official Department of Defense line at each morning's briefing.

A military Media Center with international phones, fax and telex was provided along with a thatch-covered mini stage (with an appropriately lush background) to be used for TV standups. All in all, quite a generous opportunity to cover the war by day from a safe distance – and from the exclusive perspective of only one side of it – while being able to spend the night with a bunch of noncoms slugging back gringo beer and yakking bombs, bullets and bullshit.

But with the real shooting war over, and with much of the live-in press migrating across town to the Holiday Inn to better cover the nonstory of the Noriega stand-off, SOUTHCOM has had to take extraordinary measures to keep the media bubble machine puffing. The Media Center bulletin board took to sprouting sign-up sheets for US Army conducted tours. And what an intriguing menu: '82nd Airborne Urban Clearing', 'Noriega House Tour: Lifestyles of the Rich and Famous', 'Marine Patrols', 'Panama Canal Tours' (Provide Ur Own Transportation), 'Marine Horseback Patrol' (Transp. Provided), 'Panama City Tour' and 'Gamboa Prison' (82nd Airborne Assault).

Anything with the word *assault* in it seemed my best bet. And the 82nd Airborne's Major Baxter Ennis agreed. 'Hey, this is a great story', he assured me. 'A daring simultaneous land-sea assault on and liberation of a prison. A great example of what kind of work the 82nd can do. I've got everybody out there lined up to talk to you.' Then addressing the Japanese TV crew next to me, Ennis added, 'And for you TV guys, well, it's not live action, but there's still plenty of damage left to shoot.'

Major Ennis drove us to the prison in a yellow school bus, appropriately, given that the Gamboa detention facility looked something like an average Southern California elementary school. Butted right up against the Panama Canal and six miles away from the nearest village, the minimum security facility consisted of a clapboard administration building, a small cement dormitory for the guards, one barnlike building with two dozen cells and a 50- by 75-foot grass yard enclosed by a barbed-wired fence. It looked like the sort of place that could be overrun by your average Boy Scout troop, albeit aided by a dash of steroids or speed. But to hear about it from the officers the major had assembled for us, this isolated outpost was as impenetrable as the Guns of Navarone.

'This target was one of five coordinated objectives that we assaulted during the operation's (read *invasion's*) kick-off at zero-one hundred hours of the first night', recounted Lt Col Lynn Moore, commander of Charlie Company, 3rd Battalion, 504th Parachute Infantry Regiment of the 82nd Airborne. 'We knew we had to come in quickly and in a daring way so that the prisoners we wished to liberate would not be shot. Five or ten minutes before the assault we made three passes with the three choppers. Then at the precise designated moment of the attack we brought in three helicopters, a Cobra firing 20mm cannons and two OH-58 choppers with snipers on board laying down cover fire. At the same time, with great audacity, flying at night with goggles, we landed two UH-1's firing M-60 machine guns in the prison yard itself to conduct the prisoner rescue and landed a third 'Huey' behind the prison. That was joined by an LCN [amphibious landing craft] that pulled up in the canal also behind the prison and dropped off another sixty paratroopers.'

All totaled then, the 82nd Airborne threw six helicopter gunships, one LCN amphibious vehicle and more than eighty troops into battle against. 'Against what enemy force?' I asked Col Moore.

'The intelligence we had', he answered, 'was that the compound was guarded by some fifteen PDF [Panama Defense Forces] and was holding ten to seventy prisoners.' As it turned out, there were nineteen PDF soldiers – five of whom died in the battle – and sixty-four liberated prisoners, including seven dissident PDF officers and two Americans whose names the 82nd Airborne couldn't remember.

Apart from outgunning the PDF and outnumbering them four to one, the US forces had a few other advantages rarely found in military history. 'The entire operation was launched from Fort Sherman, just up the canal', Col Moore remarked. 'All of the units involved in the attack had been training there at the Jungle Warfare School.'

'You mean your forces had come from only a few miles away and had been planning this attack before the invasion?' I asked.

'We had been looking at this target for at least two months and overflying it almost everyday. Since the build-up of hostilities here, General Thurman has demanded we keep two, not just one battalion always in training at the Jungle Warfare School.'

'So you simulated this attack at the training school just up the canal?'

The Colonel gave me that special smile reserved for civilian naifs. 'No, we did better than that! Three or four nights before the attack, as part of Operation Sand Flea, we landed our company right here behind the prison and went on foot maneuvers all through here to check out the target. Almost got into a firefight with the PDF right then!'

'Three or four nights before? Was that *before* or after the US Marine was killed by the PDF?' I asked, referring to one of the incidents used by the Bush administration to justify the invasion.

'Um. .. before. . .'

But Col Moore was cut off by a female pentagon flack in civvies with a walkie-talkie. 'I know what you are trying to get at', she said to me curtly. 'This

area here is a Pink Zone; it's Panamanian territory, but we have the right to maneuver. And the operation the colonel was referring to was part of ongoing exercise of [Canal] Treaty assertiveness ordered by President Bush last May.'

Captain Derek Johnson who led the troops in the field at Gamboa was more to the point: 'Operation Sand Flea was remarkably similar to the assault itself. We always try to do a rehearsal. But to be honest, I never dreamed we'd actually get to practice on the real target itself!'

'Well, with your rehearsal just a few days before', I asked, 'and with your choppers making three passes over the prison compound just minutes before the attack, didn't you lose the element of surprise?'

'No way', Captain Jonson retorted. 'The PDF inside here were not even tipped off by the choppers because we had made so many overflights, so many maneuvers, so many dry runs, they had become totally desensitized to our presence.'

This 'daring air-amphibious assault' on Gamboa prison is a metaphor for this whole war against Panama. The US Army invaded a country of 2.2 million people defended by a dispersed 15,000-man force (of which only 3,500 were combat soldiers) – and invaded it from longstanding bases inside the country itself. Not only were half of the 25,000 invasion troops here to begin with, but US forces had the opportunity to openly survey and assess its 'enemy' for months – really years – in advance and to conduct dress rehearsals on the real – not simulated – targets. Logistically, the Pentagon was able, with no risk and complete impunity, to fly in equipment and troops far in advance of the invasion and have most elements in place when the green light was given. The ferocious attack on the PDF's downtown Command Headquarters, for example, was staged and launched from the Quarry Heights base only 600 yards away.

On the fifteen-mile ride I took between Quarry Heights and Gamboa prison, the road was bordered by the US Albrook Air Base (loaded with gunships), the sprawling US Army Supply Warehouse and the Fort Clayton infantry base. It's almost as if Noriega's PDF was the noisome intruder on what was de facto US territory and not vice-versa.

Which is why the Bush administration is having such a tussle of a time convincing the world that the newly installed government of Guillermo Endara is anything but a puppet regime. After all Endara and his two vice-presidents, Ricardo Arias Calderon and Guillermo 'Billy' Ford had to swear themselves into office at a US military base the night of the invasion.

An attempt to further legitimate the administration a week later as much as backfired in a comic-opera presidential press conference. We reporters were urged by SOUTHCOM to 'not miss' the crucial event to be held at the Foreign Ministry that was under guard by a steely display of US armor. With 200 journalists packed into one steamy room, the new president and his V.P.'s arrived ninety minutes late due to 'a traffic jam' and accompanied by an entourage of six other civilians identified as Panama's National Electoral Tribunal.

The chairwoman of the tribunal, which last May annulled the vote count in a presidential election widely thought to have been won by Endara, was now here to annoint Endara as the duly-*elected* president of Panama. Relying on 83 percent of the total vote tally, compiled exclusively from Endara's own poll-watchers, she adjudicated 62 percent of the vote to Endara and 24 percent to Noriega's candidate. While that's probably a fairly accurate reflection of reality, this improvised 'electoral process' was best symbolized by the 'credentials' the chairwoman handed Endara, who showed up with the red-white-and-blue presidential sash already on his chest: an *empty* 8 by 14 manila filefolder.

Not that Endara's supporters could care less about the unpleasant details of their sweep to power on the hood of US tanks. In the swank Paitilla neighborhood, filled with guarded seaside condos, designer homes with indoor swimming pools, and garages brimming with Beemers and Jaguars, and looking much like Coconut Grove, the Panamanian elite is celebrating the US invasion as an unqualified liberation. Around the Vatican Embassy where Noriega is holed-up (also in Paitilla), the most stylish and sleek of Panamanian youth dance to the rock music blaring from the US Army loudspeakers (set up to drive the Noriega out of his asylum) and wave silk-screened pickets reading 'Pine-Apple Busters' – a reference to Noriega's pock-marked face.

Endara and Arias Calderon and 'Billy' Ford all have one thing in common with these revelers, they are *rabi-blancos* – 'white-asses' as the 90 percent of the Panamanian population that is mestizo or black call the pale-skinned oligarchs.

But make no mistake. It's also in the scruffy hills and ravines of northern Panama City, in the crowded working-class settlement of San Miguelito, thought to have been a Noriega stronghold, that substantial support for the invasion can be found. It's in neighborhoods like this where the 70 percent of the capital's residents who earn less than $2,000 a year live. And most of them make less than $1,000 a year, and try to eek out an existence in a dollar-based economy with a cost of living that rivals that of the US. It's neighborhoods like San Miguelito that, compared with Paitilla, provide some of the sharpest racial and class contrasts in Latin America. Manuel Noriega, a mulatto raised in a down-trodden ghetto, aimed his populist rhetoric right at the kind of people who struggle for life in San Miguelito. But now, even here, no overt support for him is to be found.

I arrive at San Miguelito's 'Pan de Azucar' PDF garrison right before lunch to find a surrealistic scene. The charred and gutted skeleton of the military base that resisted the U.S attack for six hours, is now being stripped and chiseled to the bone by local scavengers. At least two dozen men, women and children armed with rebars, screwdrivers and sledgehammers are salvaging whatever miserable scraps they can from the bombed-out ruins. Zinc roofing is being ripped off a carport to be used as a new wall in a nearby shack. One man pulls a coil from the engine of a trashed and burned Toyota. María, a six-foot, black twenty-year-old in red shorts and a white T-shirt with a machete in one hand and a crowbar slung on her shoulder tells me, 'Of course I support the invasion. We had to get rid of that bastard. I graduated three years ago from an accounting course and still haven't got a job. Maybe now things will get better. They have to.'

Standing up against one of the base's smoke-blackened walls, I spot two muscular, young men in improvised uniforms blankly looking on at the strip-down operation going on around them. They are two members of the new US-formed postinvasion Panamanian Police. Nicasio says he was attached to the PDF's 1st Company before switching sides. Like his companion Reinaldo, they were both on leave the night of the invasion.

They don't really want to talk. After some coaxing, Nicasio nervously volunteers: 'At first I supported the general. But things got worse, real bad.'

'Did you have friends in your PDF company who died in the fighting?'

'Many', Nicasio answers stone-faced before clamming up again.

'Do you support the invasion?'

No answer as he looks at the ground. I ask again. Almost imperceptibly he shakes his head. I ask Reinaldo how long he was in the PDF.

'Eight years and ten months.'

'Why are you in the new police instead having fought?'

'I was off base that night. I had nothing to fight with.'

'But would you have fought?'

Now with the first sign of some confidence he answers: 'If I had had a rifle, yes. I would have fought the gringos. But I wouldn't be fighting for the general. It's just that, like anywhere else, it's always better if your own people run things. This is Panama and we Panamanians should be the ones giving orders.'

At the entrance to San Miguelito, meanwhile, US troops were forking out bundles of bucks from behind a makeshift roadside stand for turned-in weapons. Fifty dollars for a pistol or a grenade, $150 for an AK-47 or M-16, $500 for a bazooka – no questions asked. Next to the stand, dozens of rifles and cases of ammo were stacked up in front of local gawkers. A near party atmosphere prevailed as a number of men had already exchanged their rewards for beer and the brew was flowing freely. One sullen woman walked up and pulled an automatic pistol from her purse and handed it to a bespectacled GI. After a quick glance he laughed and yelled over to the paymaster: 'What do we give for B.B. guns? Five bucks?'

'Nothin' was the immediate answer. A Panamanian translator broke the bad news to the woman, who grimaced and stormed away.

After my trip to San Miguelito I met with the director of the prestigious Central American Studies Center, Marcos Gandasegui and a black university professor who asked to remain anonymous and whom I'll call 'Eusebio'.

'Why', I want to know, 'does there appear to be so much support for the US invasion in a country whose political history has been marked by resistance to the US?

'It's painful but true that our people came out in great numbers to collaborate with the invaders, turning in members of the Dignity Battalions and so on', Eusebio answered. 'Noriega thought that a US invasion would galvanize people around him and against the Yankees. But he was completely wrong. He united people to oppose him and to, at least temporarily, support the invasion. Noriega had very little support outside of the PDF, and even there he was weak. He did embody some very legitimate nationalist ideals, but his antidemocratic methods and the incredible corruption he encouraged undermined him. This people of ours has a grand anti-American tradition. The trick now is to find out where it is, search it out, dust it off, and recover our historical memory.'

'The support you see is only relative', Gandasegui added. 'The people you see out in the streets greeting the US soldiers are of course the ones who support them. Panamanian Radio has been calling on people to gather in front of the Vatican and demand that Noriega be turned over. But how many people have gone there? Just a few, maybe a hundred. The others are inside their homes. People are afraid, scared. They see thousands of soldiers and heard the fighting and bombings. But also, the Panamanian governments during the 1980s were really antipopular. The population had no sympathy for Noriega politically or economically.'

'Support for the invasion is wide but very thin', continued Gandasegui. 'There are two major currents in Panamanian politics. Nationalists and what you can call *transitistas*, those economic elites tied to nonproductive transit-based enterprises or banking. The winners in this invasion, for the moment, are clearly these traditional business sectors. You know one of the main reasons the US invaded Panama was to destroy the PDF and create a new army that mirrors US interests and is controlled by the US. When the Canal reverts back to Panama in 2000, the US will be comfortable with who's in charge of defending it. The big question now is if the US, beyond dismantling the PDF, will go ahead and destroy our other nationalist institutions: our educational system, our trade union movement, our popular movement? All that remains to be seen. When things normalize in the next few weeks, some hard realities are going to sink in. People will be expecting change and improvement, but the sort of economic program that the Endara government favors, one in accord with the IMF, one that cuts back public employment, one that hits the poorest classes the hardest . . . to implement a program like that can bring unpredictable results. There are many challenges ahead.'

One of those challenges may come from a wave of popular anger once Panama psychically recovers and assesses the full human cost of the US intervention. Noriega may be gone, but at a premium price. In the central neighborhood of Chorrillo, literally in the shadow of the SOUTHCOM base, six square blocks of completely flattened civilian homes bear testimony to the US firepower that was unleashed against the PDF's Command Headquarters. Though severely damaged from the US onslaught, the *Comandancia*, unlike the dozens, maybe hundreds of homes around it, is still standing. More than a week after the attack, decomposed bodies are still being fished out of the rubble as buzzards circle in the same airspace earlier occupied by the attacking US aircraft.

Hundreds of ordinary Panamanians have thronged the streets to watch the US troops empty the contents of the PDF Command or to stare at and even take pictures of the awful marvel of mass destruction that lies before them. In this neighborhood, there is no celebration, no rejoicing, but rather somber meditation. Roberto Lozada, leaning on the burnt-out pump of the gas station he used to work at shakes his head. 'Too, too many people died here . . . innocent civilians. I don't know who to blame. Noriega or the gringos, or the Dignity Battalions that went mad and started shooting and burning. But even they were fighting without an ideology, fighting for a false nationalism, because that fucker Noriega didn't really fight for the canal. He didn't really fight for our sovereignty, but only fought for his own enrichment. Now the authorities of the moment say they are going to save the country. But we've been hearing that shit forever.'

As Marco Gandasegui said, the US Army *is* the source of all power in today's Panama. But except for a decade interlude during the populist rule of Omar Torrijos, it always has been. Panama was cut from the whole cloth of Colombia in 1903 by the US solely to allow the building of the canal.

The only institutions of significance in Panama have always been gringo: the canal company, the US military bases, the US-based fruit companies, the banks, even the currency, which is the US dollar. Only the Canal Treaty negotiated between Torrijos and Jimmy Carter promised that one day – precisely on the last day of this century, Panama would be fully sovereign.

In the meantime, Panama has become a convenient theater for George Bush to stage a shoddy political morality play, picking up a bundle of domestic political points along the way. For Panama is undoubtedly the last place in the region where the US could get away with rapidly knocking out an unfriendly regime with very low cost in *American* lives – though this operation has killed hundreds of Panamanian civilians and wounded a thousand others. A US military incursion into El Salvador or Nicaragua would be quite a different matter than in Panama, where the US already was the dominant power, except for the detail of a small national armed force. Trying to extract maximum domestic benefit from an action that has drawn international scorn, the Bush administration has also systematically exagerated Noriega's drug dealing, hoping to create with his overthrow the perception of a significant victory in Washington's other unwinnable regional conflict: the war on drugs.

Panama in the meantime, far from being liberated, has merely been returned to the *status quo ante* of the pre-Torrijos days. The red-and-white national license plate logo tacked on every motor vehicle that reads 'Panama 2000 – Total Sovereignty' will now loom in front of the eyes of Panamanians as a mocking, constant reminder that Panama once again exists only as an unfulfilled promise, not as a nation.

Village Voice
9 January 1990

5

SORROWFUL SEPTEMBER

SANTIAGO, CHILE: SEPTEMBER 1990. September is always a tough month for Chileans. A month full of painful, divisive anniversaries. This past September of 1990 was among the worst. It marked the twentieth anniversary of the election of the world's only democratic Marxist president, Salvador Allende. The seventeenth anniversary of his death when the air force bombed the National Palace and the army seized power. Making it also the seventeenth anniversary of the 'liberation' of Chile by General Augusto Pinochet – backed by Henry Kissinger and Richard Nixon. It was also the 180th time Chile has celebrated its national independence. And therefore, time for one more Prussian-style, full-dress military parade – this September for the first time under democratic rule in seventeen years.

September has been thirty agitated days of ceremony and counterceremony, of demonstrations and counterdemonstrations, of digging up President Allende's unmarked grave and reburying him in a glorious monument, of unearthing mass graves and searching for new ones, of – in some cases – venerating the dead and – in others – of applauding their executioners, of offering support for the new civilian government or in lamenting the deposed dictatorship.

I share in these anniversaries. Exactly seventeen years ago I saw my office in the National Palace, where I worked as a presidential translator, blown apart by rockets fired from Hawker Hunter jets. Refused protection by my own American Consulate, forced into hiding, and assisted by Mexican diplomats, I was able to leave Chile a week later under UN protection. A few of my friends' faces were lost to me forever, reappearing only as celluloid ghosts nearly a decade later in a Costa-Gavras film called *Missing*.

But no one can have more sorrowful September memories than 41-year-old Alejandro 'The Redhead' Bustos. Because it was in the predawn of 17 September

1973 that Bustos was executed by firing squad.

Three days after the military coup, Bustos was told, along with four other members of his farming co-operative, to present himself that afternoon at the local police station. When he walked into the small, rural post he immediately recognized not only a number of town policemen he had known for years, but also a handful of some of the most powerful local landlords and businessmen standing by their side. 'The other four people who had been called in were already in the cell, beaten and bloody', Bustos retells his story to me in his sparse, cement-floored living room in the agricultural town of Paine, on the southern outskirts of Santiago. His tale unfolds, give or take a detail, just like that of thousands of other horror stories in Chile, dozens of which I have recorded over the years as a reporter, always from the mouths of relatives or eyewitnesses. But never before from the survivor of one's own murder. 'They started questioning me right away. José Retamal, a cop I had known for years, wanted to know where we had hid the guns he knew we had. I told him the truth. We had no guns.'

Bustos was then stripped, had his hands tied with wire behind his back, and twice beaten unconscious. When he awoke he was questioned again. 'Then they told us we'd never get the hell out of there and before I could answer I was smashed in the face with a rifle butt and passed out again.' At 4 a.m. Bustos and his comrades were rustled from the wet floor of their jail cell, and thrown into the back of a pickup truck – part of a mongrel caravan of police vehicles and private cars driven by the landlords. The five prisoners were taken to a river bank and lined up. 'I realized what was about to happen and I gave my soul over to the Virgin. "Put your hands up!" yelled Sergeant Reyes. Before we even got them up they blasted us with machine guns. I fell to the ground; Ramirez fell on top of me and bled all over my face.' Two police and two of the civilian businessmen came over to the clump of bodies. 'They must have seen the blood all over my face. Reyes said, "This asshole's had for. We blew open his head." They grabbed my feet and arms and threw me into the canal but I clung to the weeds on the bank. While I pretended to be dead they went over to finish off the others. They smashed their faces in with rifle butts and cut their throats with bayonets. Ramirez was screaming so they cut out his tongue and eyes.' Bustos, with three bullets in his shoulder, eventually crawled to safety. 'The only thing that kept me going was desire for revenge.'

The other four less-fortunate victims are merely statistics among as many as 5,000 others who were summarily executed or 'detained and disappeared' during military rule. An estimated 100 of them were from Paine alone – an astonishing number of casualties for a town of barely 20,000 people.

Just a short walk from Bustos's house is 24th of April Street, a 200-yard stretch of dirt lined with brick and tin shacks. On 16 October 1973, exactly one

CHILEAN AIR FORCE CADETS PARADE
IN FRONT OF GENERAL AUGUSTO PINOCHET

month after Bustos's brush with eternity, 24th of April Street was blocked off
and surrounded at three in the morning by troops, police and armed civilian
death squads. Among the twenty-four families that lived on the street, thirteen
heads of households were carted away. Their crime: living on land that had been
expropriated, legally, during the agrarian reform of the previous decade. The
police provide no record of their arrest. No court registers any trial. Seventeen
years later no bodies have yet been found. The locals now have a different name
for 24th of April Street: the Street of the Widows.

   And though General Augusto Pinochet's dictatorship failed to win renewal
in a 1988 plebescite, though the midnight murders and kidnappings are all in the
past, though freely elected president Patricio Aylwin inaugurated constitutional
civilian rule and a 'transition to democracy' six months ago, and though a new
government panel promises to clear up once and for all the truth about human
rights violations in Chile, the widows of Paine still live in indignation and fear.
Not only has their miserable economic condition remained unchanged, but the
men who took their husbands away – some of the same men who shot 'Red-

head' Bustos – remain unpunished. Now, and most likely forever. Some of the police are still on active duty. Others live gracefully on pensions. The civilian death squad members are still the richest and most powerful men in town. And everyone I speak to in Paine knows their names. Knows what they did. But can do nothing about it. Sonia Valenzuela, one of the widows, says, 'They still threaten us. They drive by in trucks at night and yell that we will die like dogs.' 'Redhead' Bustos says coolly, 'There will be no justice here except for my revenge. One way or another, the moment will come. I'm just waiting for my kids to get old enough so they no longer need a father. Because here there will be no justice. There will only be impunity.'

Impunity, indeed. And Paine is only a microcosm of the nation around it. Like 'Redhead' Bustos, Chile has miraculously survived its own massacre. But now it must live out its days watching its executioners not only free, but often flourishing. Chile is no longer a dictatorship. But neither is it a democracy. Civilians are in office. But the military still holds power – at least a good chunk of it. General Pinochet himself still commands the Chilean army. This incomplete transition is the political price paid for initiating any sort of exit at all from military rule.

In the mid eighties the political left in this country (which under Allende's government had topped out at 50 percent of the electorate) joined by factions of more moderate groupings, attempted to fashion a wave of street protests into an organized campaign of civil disobedience. The most militant sectors of the opposition pushed for a 'popular rebellion' and low-level guerrilla war flickered. But by 1987, this strategy of 'rupture' had failed. Leadership of the antimilitary political forces was de facto ceded to the center-right Christian Democrats (about a third of the electorate) who had initially supported Pinochet's coup but had since moved into opposition.

Confrontation with the military was replaced with negotiation. The civilian opposition, almost in its totality, agreed to participate in the 1988 plebescite that would either extend Pinochet's rule for eight more years or open the way to elections and civilian rule. Pinochet miscalculated and lost the vote. But by then his civilian adversaries had accepted the restrictive constitutional framework imposed by Pinochet in a fraudulent referendum ten years before.

Today, the civilian government is a coalition led by the Christian Democrats that includes members of former President Allende's Socialist Party. But after submitting themselves to a process of 'renovation', the Socialists, and the bulk of the Chilean left, have renounced not only Marxism and democratic socialism, but seemingly *any* long- or short-term alternative to the free market status quo. Moreover, the constitutional framework of the government is that written by the military regime:

- Military commanders, including Pinochet, cannot be changed or removed by the civilian government until 1997. Military budgets are guaranteed independent of congressional appropriation.
- The 1978 Amnesty Law exempts all military and police from prosecution for human rights violations.
- The separate CNI secret police – notorious for torture and cold-blooded murder – were allowed to be 'absorbed' back into the army, taking their files and dossiers with them.
- A judicial system, led by a Supreme Court that congratulated the dictator after he had abolished the rule of law, remains intact.
- 20 percent of the new Senate was appointed by Pinochet, giving the political right veto power in the legislature.
- 95 percent of the country's mayors are Pinochet appointees.

Worse, there is a growing notion that not only are the government's hands tied, but that it just might enjoy the bondage. 'Pinochet is a convenient bogeyman to keep around', says one political scientist recently returned from fifteen years in exile. 'As long as he's around, all the country's problems can be blamed on him. Also, the specter of a military threat is an excuse for the Christian Democrats to maintain as conservative a government as they can. They have no intention of making any real changes in Pinochet's economic model and they are just delighted to keep the left and the masses on a short leash.'

The government's caution during its first half-year in power, its cordiality with the murderous military machine, its 'excessive realism', as one political columnist called it, does seem out of sync with popular sentiment. A recent survey by a conservative polling outfit revealed that 69 percent of all Chileans want Pinochet to resign immediately. When, twice this month, Pinochet was called to the National Palace for a meeting with the president, thousands spontaneously gathered outside. Held back by police barricades, they chanted:

> Pinochet, take a flying jump,
> Pinochet, you mother's cunt!
> Pinochet, go out for a pass,
> Pinochet, fuck you in the ass!
> Pinochet, and that's not all:
> Pinochet, go cut off your balls!

Yet, when the general this past month offered the new government a tailor-made chance to dump him, in accord with his own military constitution, the

Aylwin administration balked. Speaking to the Santiago Rotary Club and responding to rumors that the Chilean armed forces might have to undergo a democratization like that of the Wehrmacht after the defeat of Hitler, Pinochet branded the current German army as full of 'homosexuals, drug addicts, pot-smokers, longhairs and trade-unionists'. Further, in expressing nostalgia for the German army as it was before May 1945, Pinochet touched off an international incident of considerable proportion.

The German Chief of Staff retorted that 'an oak tree doesn't bend just because some pig rubs its rear end up against it.' The Aylwin government's response was more measured. After a bit of public harrumphing, the matter was dropped. Aylwin eschewed a constitutional provision that allows impeachment of Pinochet – the *only* way of removing him – for interfering with affairs of state. When one congressman of the Christian Left proposed initiating impeachment measures against the former dictator, he couldn't get the minimum ten signatures required, even though the supposedly anti-Pinochet forces hold some seventy seats in the lower house of Congress. Two weeks ago, while visiting Ecuador, President Aylwin seemed to have come full circle from his campaign promises to squeeze out General Pinochet. When asked by a reporter if he thought it was 'an error' to allow the general to stay on as army chief, Aylwin responded: 'I disagree.'

Ruby Weitzel, a diminutive, bespectacled, middle-aged Chilean journalist, sits in a small room inside the high-ceilinged offices of the Roman Catholic Vicariate of Solidarity – the Church human rights office. In a small spiral notebook, the type used by a schoolchild, she keeps a hand-written account of the mass graves that have been unearthed in the past three months. Since June, when twenty-one bodies were pulled out of the desert earth at the site of the Pisagua concentration camp, Chilean TV viewers have been jolted by almost weekly images of Pinochet's gruesome legacy being exhumed in one site or another.

Ruby reads me the list: twenty-one bodies in Pisagua; three in Colina; eighteen executed peasants found in Valdivia; four Communist leaders dug up in Concepcíon; thirteen maimed and incinerated remains in Copiapo; one body so far in a silver mine in Tocopilla; a teacher's cadaver in Coronel; three farmers in Talca; and, of course, in Paine, five bodies so far plus fourteen sacks of remains, thought to be from Paine, just discovered in the State Morgue, though they had been there since 1974.

Throughout the country excavations continue. A National Commission of Truth and Reconciliation, appointed by the president, has taken human rights testimony from some 4,000 Chileans. Several special magistrates have opened up judicial investigations around the mass grave sites. 'For the last sixteen years nothing was done for us', says Ruby, whose brother was disappeared in December 1973. 'So now we are beginning this process. But so what? So what? It will change nothing. The murderers won't even as much as be questioned.'

Ruby's pessimism is well-founded. The Truth Commission's mandate is only to turn over a complete report to the president, who may or may not make all of it public. The judges conducting the investigations know that any arrests they order will be overturned by the Supreme Court. In any case, standing in the way of prosecution is the Amnesty Law – or the 'Amnesia Law', as Ruby calls it. Meanwhile, the army defends its murders of civilians by claiming that they were 'wartime actions'. And Pinochet has stated publicly that 'if as much as one of my men are touched, that will be the end of the rule of law.'

So why continue the investigations, I ask.

'Because we need to at least know *how* our people died, *who* killed them, *where* and *when*', Ruby answers. 'We also want to clear the names of our loved ones so that history will not record them as the "terrorists" and "subversives" that the army said they were.'

Psychologist David Becker, a specialist in dealing with human rights victims, adds, 'With luck a lot or most of the truth about what happened will come out. Justice, as we know it, will be limited. And the failure to achieve justice can lead to other things: like violent retribution. But what we have to work for is the type of justice where at least we can clarify who is guilty and make them, and the whole of society, accept its responsibilities. This society cannot live forever not knowing where its dead are buried and who killed them. Only after that can there be forgiveness.'

But it's still an open question as to just how willing those who have suffered will be to forgive under the current circumstances. Activists like Ruby, grouped together in the Association of Families of the Disappeared (AFDD), argue that the government's human rights formula of 'Truth and Reconciliation' should be replaced by a call for 'Truth and *Justice*'. Or, as Catholic Bishop Carlos Camus says, 'Reconciliation based on erasing the past, without investigating the facts, is like putting a coat of paint over a rotten floorboard. It hides the problem for now, but later is destined to cave in. There can be no peace without a minimum of truth – and justice.'

The day after I meet Ruby is 11 September. The seventeenth anniversary of the military coup. Still a national holiday, though the new civilian government could have decreed otherwise. At noon, about 1,500 people, led by the Families of the Disappeared, gather in a downtown church to hold a memorial mass for their relatives. A visiting Mexican bishop conducts the liturgy. The crowd sings a mournful Uruguayan ballad as family members stage a procession through the church carrying picket-sign picture-posters of their disappeared loved ones.

Tears flow freely. And I'm reminded of psychologist Becker's observation that 'people often talk about the horrors that *happened*. But for the family victims these are events that are still continuing.' For five minutes the martyrs' names are yelled out by the relatives.

The mourners file into the street. And armed with a legal parade permit, something unthinkable during the dictatorship, they begin a two-hour march to the municipal cemetery. Chants of 'No to amnesty! No to impunity! The blood of the dead cannot be negotiated!' reverberate off the walls of the downtown buildings. Out of apartment house windows a few people applaud the march. Others watch in silence. As we pass a police station the chant becomes 'We won't forget or forgive! Death to Pinochet!'

By the time we reach the cemetery, the crowd has swelled to more than 10,000. To my side I see the disfigured face of Carmen Gloria Quintana, a youth activist set on fire by army troops in a highly publicized incident in 1986. A brief rally is held at Allende's tomb. Then we move toward the other side of the cemetery, toward Patio 29, where hundreds of identical black crosses, marking the graves of bodies buried by military authorities, are inscribed only with 'N.N.' – No Name.

From behind a wall of niches, like a noxious green cloud, dozens of helmeted national riot police suddenly materialize. Tear gas launchers and machine guns point stiffly toward us. A few leaders of the march go to talk to the police commanders, pleading with them to withdraw their men, reminding them that this demonstration is not only peaceful, but fully authorized by the civilian authorities. The police give their answer. Without warning, the first stomach-wrenching pops go off and the clouds of gas sprout at our feet. Chaotic scuffles break out, mourners and cops go hand-to-hand, heads are cracked, shots ring out. The sorry tableaux of repression of the last sixteen years is replayed once again as the police beat and scatter the marchers.

That night's TV news reports more than fifty arrests at the cemetery, dozens of injured, and two people wounded by police gunfire. It also reports that police broke up another authorized demonstration during the day. A group of about forty women, including a number of prominent widows, planned to release a volley of black balloons in front of the National Palace. Before they could assemble they were dragged into waiting police vans.

The next news report tells of yet a third demonstration. A march of about 100 young men, the camera showing them armed with clubs, sticks, chains and flags emblazoned with the symbol of the right-wing UDI party, fascist emblems and Chilean swastikas. After an intimidating sweep through the center of Santiago chanting 'Viva Pinochet!', the youth squads marched right past the heavily guarded provincial government offices and then staged a rally in front of the

Ministry of Defense's 'eternal flame' punctuated with raised-arm fascist salutes. Not only were the fascists illegally armed, but their demonstration was unauthorized. But the same police who had just dragged the widows away stood idly by. The civilian governor of Santiago said he would 'ask the police to investigate the accusations of a double standard.' A Chilean teacher who was watching the news with me cursed him: 'Fucker! Nothing has changed in this country. Nothing.'

Americans often assume, out of their own smugness and ignorance, that this sort of neo-Nazi outburst, that the military dictatorships and authoritarian movements that plague Latin America are a natural product of either tropical climates or poorly educated masses or a combination of both. But the young fascists who marched through downtown don't emerge from the muddy, pneumonia-plagued barrios that ring Santiago, but rather from that small sector of Chilean society that most closely resembles Beverly Hills. They come from the blessed neighborhoods of Providencia, Las Condes and La Dehesa, from seignorial homes with two or three maids living in and Mercedes and BMWs parked outside. They are educated in the finest private schools like the Saint George College, or, of course, The American School. They are the same people who like to live like Americans – at least like the Americans they see on cable TV.

So while their pretensions are those of the Rothschilds, their cultural sensibilities are those of Archie Bunker. They love neon-framed Oakley sunglasses, they think that bowling is an elite sport, they believe that a drive-in movie is the pinnacle of chic (easy to understand in a country where a car costs ten years' worth of minimum wages) and are proud that Chile's first McDonald's will open next month not in some prole hellhole, but rather will crown the most chi-chi intersection in town.

They also *look* like Americans – at least a lot more like Americans than the other 90 percent of Chile does. They are taller, fairer, healthier than the *indiocitos,* the little Indians, who live on the wrong side of the Burger Inn. Perhaps the one characteristic, however, that most distinguishes these Chileans from the average American, is that they have a *whole* lot more class-consciousness. And no guilt about it whatsoever.

On the morning of 11 September, before the downtown march, they stood vigil, thousands of them, in front of their neighbor General Pinochet's mansion. In antelope suede blazers, in full-length leather overcoats, in all-linen pants, in tweed and wool trousers and dresses, wearing cable-knit sweaters, and holding Chanel umbrellas, the wealthiest, whitest, best-educated Chileans jumped up and down, as if in some mad ritual to exorcise all challenges to their privilege, and tirelessly chanted, 'Pin-o-chet! Pin-o-chet! Pin-o-chet!' They cheered as their overgrown children harassed and pummeled any foreign TV crew stupid enough to have shown up (the logic here is that Pinochet's bloody image is the sole product of a worldwide media conspiracy).

Here, there are none of the charades of First World politics. No grandiloquent pronunciations about democracy. No pompous rhetoric about equality. No silly rationales, like justifying a vote for George Bush because he is 'kinder and gentler'. Just pure gratitude to the dictator who didn't flinch in using any means necessary to uphold and re-enforce an unequal system that benefits them. As a writer friend of mine said as we observed the histrionics in front of Pinochet's house, 'They might as well be chanting, "Thank you. Thank you. Thank you for defending our class interests!"'

It's an attitude I come face to face with over dinner that night in a home not far from Pinochet's. Leon, a 65-year-old German Jewish refugee, has been living in Chile since 1937. He is a book distributor. Not at all wealthy. But much more comfortable than the bottom two-thirds of Chilean society. 'The military were our saviors', he tells me. 'There was nothing but economic chaos under Allende. I lived through the Nazis once. To me Allende was a Nazi in a red shirt.'

It's no use my arguing with him that the Allende government, while socialist, was also elected, constitutional, fully democratic, and caused no one to be murdered, tortured or disappeared. Leon listens, and then always shifts the discussion back to economics.

'You don't know what it was like here [under Allende]. Shortages, inflation, you had to stand in line after line', he answers.

I tell him I do know. That I also lived here then. And that, yes, there were great economic problems – in great part because the people in this very same neighborhood took to black marketeering – but how could he, as a survivor of the Nazis, defend the dictatorship, the murders, the mass graves filled with simple peasants?

'They were peasants, yes. But they were Allende supporters. Communists. It was a confrontational situation. Either you or them. You can't justify torture, and there was torture; you can't justify murder, and there was murder. But today we have a decent country. Since the military made the reforms they did in our economy, this has become a country to be proud of.'

The military's economic 'reforms' – most often called The Modernization – took the form of radical privatization, lifting all barriers to foreign investment, offering up a repressed, inexpensive work force, and increasing mostly fruit exports to the developed world. It's a policy that has kept inflation down, provided a good deal of low-paid employment (much of it seasonal), and allowed Chile to promptly meet its foreign debt repayment obligations.

'But this modernity', says novelist José Donoso, 'is but an official mask. Modernity is the most annoying new word that has been forced into our vocabulary. The most awful thing that the military has done to Chile is to try to make us competitive, this uncivilized business of being better, of being the best, the most efficient. Such rot! As if we were Singapore. They forget we are still Latin America.'

The market-based economic policies of the dictatorship – accepted almost in full by the Aylwin government – attempt to rollback a hundred years of Latin American political and cultural development. The concept of being a 'citizen' is replaced by that of becoming a 'consumer'. Democracy itself is redefined from that of political participation to insertion into the marketplace. The message is a constant drumbeat: Out of the streets and into your living rooms. Turn the public into the private. Put down the placard and pick up the TV remote control. And these are concepts that Chile's new civilian rulers are more than comfortable with. The Aylwin government has taken pains to establish a 'modern' facade. No more of those messy South American street rallies and marches. Now it's government by back-room deal and announced to the public on television.

The grand Chilean tradition of making history in the streets has a formidable new rival: mass commercial spectacle. An explosion of private schlock TV channels. A rash of video rental stores – the largest chain opening more than three dozen outlets in just two years. Coca-Cola sponsoring David Bowie and Eric Clapton concerts last month. And Pepsi underwriting this week's Amnesty International extravaganza, which will play here much more as a narrow marvel of entertainment than as a significant social statement.

The euphoria that bubbled through Chile two years ago when Pinochet was defeated in the plebescite has turned to quiet resignation, often apathy. 'It's the triumph of modernity', laments Pablo, a 21-year-old student at the Catholic University. 'Of 13,000 students, there are less than 200 political activists, counting all the parties.' A pathetically low figure, considering that under military rule – three or four years ago – thousands of students would come out to confront troops and risk death in the streets. 'It hurts me to say it, but the World Cup soccer matches drew more interest among the students than the revelations of the mass graves. What is undeniable is that Chile has been politically demobilized. What remains to be seen is if it has also been depoliticized.'

But the economic base on which this political recess rests is paper-thin. Examples abound: under the dictatorship several chains of American-style supermarkets blossomed. For the first time Chilean employees appeared in neat, colorful, company uniforms, aprons and caps – a far cry from the disheveled workers you'd find in a Peruvian market. But the boxboys are barely thirteen. They have to buy their outfits. And they get *no* salary. Only tips. With the wave of privatization, private schools were folded into the public education system and given state subsidies greatly expanding the students' 'freedom of choice'. But education in these establishments is substandard. Teachers take home less than $20 a week – half the amount it would cost just to rent a small apartment.

Nikes, Addidas and Reeboks fill the shelves. But with over half the work force making less than $150 a month, a pair of these shoes can be financed over ten months – at 65 percent interest. A full 50 percent of the population lives below the official poverty line. One out of four Chilean families is classified as 'indigent'. Economist Carlos Zambrano says, 'In a neurotic quest to imitate Asia, accumulation and growth in this country have been achieved only by maintaining low salaries – salaries whose buying power has fallen 50 percent in ten years.'

The most astounding fact about Chile today is that in the face of such dire economic figures, there is virtual across-the-board political agreement that the 'economic model' will not be modified. 'The Chilean political class is prone to copy foreign utopias', says University of Chile political analyst Ricardo Israel. 'Nowadays they are copying western free market capitalism. The Chilean left has not just been 'renovated', as it claims. It has been transformed. They are no longer a left alternative *to* the system, they have become the left *of* the system.'

It was twenty years ago that the CIA and State Department were spending millions of dollars to keep the Socialists out of power, and then more millions to bombard them out of office after they got elected. Today, relations between Washington and the government that includes those same Socialists couldn't be warmer. 'But make no mistake', says Israel, 'the US position has changed very little. It's the Chilean socialists who have come to coincide with US policy. The Socialists, like all the other politicians here believe that history has ended in Chile. They are mistaken. Chile, living at the tip of the world, has made Chileans think they are special. We invent collective lies. That we are the Englishmen of Latin America. That we have the best wine in the world. The most beautiful women. Now the new lie is that we have designed the perfect transition to democracy. That's the big lie.'

19 September. The annual Independence Week military parade in O'Higgins Park. Chilean families, enjoying the last of a four-day holiday, have come out in smaller than usual numbers owing partly to a light rain. It's hard to estimate how many because they are retained by barricades and police far from the reviewing stand where the press has gathered.

Sixteen thousand men and women – a full sixth of the Chilean armed forces – are gearing up for the procession. Three battalions of navy infantry. The elite, pale-skinned navy cadets. Two companies of air force officers. Detachments of the militarized national police. Army antiaircraft regiments. Battalions of army artillery specialists. Paratroopers. Armored cavalry. Alpine mountain units. The feared Black Beret Special Forces. Squadrons of T-35 and A-37 combat aircraft, which will overfly the parade grounds. Just before three o'clock, the military commanders, including Pinochet, arrive and take their place at the official reviewing stand. The galleries behind them – holding 5,000 relatives of the military and invited guests – break out into applause.

A few minutes later, President Aylwin and then his cabinet ministers arrive in separate cars. Each one is received with boos, whistles and jeers. In their down-quilt coats and Miami Dolphins windbreakers, the children and wives of the generals hoot and howl and pump their downturned thumbs up and down. Aylwin and his entourage are, after all, civilians. Shouts of 'Pin-o-chet! Pin-o-chet! Pin-o-chet!' begin to swell. A few valiant souls respond with 'Ayl-win! Ayl-win' but are quickly drowned out.

Silence comes as the jeep carrying General Carlos Parera, former director of the overseas division of the secret police, current commander of the Santiago garrison, pulls up in front of the reviewing stand that Pinochet and Aylwin share. The general breaks decades of tradition and does not ask the president for permission to begin the parade. Instead he gives a silent nod to his superior commander, Pinochet. Pinochet, the man who ordered jets to bomb the government palace, to set it on fire and consume the elected president and the constitution. Pinochet, the man who padlocked Congress, outlawed politics, penned up unionists and housewives in his concentration camps, and sent his troops and agents to kick in the doors of thousands of his countrymen. Pinochet, whose minions blew up his exiled predecessor in Buenos Aires, whose operatives murdered Orlando Letelier in the broad daylight of DuPont Circle. Pinochet, who oversaw the summary execution of hundreds, maybe thousands, of civilians. Pinochet, who hid their lime-doused cadavers in the northern deserts and southern forests. Pinochet, who passed as many as 200,000 Chileans through his jails in sixteen years – Captain General Augusto Pinochet, former president of the Governing Junta, former president of the Republic of Chile, commander-in-chief of the Chilean army, stood erect, and smiling, flashed a salute back to General Parera. Strutting its Prussian heritage, the army band struck up the traditional 'Radetzki March', and with glockenspiels triumphantly chiming out the beat the first detachments of army troops goose-stepped by, their faces turned sternly upward and to the side in deference to their commander. The official galleries erupted in ecstatic ovation. For the first time in seventeen years, Chile's military was beginning its annual parade under democratic rule.

Village Voice
16 October 1990

6

LAST CHA-CHA-CHA IN MANAGUA

MANAGUA: FEBRUARY 1990. It's 3:45 a.m., ten hours after the polls have closed in Nicaragua's national elections, and the Sandinistas' favorite balladeer – Luis Enrique Mejia Godoy – is trying to make the best of it. On a brightly pastel-lit stage set up in the middle of the 19 July Plaza, Godoy's group is belting out a slinky cha-cha-cha, but only a handful of couples are going through the motions of dancing. The other 400 or so gathered in this dark Managua morning are all but shell-shocked. They sit or stand almost motionless, staring out – many of them through tears – at an uncertain future that has just up and hit them much as would a rotten mango suddenly ripping from its branch.

After ten years in power, after surviving the last days of Jimmy Carter, outmaneuvering two entire Reagan administrations replete with mined harbors and CIA assassination manuals, withstanding covert and overt attacks, militarily defeating a contra army buoyed with a half-billion US tax dollars, confronting a political opposition directly financed by the United States and a paralyzing economic and trade embargo, these mostly young revolutionaries have just seen their Sandinista government get voted out of office in balloting they were sure they would win.

So sure, that the platform and massive sound system that is carrying Godoy's performance was set up before the polls closed in anticipation of an all-night victory celebration that was to draw out maybe 200,000 revelers. But the depressed clumps of Sandinistas that are barely breathing in the square are testament to a celebration party that never really happened. Moreover, to an entire revolution that was never *allowed* to happen.

From even before they formally took power in the 1979 insurrection against the Somoza family dictatorship, the Sandinistas became the target of an often fanatical hatred on the part of succeeding American administrations. And what's hurting these kids in the plaza the most tonight is the knowledge that they not only lost the election to the opposition UNO alliance and to the former Somoza collaborators and contras that people its leadership, but also that they have seen as many as 50,000 of their own generation die in the contra war only to wind up directly losing to President George Bush. It burns in their guts, the same way it will in those of many Americans later this week when they'll see Dan Quayle hailing the Winds of Freedom sweeping through Central America.

Indeed, the headlines being printed at this hour say that the rather dull matron of the Nicaraguan Right – Doña Violeta Chamorro – has emerged as the winner in the Nicaraguan vote. But the world knows the ultimate victor is Washington. And the lessons of this campaign will not be lost on other Latin Americans pondering an escape route from misery and underdevelopment. Simply, if that route requires breaking out of the American orbit, then we'll mine you, bomb you or invade you until Congress gets queasy. Then we'll just choke you out, embargo and blockade you, wreck your economy, set off an inflation rate of 30,000 percent, put 20 percent of the population out of work, make sure that the schools, clinics and roads you fought for can never be built, and then, when domestic discontent begins to simmer, we'll unload truckloads of dollars at the door of your political opposition. This was US policy in Nicaragua. And tonight it proved a winning policy.

Less than two miles from the grim scene at the plaza, the beneficiaries of that policy, Chamorro's UNO coalition, are blowing the corrugated roof of their Bambana restaurant. Shouts of 'Tomorrow Havana! Tomorrow Havana!' ring out from the crowd so tediously and dreadfully reminiscent of the blood-oath rallies of Salvadoran Major Roberto D'Aubuisson's ARENA party. Having economically and socially presided over Nicaragua for decades, no … centuries … till the Sandinistas came to power in 1979, these people think it only *natural* they should rule once again. Just as natural as having their campaign openly financed with US$10 million. Just as naturally as they now expect to have the US trade embargo replaced with a Panama-style billion-dollar bail-out as soon as they take office on 25 April. And the US money, denied for a decade to the Sandinistas, that would have been used to open the promised schools and hospitals, will now be available 'for the creation of a full market economy' as one top UNO official vowed.

Unlike in the neighboring 'emerging democracies' of El Salvador so admired by UNO and where voting takes place in the shadow of thousands of government troops, cops and death squads, Nicaraguans voted in this election with literally *no* military or police presence in the streets. This was, however, the mostly closely scrutinized election campaign in hemispheric history. In this tiny country of less than 4 million souls, more than 5,000 official and self appointed

DANIEL ORTEGA TRIES TO RALLY SANDINISTA SUPPORTERS
IN THE WEEK FOLLOWING HIS FAILED RE-ELECTION ATTEMPT

'election observers' and journalists poured in over the last week.

The city was awash in a sea of specially marked speeding vans, rented cars, Land Cruisers and tourist buses packed with the mongrel foreigners, observers, election experts and political groupies of every persuasion. As an unmistakable warning to a small nation like Nicaragua that it exists only at the pleasure of much more powerful global forces, anyone and everyone who has ever had as little as a passing thought on Central America showed up to contribute whatever special talent they thought they had to the final dramatic battle that would de- fine the future of US–Nicaraguan relations: American academics with their lat- est books under their arms; former and present advisers to the contras in their Miami-bought Ray-Bans; Jimmy Cliff and Jackson Browne, who have performed at the Sandinista rallies; Bianca Jagger with a camera crew of unknown origin in tow; Ed Asner, who one of the morning papers identified as Lou Grant; Euro- pean and gringo 'Sandalistas' holding press passes from magazines no one has ever heard of; globs of American congressmen hungering to take credit for per- sonally overthrowing World Communism; a half-dozen or so former Latin American presidents; enough priests, missionaries and church-workers to start a whole new Reformation; Salvadoran and French representatives of the Socialist International; packs of pallid gringo bureaucrats here to nurse along and handle the opposition candidates; something called the International Democrat Union that brings together US Republicans and Guatemalan goon squads all claiming to be 'impartial' observers; Japanese members of Parliament; Scottish Tories; the mayor of Berkeley, California; human rights commissioners from San Francisco; pollsters and survey takers who conducted thirty-one national samples in the past months; something called the Commission on Nicaraguan Pre-Election Polls, which has been monitoring the opinion monitors; Vietnam Veterans for Peace in neon pink T-shirts; and even the ubiquitous P. J. O'Rourke from *Rolling Stone* (who began writing the same piece he always does as soon as he hit the Sandino airport and, after less than two minutes of baggage delay, was heard to mutter loudly, 'Typical Communist luggage service'). In short, the Nicaraguans are lucky that the American Medical Association had never taken a position on Central America lest the Union of Democratic Proctologists had sent a delega- tion of Asshole Inspectors down here.

Going into the vote, nearly every major independent opinion poll showed the Sandinistas maintaining a huge popular advantage over UNO. And they tended to show that a majority of the Nicaraguan people identified the Sandin- istas as a sincere patriotic force, pitted against an opposition that represented the political, military and economic interests of the United States. On the eve of the vote, Sandinista militants were confident that, for perhaps the first time in his- tory, an incumbent government would be reelected even while running on a record of astronomical inflation, a full-scale economic recession and a decade-long war because the Nicaraguan people had correctly perceived the US and its allies, not the government, as the source of its misery. 'UNO's ties to the contras, the bald-faced US funding of UNO, and the reemergence of Somoza-era politicking was the perfect formula for lighting a fire under the ass of every disgruntled, disillusioned, jaded, burned-out one-time supporter of the Sandinistas', said one Sandinista journalist two days before the vote. 'All of a sudden we were offered the golden opportunity of hitting the streets once again in the campaign and taking on directly the US and the contras! It's a hell of a lot more fun and a much more satisfying challenge than standing in line for three hours in the sun waiting for a liter of cooking oil.'

So what went wrong? Ironically, the man responsible for conducting the one opinion poll most frequently cited during the campaign as evidence of an impending Sandinista victory had been warning all who would listen that his own survey – and others like it – was flawed. Thirty-seven-year-old social psychologist Marvin Saballos runs the Nicaraguan company that was contracted by the politically conservative US-based Univision Spanish-language TV network to conduct a nationwide voter survey in the last phase of the campaign. Its major findings: Sandinista President Daniel Ortega was favored 53 percent to 35 percent over UNO's Chamorro; 54 percent believed that Chamorro was too close to the United States and 45 percent branded her an outright 'US puppet'.

'There were a whole series of technical as well as political factors that made all polls unreliable', Saballos explained as he watched the UNO celebration from a corner in its campaign headquarters. 'With the extreme polarization that characterized the country, I supposed people would tend to give answers that were related to who they thought was asking the questions. This polarization, marked partisanship, and overall lack of experience in participating in polls, made it impossible for many if not most Nicaraguans to believe the survey taker was really an independent agent and not fronting for one or another political group.

'I think we can see tonight that the determining factors in the Sandinista defeat *were* the economy, the war, and the political attrition suffered by the Sandinistas after ten years in power. Our research shows that what put UNO over the top was what we call a "punishment vote" – much more antigovernment than consciously pro-UNO. I don't think it is at all clear if the population fully understands the consequences, the changes in their lives that might be brought about by the change in government, because it approached this election in a much more emotional rather than programmatic way.

'This campaign began last year with a huge block of undecided voters. But they progressively moved toward UNO because of three issues. First, the Sandinistas called off the truce in the contra war. Even though the contras themselves lack much popularity, the thought of more war was even less attractive. Second and third were the US invasion of Panama and the subsequent government call up of reserve forces. On the one hand, the US takeover of Panama stirred nationalist sentiment and favored the Sandinistas. But on the other hand, it revived the specter of yet another long military conflict – this time directly with the US – a fear that was heightened when Ortega mobilized the reserves. The whole Panama episode generated great anxiety that was identified in the public mind with the Sandinistas.

'The Sandinistas had a good chance of having won the election if all of the corrective steps they took near the end of the campaign had been taken earlier. The amnesty, the suspension of the draft, the other measures that reduced the tension of the war, the palliative economic measures and so, all came too late. Just too late.'

It's now dawn on the Monday morning after. The national election council has just announced that with half the votes counted, UNO leads the Sandinistas 54 percent to 41 percent. Chamorro claimed victory several hours ago. The government camp is all silence. In the Olaf Palme Convention Center, a thousand reporters (many of them locally based freelancers supportive of President Ortega) looking drawn and exhausted in the first morning light lounge in the cavernous Plenary Room. Daniel Ortega is due to speak and a rumor sweeps the room that he won't concede, that instead will reveal how UNO has 'manipulated' the vote count. Then at 6:20 a.m., Ortega and some three dozen top leaders of the Sandinistas – a few in guerrilla uniform others with red and black kerchiefs around their necks – boldly stride to the podium. Their jaunt, their defiant manner, their fists held high in the air electrify the assembled press and government supporters, who spring to their feet and greet the Sandinistas with a thunderous, three-minute standing ovation. Ortega and entourage receive the applause grinning and waving high their arms. They look nothing like losers. Ortega's tone is firm. But a minute into his forty-minute talk, it's evident that this will be like no other speech he has ever given. 'We Sandinistas have learned to steel ourselves in the moments of greatest adversity. ...' This is unmistakably to be a concession speech; but one that will make no concessions. 'As a candidate I was sure, I was convinced. But as a Sandinista leader I was not just defending my candidacy, but also our stated political project: political pluralism, a mixed economy, our national independence and sovereignty, Nicaragua's right to live in peace and with dignity. We have never clung to power. We were born poor and will be satisfied to die poor. Our strength was spent in this contest in a challenge to find the creativity and imagination needed to better the lives of our people.'

This man is no Dan Quayle. And the press knows it. Even some of those who have been tough on Ortega in print. Not a few reporters are by now openly sobbing. Not, as some hack like O'Rourke will write, because they are blinded by ideological loyalty to the Sandinistas. But because they so infrequently are able to cover a politician who transmits the sort of principled and deep-seated integrity undeniably present in this chamber, this morning. Or at the very least, in sharing what must be Ortega's frustration in never having been able to placate the irrational fears of Washington.

Ortega pauses. The man so often described as 'wooden' is now fighting for self-composure. 'A few minutes ago we looked at the vote tallies', he continues, 'and the numbers and percentages mark a clear tendency ... a tendency that, barring some mathematic miracle, isn't going to change.' A gasp, and the odd whooshing sound of hundreds of reporters scratching this concession of defeat into their notebooks all at the same time. 'In this historic moment, I can say this is the victory of which I am most proud as president and as a Sandinista. The victory of having opened up today a new path, a path of a democratic Nicaragua, a Nicaragua without any more war, without any more contras, and we must be proud that in having turned this dream into reality, we did so peacefully, civilly, and we are proud that all of us are ready to accept and abide absolutely by the popular will expressed in today's voting results.'

Ortega again thrusts his hands high, his fingers outstretched in a victory salute, a broad smile on his face while the bars of the Sandinista Hymn fill the room and hundreds, thousands of camera flashes blaze his face. The song ends. Ortega and his comrades give one more waving salute and turn to walk off-stage. A barrage of 'Viva el Frente Sandinista! and Patria Libre o Morir! is launched from different pockets in the audience. The slogans ricochet once off the conference room walls and die. And then it is all over.

Village Voice
6 March 1990

7

FORGET IT, JAKE.
IT'S ONLY BAGHDAD.

BAGHDAD: DECEMBER 1990. The first real conversation I had with an Iraqi took place as I was laid out on a gurney, my head hanging down over the back of it, my eyes struggling to focus on the upside-down image of his face. A sudden attack of vertigo had landed me in the Al Yarmook public hospital my first morning in Iraq. And as the doctor summed up his prognosis ('A few hours, maybe a few weeks in bed') he asked me, 'Are you a guest here?'

Oops. There it was. Less than twelve hours in-country and the G-word pops up. I opened my mouth to answer but nothing came out. I mean, *Guest* is a complicated word around here. I *was* a guest in the sense that I was travelling with an invited delegation of religious peace activists, but *not* a Guest, hopefully, in the more permanent sense the Iraqi government had come to use the term these past months: that is, *guest* as in *hostage*. Reading my silent but visible confusion, the doctor rephrased his query: 'I'm asking if you are free to come and go?'

After my affirmative answer I was politely and competently treated (at no charge) and ambulanced back to my lodging at a nearby honeymooners' resort complex – a tacky 'tourist island' full of prefab villas temporarily renamed and retooled as the World Peace and Friendship Camp. I got back just in time to catch dinner while an Arab duo armed with Yamaha keyboards and electronic drums banged out 'Lambada' and 'Feelings' to a cafeteria full of rather bewildered international clergy and 'peace workers' – the most prominent of whom, Muhammad Ali, was entertaining his table with card tricks.

This odd entrance into Baghdad was bizarre but, as it turned out, appropriate. Indeed, to come to Baghdad under any circumstances is to enter what one Palestinian writer calls an 'unreal society'. And under present conditions, doubly unreal. As never before in history have two such massive armies faced off against each other across a few klicks of sand without firing a shot. It took halfway through World War II, eight years into Vietnam – and in both cases, tens of thousands of casualties – to reach such large-scale troop mobilizations on contending sides. And as during that month of September 1938, when all eyes were cast on Munich, once again today the world holds its breath waiting for war, or peace, or neither. As the clock ticks toward George Bush's 15 January deadline, both sides seem to be sleepwalking toward Armageddon.

The dreamlike quality of this journey had actually begun the afternoon before in Jordan's international airport. A messenger from the Iraqi embassy had delivered the Iraqi Airways tickets to the thirteen members of the peace delegation to which I had attached myself – and they were one-way tickets. Worse, we would be coming into Iraq on the very day that the UN Security Council was voting George Bush a green light for war. Our luggage was hand-inspected three times before being checked through. And before entering the Iraqi jet, we found our suitcases piled up on the tarmac in front of conveyor belts emptying into the plane's belly. Each passenger had to individually load his or her suitcase aboard – any unaccompanied luggage left on the ground would be a suspected bomb. And at the door of the aircraft, a final body pat-down before being seated. The hour-long flight from Amman to Baghdad was just short enough not to allow you to unwind from the carousel of security checks and just long enough to let you soberly ponder from where, if anywhere, the internationally embargoed Iraqis might be getting spare maintenance parts for their American-built jetliners.

Upon our arrival at dusk, the Saddam International airport loomed like Jean-Luc Goddard's Alphaville in the desert's dying twilight. The international embargo had left its maze of runways, its immense parking lots, its sprawling passenger terminals almost bare under the surreal orange glow of the sodium lamps. Apart from our planeload, in a scene that would delight Fellini, the only other inhabitants of the modern airport were one roomful of Vietnamese 'guest workers', all dressed in identical green windbreakers, all waiting patiently to leave.

Our delegation, organized by the ecumenical Fellowship of Reconciliation, was bringing in eight tons of donated medicines and infant formula and that's why we were met by a knot of official hosts. These middle-aged men were ostensibly from the Iraqi Organization of Peace, Friendship and Solidarity, but their sharply cut dark suits, their neatly trimmed moustaches, their officious bearing and their reluctance to do much of anything other than efficiently pack us off to quarters at the Peace Camp suggested they might just be on loan from a different, generally less amicable, state agency.

For the next week, these same hosts, who always dined at separate tables from us, who never told us in advance what the next day would bring, led us on a tour of Iraqi society. It was an eccentric excursion marked by both its attempt to strictly control what we would see and its utter failure to do so as gross inefficiency and inexpertise brought the whole experience perilously close to a full-time clown show.

A visit to the imposing Martyrs Monument, two ten-story silver sabers arched over a macabre spill of captured Iranian army helmets, produced a demonstration of 300 ten-year-olds in combat cammies and military formation shouting, in English, 'Saddam Yes! Bush No!' But the event degenerated into wonderful chaos as one American clergyman started handing out Tootsie Rolls, leading the youths to break ranks and switch their chant to 'I love you! I love you!' A foray into the countryside, billed as 'people-to-people contact' turned up less than a dozen peasants, who were far too busy loading this year's 'abundant rice harvest' to strike up any substantial conversation but had found the time to 'spontaneously' prepare a bountiful mid-day banquet for the foreign visitors. A run through the art museum revealed a gallery full of angry paintings of Uncle Sam having his heart torn out and balls cut off. A call on the Iraqi Women's Federation informed us that 'illiteracy has been stamped out' and that 'full equality between men and women has been achieved'. In sum, Saddam Hussein may have built his political career on exterminating Communists, but apparently not without first taking the immersion course in Stalinist PR.

It was hardly necessary, however, for our minders and handlers to choreograph our stay as Iraq unfolds, on the surface at least as a stunningly uniform, seamless society. We had hours of time each day to roam freely through Baghdad, without any accompaniment, and yet it was near impossible to find any significant range of public opinion, God Forbid, any dissidence. Admittedly, my Arabic is at a comparable level to Dan Quayle's grasp of Babylonian society. But in meetings and chats through improvised interpreters as well as in English, no one had an opinion that differed from that of Saddam Hussein, actually Mistersaddamhussein as he is unfailingly referred to.

A 1990 Middle East Watch human rights report concludes that 'Iraq under the Baath party has become a nation of informers. Party members are said to be required to inform on family, friends, and acquaintances, including other party members. . . . Teachers reportedly ask pupils about their parents' views, with the result that parents feel obliged to disguise their thoughts in front of their children.' Public insult of the Iraqi state or of the president can be considered capital crimes.

And as a reminder to those who might forget just who's in charge, Saddam is omnipresent. In fact, Baghdad is one place where you never have to ask the name of any important public building. It's the Saddam Airport. Saddam University. The Saddam Central Teaching Hospital. Nor is it a place where you ever have to ask your way. As long as you go to the nearest Saddam poster and turn left, you're never lost. Saddam photos in every public office, in almost every shop window. Whole stores that sell nothing but varied dozens of framed Saddam photos and paintings. Ten- and twenty-foot-high hand-painted Saddam portraits on nearly every street corner. Saddam in military uniform, in a white linen suit, in desert robes, Saddam commanding troops, reading a book, studying a map, digging a trench, smiling in ski glasses, puffing contentedly on a cigar, lounging bare-chested on a Kurdish rug like a *Playgirl* centerfold, riding a horse with his red-checkered *khafiya* flowing in the wind. Saddam in seemingly every conceivable pose and get-up except maybe a belly-dancing outfit from *A Thousand-and-One Nights*.

Functioning below Saddam's benevolent street-corner gaze is a vibrant 1,200-year-old city of 4 million people whose disposition toward war or peace is anybody's guess. 'People here are hardly free to choose whether or not to fight', said a religious leader of one minority community. 'But it makes no difference, really. Some out of respect, some out of fear, or maybe both, but if called upon to fight, they will.' Yet along the broad modern avenues shaded by palms, cypress and eucalyptus, among the clean, relatively prosperous one and two-story adobe brick and stucco residences that line the Tigris River, around the gargantuan public structures that squat like overblown Palm Springs shopping malls and nearby the wondrous aquamarine-tiled mosques, there is little sign of war preparedness. A few ak-ak batteries near the airport and around Saddam's downtown offices, a good number of unarmed soldiers on temporary leave chowing down on massive fish dinners along Saddoun Street, but nothing you could call a war-footing. Though regional correspondents remind you that during most of the eight-year war with Iran, Baghdad was also able to maintain this tenor of normal urban life.

Saddam's invasion of Kuwait and Bush's political calculations may, indeed, eventually lead to an apocalyptic climax and the pulverization of Baghdad. But for the time being this city is gripped by a consumerist fever. Kuwait, formerly disparaged by its poorer neighbors as the 'world's largest department store', has been stripped bare by Iraqi troops and the booty has flooded the alleys and nooks just off the central Rashid Street *souk*. Gold Parker pens for $25, half-pound solid gold Rolexes with the likeness of the Kuwaiti Emir on the dial for under a grand. Japanese radios, tape-players, CDs and computers trading for bargain-basement prices. Bakeries forced out of the bread business by flour shortages have been reborn as discount electronic goodie shops. Saddam has capitalized on simmering popular resentment of Kuwaiti opulence and has created for the time being a tangible, commercial justification for his invasion beyond the usually cited historical reasons. And not just for the Iraqis. One Italian reporter, who excitedly flashed me her just-bought Omega, complained she was having trouble finding Italian 'hostages' to interview, as they were spending most of their time in the streets buying up Valentino suits.

Though, that really isn't a fair example. The easiest people to talk to in Baghdad were, in fact, the thousands of Western hostages. And some clarification of that term is in order. They are prevented against their will from leaving Iraq. Dozens, maybe hundreds of them, those that the media called 'human shields' are housed in the so-called 'strategic sites'. But they are not hostages in the way the fifty-two Americans were held in Iran a decade ago. They are not accused of being spies, nor of doing anything wrong, nor are they threatened or abused, other than having to, in some cases, share the same impoverished living standard of rural Iraqis. I am not underestimating their suffering or anguish, but trying to accurately portray their condition. As implausible and outrageous as it sounds to our ears, the Iraqis at least half-believe it when they call these detainees 'guests'. The overwhelming majority of hostages, at least in Iraq as opposed to Kuwait, are free to do anything they want, like shop for Valentino suits, as long as they do not leave the country.

Inside the American ambassadors' residence, naturally in one of the most pretentious of Baghdad's neighborhoods, fifteen American civilians have been holed up for weeks, some for months, the night I visit them. Potential fodder not only for a Hussein-Bush bomb-fest, they also served as appetizers for the voracious commercial appetite of the American press. Long before my visit they had decided to forego any new press contacts and refer all reporters to one designated spokesman. But they make an exception for me only in exchange for an ironclad promise I will in no way identify them.

A paperback lending library has blossomed on the ambassador's old credenza. Folded laundry is stacked on the living room floor. Crates of soft drinks and beer are stashed in the corners. Over a delectable dinner of roast chicken, mashed potatoes and gravy, served on the Embassy's gilded china, and fueled by industrial amounts of Heineken, a half-dozen of the hostages speak freely with me for over two hours. And it is a disorienting, frustrating experience, every bit as dizzying as my earlier bout of vertigo. I find myself pinballing among poles of compassion, pity and rage. At one moment, the hostages give me tips on where to go during the day to pick up cheap cameras and rings from the Kuwaiti-supplied black market. A moment later they tell me their fears that some 'raghead' will jump the walls of the compound and bazooka them.

One man expresses anger at the Bush military build-up, saying that 'those 500,000 American troops out there make me feel like shit! They can't do what a few scroungy women can, namely get us the hell out of here.' That being a reference to the success that a delegation of British wives had in securing the release of their husbands.

There is palpable disgust in the room for what they consider high-profile symbols of the peace movement, for Jane Fonda, for Ted Kennedy; even old Jerry Brown is dug up to take a verbal licking. And yet there is authentic gratitude toward the individual peace activists who are accompanying me at dinner and who promise to do what they can to get these Americans back home.

All of the absurd contradictions of US policy toward Iraq over the last decade as well as the quirks and inconsistencies of late-twentieth-century American Ideology are distilled in this one closed dining room and, frankly, chill me. Here is a bunch of guys, mostly construction engineers and technicians, who speak freely of the way the US courted Saddam throughout the eighties. They are infinitely better informed than the American public in general as to how the US has employed a moral double standard with Baghdad, how in 1983 the US favored Iraq with $1 billion in agricultural credits, how Reagan encouraged the French to sell missiles to Saddam and urged the Saudis to finance him, how US satellites provided him military intelligence during the war with Iran, how American lives were endangered when the US sent its navy into the Persian Gulf in 1987 to allow the free flow of Iraqi oil exports, how our government didn't as much as shrug when an Iraqi missile blew away thirty-seven sailors on the USS Stark, how good relations with Iraq continued after Saddam dumped poison gas on the rebellious Kurd minority and how just before the outbreak of the current crisis the very same George Bush vetoed a measure that would have punished Saddam for using farm credits to buy weapons of war.

These same men also admit that working in Iraq as they did, really in any capacity, means working for Saddam Hussein. And they say they did it for adventure, for high salaries, for overseas tax breaks, for the least glorious and most pragmatic of reasons. Fine. And they tell me they love the Iraqi people, as I'm sure they do. And that they know the Iraqi people want peace, as they most probably do. But then they turn around rather glibly and invoke mass death, telling me, 'We have got to stop Saddam. If we don't it will be the mistake of our generation. . . .' 'This situation isn't analogous with the European front during World War II, it's synonymous'. . . . that 'We want out of here but let's get off the dime and finish this job'. . . that 'We who are the dead salute you. Let's just nuke'em and not waste 20,000 of our boys on them'. . . that 'Either this guy gets out of Kuwait or we go for orange skies.' No surprise that people being held captive should wish the worst for their jailers. But what flabbergasted me was that not a single one of these Americans suggested that Baghdad be razed in retribution for their captivity. Rather, these men, all of them able, until last 2 August, to display supreme moral flexibility in working on behalf of what they freely describe as a dictatorship, now cloaked their desire for revenge in the language of principle, as if they had lived the entirety of their lives anxious over the integrity of Kuwait's borders. Just as George Bush threatens war against his former ally in defense of cheap oil – but in the name of international law. Both in Washington and here in the ambassador's dining room, be it the millionaire president or a handful of innocent civilians caught in the web of his policy, there is the same, shared, American arrogance of redefining self-interest as Righteousness. I wait all through dinner for at least one of these hostages to just say 'no'. No, this isn't worth the lives of American soldiers, no, it isn't worth the lives of my Iraqi co-workers, neighbors and children, ultimately, it isn't worth *my* life. But those words never come.

Dinner over, one of the younger Americans offers to drive me back to my lodgings. In a hallucinatory sequence, the Iraqi soldier standing sentinel outside the diplomatic residence moves out of his guard box as we back the Land Cruiser out of the iron-gated driveway, steps into the middle of the street to stop any oncoming traffic, and then snaps a respectful salute to my hostage-driver, who waves back.

I fall asleep that night listening, almost trancelike, to the Voice of America's half-hour 'Radio Postcards' show; thirty-second taped messages from hostage family members back home, a shortwave buffet from suburbia's small world of pecan pies, orthodontists, tales of lonesome pets, trips to Vegas with Uncle Bob, Thanksgiving dinners with missing loved ones and advice that the only salvation is to be found through prayer.

When I get to Naji Al-Hadithi's cavernous eighth floor office atop the Ministry of Information and Culture the next evening, he is loudly clicking a string of reddish amber worry beads. But he's not praying. He's giving stern orders over one of the multicolored telephones that crowd his desk along with a Grundig shortwave. As the nation's Director General of Information, the 45-year-old Al-Hadithi is Iraq's undisputed commander-in-chief in the international propaganda war. He oversees the totality of the country's information apparatus, he personally schedules Saddam Hussein's press contacts, and is one of the president's most loyal and intimate strategists. He has life-and-death control over what access foreign reporters are given inside Iraq, and also serves as editor-in-chief of Iraq's state-run English- and French-language dailies. He is also the most eloquent voice the Iraqis have in speaking to the outside world. Having worked in London as a senior embassy press attaché, he has an up-close understanding of the Western media and masters a disarming, colloquial English.

As we begin our talk, which lasts nearly three hours, a TV monitor to my left broadcasts the evening news: violent images of West Bank Palestinians being noisily beaten. When Al-Hadithi gestures to an aide to turn the volume down, I notice the watch on his left wrist: a one-inch-wide, solid-gold band, the dial adorned with an image of Saddam. His manner is confident, almost buoyant.

If war is to be avoided, I ask, who will give up what? Will the US ever agree to Iraq's demand to link the Palestinian issue to the Gulf crisis? Will Iraq ever withdraw from Kuwait? Before Al-Hadithi can answer he is interrupted by an assistant who bustles into the room to show him a mock-up of the government's latest propaganda poster. Like an inside-the-beltway spin doctor, Al-Hadithi whips out a pencil and forcefully marks up the draft. The heroic Iraqi mother pictured next to Saddam is to have her hairline lowered a fraction of an inch.

'Look, we are not here to be *lectured* to as underdogs and dragged to talks full of preconditions', Al-Hadithi answers. 'Kuwait, maybe is Iraq's land, or maybe it is Arab land. But it is certainly not American land. Both parties must enter talks with good faith. The world events of the last two years tell us that there is no longer any problem that cannot be solved through dialogue and negotiation.'

Then why, I ask, didn't Iraq solve its dispute with Kuwait with words instead of troops?

'We did talk! We talked and talked right up to 2 August. We sent one delegation after another telling the Kuwaitis that what they were doing [with oil and financial policy] was harmful to Iraq. For the last seventy-six years, since Kuwait was carved out of Iraq, we have had no formal borders with it. Only our government offers to finally negotiate a clear demarcation of the borders. But they didn't listen. Instead they were stealing Iraq's oil, they were glutting the oil market, driving down our currency. In May we gave our first warning to the Emir when he was here for a summit. Then in July, Saddam told the Kuwaitis that we will not let our people be starved, that we prefer to cut our own throats before allowing ourselves to be starved.'

On the TV a new program has begun. A middle-aged male singer in a tux and with an ecstatic grin sings praises to Saddam while clapping his hands. His song is inter-cut with clips of a robust Saddam striding into an auditorium while thousands of uniformed schoolgirls shower him with confetti. Meanwhile, I suggest to Al-Hadithi that, possibly, Iraq, by invading Kuwait, has succeeded in cutting its own throat, giving the US and its allies a reason to make war.

'Ridiculous', he snaps back. 'Kuwait in no way affects US interests. So you might say the UN has passed a dozen resolutions against us. Well, there are *dozens* of such resolutions that have been lodged against Israel's occupation of Palestinian land and no one has bothered to implement a single one of them, much less make war over it. Then there's the oil argument. OK! So we do control 20 percent of the world's oil. Until 2 August we were exporting a third of it to the US, even though we knew you had a hostile policy toward us. You know we cannot irrigate the desert with our oil. We cannot drink it. All we can do is sell it. We have never used oil as a political weapon. When your new friends the Saudis escalated oil prices in 1973, Iraq opposed the move! Let me remind you that in this world it is the US that controls half of the grain market, it is the West that controls most of world technology, and you are always using food and know-how as political weapons in the Third World, so we are not impressed by your arguments over control of oil.'

And the regional threat that Iraq poses?

'Why fight with us?', he answers. 'We are not fanatics. We are not Communists. During the war with Iran you saw us as your friends. You say you sent troops to the Gulf to protect the Saudis. But we are not stupid. If we had intended to invade Saudi Arabia we would have done it when we entered Kuwait. Why in the world would we wait for US troops to arrive before attacking Saudi Arabia, which in any case we never intended to do.'

The TV is showing the English-language news. The tape footage is all of official events. Every camera angle manages to include a background poster of Saddam. It's now more than two hours and several shots of thick sugary coffee into our interview. It seems there is only one more relevant question. When Iraq speaks of its readiness to fight if necessary, does it understand what it's up against militarily? Does it really think it can take on the US forces?

Al-Hadithi lets out a bellow. 'I love it when Americans say Saddam is isolated and doesn't understand the threat. Go to any Iraqi's home and you will find three, four radios. They all listen to VOA, BBC and so on. The whole population knows fully what's going on. If they know, imagine what Saddam knows.' He pauses, sits up squarely, and picks up a pen to punctuate the point he is about to make. 'If George Bush makes the grave mistake of attacking Iraq, we Iraqis will be fighting back on our own land, defending our own homes, our own children. We are not a small village, we are not Panama nor Grenada, Mr Bush himself says we are the world's number 4 military power. We would enter the war with 1.2 million men in the army, other millions in militias.'

'On the other hand', he continues, 'the Americans will be fighting in a strange land. And we are not neighboring countries. Really this would be a war between the *nation* of Iraq and the *army* of the United States. That makes a big difference. During the war with Iran, our soldiers went home on leave every three weeks. What will American soldiers do? They are already bored in the desert. And if they have to fight, what will they tell themselves they are fighting for? To defend democracy in Kuwait? Come on. I know, you are going to say the US has air superiority. We know that. So did the Iranians. In fact, they had a modern, US-supplied air force. But we know a conflict like this will be settled on the ground. We are the defenders. In military terms, an invader needs a three-to-one advantage. We have over a million men in arms. I don't think the entire US army is that big. And here we accept sacrifice. Do you know that during the war with Iran we lost 53,000 men just to regain one small city, one small city that was part of Iraq: 53,000 men we lost to win back Al Faw because it was ours, a place Americans have never heard of. 53,000 men is what you lost during the entire Vietnam War. Do you think Mr Bush can afford to lose 53,000 men to defend some hole in the Saudi desert? Do you think he can make that sort of sacrifice? Do you think the people of the US will accept that sort of sacrifice?'

A few days later, as I prepare to leave Baghdad news comes that the Western hostages have been allowed to go home on a fleet of chartered jumbo jets, yet there seems to be no let-up in the march to war. I take a last walk through the crowded northern suburb of Kadhimiya as what I fear will be a farewell forever to Baghdad. A buzzing gold *souk* and general goods bazaar – stuffed with spices, dried figs, socks, shoes, scarves and toys – fans out in the twisting alleys and side streets around the sixteenth-century Golden Mosque. This temple is one of the holiest places in Iraq, a necropolis for family members of Caliph Al-Mansur, the founder of Baghdad. Hundreds of thousands of Iraq's politically unrepresented majority Shias are jammed into this ancient quarter of the city, to which the British added roofed verandas and gallery arcades. Unlike the capital's more modern downtown, where women strut in make-up and mini-skirts, here they shroud themselves in traditional black robes, their eyebrows and lips marked by hand-etched tatoos. In the corner tea shops lit with green fluorescent tubes, old men sit around rough-hewn tables and puff on huge, bubbling water pipes. The shopkeepers, the pedestrians, even the paratroopers greet the American visitor with a nod and a 'Hul-lo'. These people are what leftist intellectuals call the Arab Masses. These are the people whom Al-Hadithi guarantees us will fight to the last nail. I have no idea if they will or not. I do know, however, if war erupts, they will be its victims. And for what cause?

This conflict has never been about democracy or sovereignty. At its center is oil. The political elites that rule Saudi Arabia and the Gulf emirates do so only by the good grace of the developed, oil-addicted First World. They are kept in power and lavished with arms and favors in return for their acquiescence in supplying oil reliably and relatively cheaply, in accord with the needs of the industrialized world. Iraq's takeover of Kuwait raises the horrifying specter of a regional power that could blunt the US-European hegemony over what should, by rights, be Arab oil.

Further, the US deployment in the Gulf seems to be a last-gasp attempt by the world's foremost debtor nation, the United States, to exercise its waning imperial muscle in what the rest of the world hoped would be the beginning of a post-imperial age. As the editors of the Washington-based *Middle East Report* have noted, 'George Bush responded to Iraq's aggression like Saddam Hussein responded to Kuwait's stubbornness; by choosing a military over a political solution, by overreaching, by taking steps that are now difficult to reverse. The symmetry of their behavior is striking.'

Caught in between these two men are the people of this city, which was founded in 762. It is in this region that the Sumerians first invented writing. It's where the world's first urban culture was born. Babylonian King Hammerabi gave the world its first formal code of laws almost 4,000 years ago. The Abbasids invented algebra here. While Europe slipped into the Dark Ages, the Arabs drew the first map of the world. And throughout their history, these people have been over-run time and again by foreign invaders. By the Mongols, by Tamerlane and in the mid sixteenth century, the 400-year-long night of Ottoman rule commenced. Then came the British, who during their 35-year rule arbitrarily redrew the maps and propped up the monarchies that have helped spark today's conflict. And yet these people have survived.

Al-Hadithi *is* correct in saying that war here would be between the US Army and the Iraqi nation. And this mass of humanity around me is that nation, half of them under twelve years of age. And when the bombs fall, it will be on them. And certainly not on that small, pristine world of shopping malls and theme parks that wafts in and out every night on the airwaves of the Voice of America. Certainly, these Iraqi civilians are the enduring hostages of this conflict. They are permanently stationed at Ground Zero. No one will come to airlift them out on chartered 747s. Who will object to their deaths when the bombs begin to fall next month?

Village Voice
1 January 1991

8

ROLL OVER, CHE GUEVARA

HAVANA: MAY 1991. Sixteen-year-old Kanek was on the verge of tears as he caught up with me at midnight on a friend's terrace party, just three nights after Fidel Castro had marked the thirty anniversary of the Bay of Pigs. Once again 'El Lider Maximo' vowed that Cuba would 'fight to the last man' in the struggle for 'socialism or death'. Nervously fidgeting with his ponytail, Kanek told a tale that none of the adults present wanted to believe, but that all knew was true. Kanek was, after all, an unimpeachable source. His full name was Kanek Sanchez, grandson of Ernesto Guevara – Che Guevara – the veritable icon of revolutionary duty and purity.

About 400 Havana teenagers, most of them – like Kanek – long-haired rockers, had gathered at the Miramar neighborhood Cultural Center earlier that evening to hear a heavy metal group called Venus. In the stifling tropical night, Kanek said, one youth took his shirt off. The center director told him to put it back on, he refused, and within minutes a squad of eight uniformed cops had confronted the bare-chested boy, warning him to get dressed. Shouts escalated to scuffles, and at least sixty officers poured into the concert site, then staged what we in the States have come to call a 'police riot'. Tear gas, clubbings, police dogs, even a few pistol shots in the air, at least twenty-one arrests, and a few kids dispatched to hospital emergency rooms.

'Long hair was supposed to mean something in this country', said Kanek, stunned, sullen and still sinking. 'Fidel and Che wore it long in the mountains as a sign of something. But when we do the same we are scorned and now beaten. I didn't think I'd ever see anything like this in Cuba.' The dozen or so adults – writers and journalists – who gathered around Kanek, all of them one-time Fidelistas, however, showed no surprise, but only soul-eating grief over the young man's firsthand account. For some time now they had been expecting an incident like this. While they could only hope it would not spark more generalized turmoil, neither could they guarantee that these coming months would not become Cuba's long, hot summer.

Since I had last been in Cuba the year before, in 1990, I had been hearing that 'la calle está caliente' – 'the street is hot', social tension is mounting. Yes, not withstanding the After-the-Wall bombastics of the Florida Republican Party and its Miami exile community base, Cuban Communism had survived the first year of the New World Order. Caribbean socialism's more nationalistic essence, its more benign face – compared to the Czech and Polish variants – had so far prevented it from melting down into one more marvelous marketplace.

But the disappearance of Cuba's Eastern European trading partners and the spiraling economic turmoil in the Soviet Union have landed staggering body-blows to the island nation's economy. Soviet petroleum deliveries are down at least one-third and the rickety Cuban productive machine seems to be grinding toward a dead halt. Fidel Castro is calling it a 'special period'. Ordinary Cubans are calling 1991 the roughest economic times since the onset of the American trade embargo thirty years ago. Most ominously, for perhaps the first time in the history of the revolution, fewer and fewer Cubans see any longer see any light. The egg ration is down to about one every other day. Most Cubans are receiving about one pound of chicken per week while beef has become mostly a rumor. There is no soap, no tooth paste, no rubber for resoling shoes, and the purchase of clothes is restricted to two articles every two years.

In a society that has kept a three-decades-old promise to provide everyone with a job, official unemployment now threatens tens of thousands of workers. When their urban worksites close in the coming months, they have been told, they can either move to the countryside and join agricultural brigades or opt for one month's salary worth of severance pay.

Fuel is scarce. On the streets of Havana, swarms of bicycles, whiz by as Fidel has imported a half-million of the two-wheelers. 'I don't mind riding my new bike the five miles or so each way to work', one middle-aged intellectual told me. 'The only problem is that riding it you work up too big an appetite', he continued, only half-joking. His wife, a computer programmer, very seriously added, 'By two in the afternoon, work just about comes to a halt in my office. The next three hours are filled with talk about food. How we made do the night before, how we will fix what we have for dinner tonight. There's just this anxiety about food like never before.'

That economic anxiety translates, inevitably, into unprecedented political uncertainty. And most uncertain of all, are Cuba's youth. More than half the island's population has been born since Castro came to power in 1959. And they are the hardest hit by the crisis.

THE ONLY GAME IN TOWN:
LOUNGING ON HAVANA'S MALECON SEAWALL

Universities that were wide open a decade ago, last year accepted only three out of ten applicants. This year the ratio will fall to one in ten. Yet even the Communist Youth newspaper recently published a long reportage – entitled 'Me, a Worker?' – admitting that Cuban youth as a whole reject the notion of a working-class career. In the meantime, *all* Havana students who want to go to college must now spend the entire three-year high school period in rural-based schools, where half the day is spent tending crops. 'Look at my future: either unemployed or working a rice field', said Ramiro, a nineteen-year-old engineering student. And his pessimistic view accurately reflects the gloom that has settled over Cuba's teenagers. To many of their parents, the Cuban Revolution was always a promise to be fulfilled. But to this new generation, the revolution is increasingly thought of in the past tense. The revolution has, indeed, given them and their families free health care, cheap rent, universal education: it has staved off the nightmare scenario of hungry beggars that haunts the rest of Third World, and it has given the island of Cuba national dignity.

But the revolution, and its leaders, can no longer guarantee these kids a future. So many have gone back to the past. Cuban society is experiencing a sort of re-run from Europe and America's sixties. If there is one dominant fashion in the Cuban youth culture today it is the pose of rebellion. In some high schools, as many as a third of the males wear long hair, forced to tuck their ponytails into their shirt collars. More and more young people proclaim themselves as 'Rockeros' – pasting pictures of Bon Jovi over those of Marx, listening to Metallica instead of the speeches of Fidel. Rock T-shirts and cassettes trade briskly at the price of a month's salary each in the underground economy. Most notable, among the youth there is a manifest rejection of the system-as-is. What was unthinkable three or four years ago is now commonplace among Cuban teens: vociferous criticism of Fidel Castro who is viewed by the young as an old man completely out of touch with their needs. To the horror of Cuban authorities, the battle over the island's future may be shaping up along generational lines. Youth might just start doing crazy things – not out of the question in a place where there is so little to do in any case.

Saturday night at 10 p.m.: downtown Havana has the look and feel of a somnolent, provincial backwater. The streets are nearly empty of cars. There are no shops. The few bars and cafes that exist accept only dollars and are for the exclusive enjoyment of foreign tourists. In this 'special period' fewer busses are running, most live theater has closed down, a few cinemas still draw small crowds, but most nightlife is restricted to small groups of family and friends hanging out on porches and street corners. 'We may just be witnessing the assassination of daily life in Havana', says 45-year-old writer Carlos, who has taken me, his seventeen-year-old son Gaspar, and his friend Kanek on a drive through Havana.

'It's especially bad for the young', Kanek says. 'The only places to dance and listen to music in Havana are a handful of fifties-style nightclubs. They are formal, expensive, very hard to get into and not to the taste of the young.'

What most Cubans, young and old, do at night has little to do with his grandfather Che's vision of New Socialist Man: they watch television – trash television at that. Indeed, when Cubans aren't talking baseball or telling Fidel jokes, they are comparing notes on the outrageously sappy Brazilian soap opera *Roque Santeiro*. 'Every night at ten, the world comes to a stop here', says Carlos. 'The only thing people seem to want to know about is *Roque Santeiro*. And now the government is showing first-run American movies on TV not twice a week, as it did up to two months ago, but six times a week! Is that what we made a revolution for?'

We get out of the car at the Coppelia ice cream plaza on Havana's central 23d Street. Long lines snake through the square and lead to a half-dozen sales counters. Around the edges of the park clumps of teenagers, many of them rockers, hang out and talk and smoke. Among them are what the Cubans call *freakys* – more extreme rockers, punks, really. 'There used to be more of us out here', says Gaspar. 'But for the last year or so, the cops hassle you. They ask for ID and then fine you thirty pesos for jay-walking, stepping on the grass or any irregularity they can find in your papers. I know one kid who was stopped on his skateboard by cops who demanded he show them a drivers license for it!' Gaspar laughs and then adds: 'If you walk out in the street with a radio, or a boom box or a cassette recorder, the cops can stop you and demand you show a receipt to prove you haven't stolen it from a state entity.'

Carlos, his father, who has spent his life in the Communist Party, only grimaces. 'What can I tell you? This revolution has never devoted a minute's thought to providing entertainment or an outlet for kids.'

On most Saturday nights, one small courtyard, dubbed Maria's Patio, shelters the rockers and offers the possibility of a music concert. 'But only the possibility', says Kanek. 'More than half of the concerts fail because of technical problems, you know, equipment that doesn't work.' Kanek and Gaspar complain that the state, which rations out the purchase of equipment, provides no facilities for rock bands. 'Salsa is OK, New Song groups no problem, but there's never a single piece of equipment for rock bands. They say we are deviationists', he says. There was a popular rock show on Radio Ciudad Habana, but it was recently pulled.

By now we have pulled up along El Malecón, Havana's well-lit, five-mile-long seawall and promenade. Like a giant Art's Drive-in, hundreds of young couples lounge on the wall, pass bottles around, listen to music from their open car doors; a few dance, but most just sit around.

One of the most persistent rumors that swept Havana at the beginning of the year was about a another car ride through the city, much like the one Carlos has taken me on. The most common version of the story was that Communist Youth leader Roberto Robaina drove while Fidel rode shotgun. An hour passed in silence. Then an impatient Fidel turns to Robaina and says, 'What's the point of this? All I see are a bunch of kids hanging out.' Robaina then supposedly hit the brakes, pulled over and smiled, saying to Fidel: 'That is the point. These kids have nothing at all to do.' Fidel stroked his beard, nodded and – the story goes – immediately allocated $1 million for the opening of a series of discotheques to be run by the Communist Youth.

The story may be apocryphal. But that first discotheque has just opened. We drive up to the faux Moroccan-style 'Little Castle of the Youth', which sits right where the Malecón makes a turn behind the Riviera Hotel. 'Welcome to Communism Lite', sneers Carlos. Gaspar and Kanek look like we've just arrived at the dentist's office. A half-dozen Communist Youth bureaucrats stand behind a waist-high door across the front steps. A disappointed knot of twenty spruced-up kids mill on the outside, having been turned away. They explain that 250 people a night are allowed in – but that entrance tickets go on sale every morning at 7 a.m., for which you have to stand in line. One ticket per person. And currently, tickets are sold out a month in advance. Black market tickets are scalped for ten times the dollar–peso tariff.

After fifteen minutes of cajoling the doorkeepers and dropping every name in the *nomenklatura* except maybe Fidel's, I'm allowed in for a brief walk-through. Here is Lawrence Welk's idea of a wild and crazy disco complex. The bright-lit family pizzeria just inside the doors has run out of food and is closed. There's an outdoor roller skating rink, but that's for daytime use only. A 'Video Room' houses seven color TVs and Atari computer games, but they are not working either. The disco dancefloor, however, is jammed. On a technical level, the disco is first-class. Nice strobes, a wondrous light-organ, a deliciously air-conditioned room temperature, even dry ice clouds rolling out of the walls and hanging over the floor.

But this is beyond square. First, of all, they let parents in. So most of the kids are dancing with their mother or fathers. The music itself is some gawdaful reject from *Saturday Night Fever*. And, of course, no alcohol, in fact, nothing at all to drink. Just to make that point, my guide tells me with a Church Lady smirk that the Little Castle will be closing in five minutes – at 11 instead of 1 a.m. tonight as a precautionary move – because two boys had been caught earlier smuggling in a bottle of rum.

We get back, early, to Carlos's house just as his wife, mother-in-law and two neighbors are watching the final scenes of tonight's episode of *Roque Santeiro*. I spend the next three hours in the still air of the balcony talking to Willie, Gaspar and four other rockers. One's father is an army general, another a judge, the other two have at least one parent active in the Communist Party.

What strikes me about these kids is their idealism. Their rocker identity is central to them, but much more like it was in the US twenty-five years ago than it is today. None of these six teens believe in the Communist Youth, yet they are the true 'vanguard' of their generation. They are well-educated (spectacularly better educated and more articulate than comparable American sixteen- and seventeen-year-olds), and their nonconformism, more than a flight from reality, is rather a desperate demand, a passionate plea to be *included* and heard in a society they deem closed and obsolete. And they seek neither apocalypse nor revolution, but rather a good dose of reform. In that sense, they are more reminiscent of the early days of the American Rock Generation, circa 1963–64, than they are of that generation's infinitely more cynical, MTV-ized offspring.

'What unites us is not just the music', says Gaspar, 'but it's a whole way of seeing the world.'

'We don't want radical change', says Kanek. 'What we want is understanding, freedom, freedom of expression, we want to be treated at least as well as the tourists are treated. We want to be accepted as we are. People ask us if we are revolutionaries. We are revolutionaries because we have been taught to believe in the desirability of change and we still believe in it. We aren't revolutionaries the way the government wants us to be, because they want people who are stagnant. That kind of revolution is for people who have shit in their heads.'

'The government says it's afraid to open up in the face of hostility from the enemy, the Bush administration and the Miami Cubans. . . .'

'Well, that's true', interrupts Juanito. 'Look at all the people who got fooled in Eastern Europe. They are sorry now.'

But Kanek continues, 'Look, I think the way I do with or without freedom of expression. You don't gain anything from keeping the lid on.'

'That's right', agrees Gaspar. 'If you say that opening things up leaves room for the enemy, it means you don't trust your own work, that you don't trust us. If after thirty years Fidel and his people can't rely on what they have built, if they are afraid of their own people after thirty years of monopolizing their attention, then what is the use of defending any of this?'

That's the same sentiment I hear the following day when I visit the communal apartment of a five-member rock group. In a high-rise apartment with a commanding view of the bay, the group lives together and pools their money toward the black market purchase of sound equipment. Apart from the surrealistic murals that cover the walls, and a seeming gallery of Che portraits and photos, the apartment is almost bare. Furniture, clothes, even books have been sold off over the years to make piece-meal buys of amps, tubes, wires and speakers. And yet, what equipment the group has managed to collect still looks, frankly, like a heap of junk. On the day of my visit, one young band member is trying to rewire a microphone that looks like a Walter Winchell hand-me-down. A small boombox is tuned to a Miami FM station, the anemic signal threatening to fade at any moment. Next to it is a small Casio keyboard, picked up at the bargain black market price of $500 because its only flaw is a burnt-out power supply. 'In six years we have managed to put on two small performances', says Ernesto, the 25-year-old band leader. 'We just can't get the equipment all working at the same time.'

A devotee of Iron Maiden's music and Jim Morrison's persona, Ernesto even physically resembles the latter. 'The person I most identify with is Morrison', he says while laying back bare-chested on a mattress thrown on the floor. 'Like him, my father is also a military officer. And my dad told me, you can either be my son or you can play music. I chose music. But Morrison did his first record at age twenty-six. I'll be twenty-six next month, and then thirty-six and forty-six, and I'll never be able to record in this country.'

'This government fears rock', he says. 'Some say rock is feared because it is a cultural deviation, American cultural imperialism. But that's pure shit. Our ballet is French, our opera is Italian, government functionaries love to wear American jeans and tennis shoes, and they are the ones who fill TV with American movies. So don't tell me they fear our music because it's American. They fear it only because it sings of the desperation that is in our hearts.'

His thirty-year-old brother Sergio, after more than a decade as a 'special operative' of the Ministry of Interior and in defiance of his father, who holds the rank of general in the same ministry, quit his police duties ten weeks ago to become full-time 'manager' of the nearly nonexistent rock band. 'I was born and educated in the revolution and told that socialism was irreversible. Now it has collapsed around the world. For years I argued with my brother here. I saw the world one way, he saw it as it really was. But when I was given orders this year that I disagreed with, I quit the ministry. I said, Fidel is only human, and he can also make mistakes. I don't regret my time in the service. Everyone has his ideals, and so do I. I didn't join the ministry to defend Fidel or his brother Raúl. I did it to defend ideas, to feed children, to house the poor. I entered it like Che would have.

'We are destroying the most beautiful revolution in history. Fidel said so many times, "No concessions to the imperialists!" And yet all our hotels are now reserved for capitalist tourists! Now I'm afraid that things will break open here. I know if tomorrow 10,000 Cubans come protesting into the street among them will be provocateurs and foreign agents and what have you. But 9,000 of them will be completely innocent, just fed up with too many privileged bureaucrats, too many fat ministers who have never been on a bus with their own people. I quit because I'm just not ready. I knew about Chile, where cops can't read or write and when Pinochet tells them to beat their own people they go ahead and do it. I wanted out before I was forced into that situation here. I could no longer answer the question, What am I defending?'

Not withstanding Sergio's disillusionment and fears, there is much to still admire if not defend in Cuba. For more than thirty years the Cuban revolution stood as a symbol for Latin America's poor, it offered hope that some alternative fate for them was possible. It gave sustenance to those who believed there was some hemispheric order beyond a Pax Americana. And there are no new icons of social change. If Che is forgotten and Fidel fades, then Latin American youth will face the next century accompanied only by the Ninja Turtles and Pee-Wee Herman on dubbed-over videos.

And there is still an amazingly broad consensus among Cubans to reject a return to capitalism. Socialism remains a popular concept even among the young, but socialism broadly understood as a society that subsidizes public services and emphasizes collective goals rather than individual profit. At the same time there's a palpable restlessness that some fundamental changes, reforms and rethinking must be undertaken to make the system more flexible and liveable – and that these must be enacted quickly, much more quickly at least than Fidel Castro seems willing to allow.

'And that's the real danger here, the danger is Fidel', says a father of one of Gaspar's rocker friends. 'The debate in Cuba is still not over socialism or capitalism. Cubans resolved that a long time ago. But Fidel, in his intransigence to not effect changes, is artificially polarizing the country. Cubans have seen the disaster that Eastern Europe has become and they are in no rush to imitate it. But if Fidel keeps standing in the road to change, people could get desperate enough to accept anything but the status quo. So the man who made this revolution stands today as the man most likely to undo it. If Fidel continues to tie his personal fate to the very concept of socialism itself, we could be doomed. People are feeling hopeless, that Fidel isn't offering any way out.'

A week after the police riot, word comes that one more rock concert is to be staged at another one of Havana's cultural centers. Venus and one of the other groups who performed at last week's troubled concert are rumored to perform.

When I ask Sergio if he's heard the rumor about another concert that night, he smiles. 'Not only have I heard about the concert, *Chico*, I've heard what's going to happen', he tells me. 'I've still got friends in the ministry. And the order has come down. They're not going to tolerate any more crap from the kids. Either the cops are going to be all around the concert waiting for an excuse to close it down, or it just will never happen in the first place.'

When I arrive at the tree-covered lawn in front of the cultural center at the corner of Calzada and 8th Streets at 8:30 p.m. there is no sign of any rock band. But Kanek is already there along with Gaspar. So are about 200 other Havana teens, mostly dressed in black T-shirts, some emblazoned with the logos of Megadeath, Iron Maiden, Black Sabbath and Metallica. A few *Freakys* stand off to one side, among them a young man in a stylishly slashed denim jacket and an outlandish Mohican. The three or four blacks in the crowd have adopted the style of rappers.

I see no uniformed police or any patrol cars. But a sprinkle of square-looking plainclothes police stand out as absurdly as they did at any 1968 California antiwar rally and they are quietly ignored. In fact, the gathering as a whole is unnaturally still. Kids just hanging out, waiting for something to happen. The hot evening air spiced with sea-salt and the weak street lighting add to the languor. Gaspar marks time with an update on the previous week's violent clash. He says he heard at a Communist Youth meeting that an 'investigation' of the incident was under way. But the preliminary police report, he says, claims that the concert was broken up after 'one girl took her blouse off and exposed her breasts while one boy began to masturbate in public.' Gaspar just laughs at his own story.

Kanek passes me one of the half dozen or so bottles of grain alcohol that are circulating through the crowd. 'Looks like there will be no concert', Kanek says matter of factly, noting that it's already past nine. I see lights blazing through the open door of the cultural center and ask why Kanek or someone else doesn't go in and ask what's up. 'They'd just lie to us if they'd even talk to us', Kanek says. 'You don't understand how it is in Cuba. We are just kids, not anybody important. These *comemierdas*, these shit-eaters think they have to answer to no one, let alone us.'

We kill another half-hour sitting under a lamp-post, finishing off the bottle. 'Suspended, cancelled, let's go', Kanek concludes, and stretches upward. As if a secret signal had been given, the *rockeros, freakys* and long-hairs begin to say their goodbyes to each other with hugs and two-cheeked kisses. I feel confused, between anger and sadness. I feel robbed of something that was part of me for years. Yet Kanek and Gaspar seem much more sanguine about it all. They are used to such evenings.

Kanek looks down at his watch and clucks. 'If we hurry we'll catch *Roque Santeiro* on the telly', he says. And with that, Kanek Sanchez breaks camp, much as his grandfather Che did thirty-five years before in the Sierra, knowing that the time and place of battle must be chosen carefully, and along with Gaspar and the dozens of other kids around me glides off and dematerializes into the dark, empty, humid streets of Havana.

Village Voice
16 July 1991

9

RAINFOREST CRUDE

ECUADORAN AMAZON: SEPTEMBER 1991. Ecuador's Trans-Amazon Pipeline slithers out of the soft belly of the jungle and then writhes and crawls 300 miles into the Andes, past the capital of Quito and then over to the Pacific Coast, where it spits out its primordial black venom into a line of waiting tankers. So if you start in the crowded, trash-choked outskirts of Quito and work your way backward, eastward, along the kidney-crushing, unpaved Pan-American Highway, which borders the route of the mammoth five-foot-in-diameter, rust-scaled serpent, you get ever deeper into the jungle. Ever closer to the prehistoric pools of crude that rest below the Amazon and that silently sacrifice themselves to keep the Ecuadoran economy barely afloat.

Just a few hours past the natural hot springs of Papallacta, a half-day east of Quito, around a gently sloping mountain curve and Ecuador's *Oriente*, the 30 million acres of the Upper Amazon Basin, stretches before you. Descending into the valley of the Amazon headwaters, the mountain fog and scruffy brush cede to a humid, tropical sun and a breathtaking explosion of banana tress, palms, proud stands of forest hardwoods, jacaranda, silk-cotton and cinnamon trees, verdant walls of fern and jumbles of blossoming vines and trailers.

One of the most biologically rich zones on the planet, a single acre of this land can contain up to 100 different species of trees – five times the number in the temperate rainforests of the US Pacific Northwest. This basin nurtures almost 20,000 plant species and provides a habitat for hundreds of varieties of rare fish, reptiles and mammals, including macaws, screamer monkeys, freshwater dolphins, wild turkeys, anteaters, alligators and river boas. And under this same protective canopy, as many as a half-million of Ecuador's indigenous people have woven themselves tightly into the jungle fabric, trying to hold out against industrial civilization and its inevitable byproduct – extinction.

Great swaths of this Ecuadoran Amazon have been declared 'protected lands'. Indeed, its most diverse storehouse of biological wealth, the 600,000-acre Yasuní National Park, has been declared by UNESCO a 'world biospheric reserve'. Yet when the heavily indebted Ecuadoran state and a thirsty herd of foreign oil companies cast their gaze toward the Oriente they see green of a different kind. Over the past twenty years, after discovering a crude petroleum bonanza, these companies, led by the U.S-based Texaco, have superimposed a grid of more than a dozen 500,000-acre geometrical drilling 'blocks' over the Amazon. Some 400 oil wells and pumping stations have punctured the jungle floor to lap up 1.5 billion barrels of crude, while hundreds of miles of roads, ducts and pipelines have ripped through the lush swaddle of vegetation. So far, a tenth of the Ecuadoran Amazon has been consumed directly by the oil companies. An equal amount has been lost to desperately impoverished 'colonists' who invade the forest along company roads, settle in and ravage the woods around them.

And now the final chapter in the story of the Oriente threatens to conclude before most of the world ever reads the preface. Although profit-sated Texaco is winding down its operations in Ecuador, another 3 million acres of the Amazon remain under active oil exploration. Its most intimate, complex recesses, its 'protected areas', the lands inhabited by the most fragile and precarious of indigenous clans, have been mapped and measured, staked out and sized up, prodded and probed. And any day now the heart of this jungle basin is about to be penetrated and sucked dry of its subterranean ooze. Last autumn, after a firestorm of international controversy, the Ecuadoran government flashed a definitive green light to begin oil development in what is euphemistically called Block 16, but what is, in reality, part of the world-treasured Yasuní National Park, homeland to the near-extinct Huaorani tribe

It's an assault that could prove fatal to a big chunk of the Ecuadoran Amazon and the indigenous people who inhabit it. But like much of Ecuador's history, this potentially decisive battle over Ecuador's environment and resources is shaped by powerful forces outside its borders, beyond this small nation's reach and influence.

Every day 300,000 barrels of crude petroleum are dredged up from underneath the Amazon, force-fed through the snaking pipeline, dumped into tankers and dispatched to cracking plants world-wide, after the Ecuadoran state takes its cut in revenues, hopelessly trying to pay off a foreign debt that has multiplied sixty-fold since the oil boom of the seventies. A full half of the Amazon crude winds up in the United States, transmogrified into Regular, Unleaded and Super where it is then pumped, once again, into our gastanks, guzzled, half-digested and then rudely farted out tailpipes and into our skies and lungs by the cars and trucks butted up fender to fender on the San Diego Freeway – vehicles that for the sixth straight year have shown declining gas mileage.

Now four US oil companies and a Taiwanese partner, led by the Dallas-based Maxus Energy Corporation, have offered their services in gratifying our insatiable gasoline addiction. With a capital investment of $600 million they are poised to build hundreds of miles of new roads and pipelines and scores of wells and pumps to tap the estimated 300 million barrels of crude that lie underneath Yasuní Park. This is an addition to ongoing oil activity in other areas of the Amazon by other multinational petroleum pushers, including Arco, Occidentel, British Petroleum and Petro-Bras.

Ecuador's disenfranchised indigenous organizations and its frail environmental groups have been locked in a desperate struggle to impede the development of Block 16. From the Ecuadoran government, the press and most political parties they have been answered with a chorus of shouts: Impoverished Ecuador has no choice other than to bleed itself dry.

It's enough to tour the Quito offices of the environmental and indigenous groups to realize why opposition to the drilling has so far been futile. First, there is the historical mistrust that many Indian groups feel for environmentalists, whom they often associate with the most conservative, oligarchic conservationists in the country. Esperanza Martinez, a part-time biologist and full-time activist explains, 'The indigenous say, "You environmentalists are out defending birds and cats while we Indians are out getting killed and losing our land."' Martinez has helped coordinate the alliance of two dozen groups opposed to drilling Block 16 from the ramshackle offices of her Acción Ecologica. The rough-hewn benches on the floor, the wood crates for files, all attest to the realism of her confession: 'We have no illusions about who we are. Real power is in the hands of the indigenous organizations.'

Marcela Enriquez, the firebrand environmental lawyer whose organization, CORDAVI, works with Indian groups to mount legal challenges to drilling, believes it's not quite that simple. 'The indigenous have a right to self-determination', she says. 'But they can also make mistakes. The Amazon and its resources are the patrimony of all Ecuadorans, of all humanity, not just the indigenous groups.'

Across town, Leonardo Viteri, the 37-year-old adviser to Ecuador's umbrella Indian Federation, CONAIE, is nervous about the interest that 'all humanity' is taking in his people's lands. Specifically, he mentions the growing involvement of US-based ecology groups in the Amazon drilling dispute. 'On the one side we have some ecology groups from the US telling us to make a deal with the oil companies', Viteri says, shaking his head. 'On the other side, we have other groups telling us to never negotiate anything. As if they had something concrete to offer us instead of just more hunger.'

Indeed, when I tell the leader of Ecuador's Amazon Indian Federation, Valerio Grefa, of my desire to see the proposed drilling areas firsthand, his first response is unabated ire. 'That's the real problem!' He shouts at me, 'One gringo after another going out there and screwing things up. I'm thinking of issuing an order that just says: No more gringos allowed out on our lands.' But Grefa finally agrees things have gotten so twisted recently by foreign meddlers that one more reporter could hardly makes matters worse. 'Go', he says. 'Go and see for yourself what oil does to our people.'

'The Mayan people think that whenever a tree is cut down, another star falls from the sky', says 25-year-old Miguel Pandam, a national representative of the Shuar indigenous group. With Leonardo Viteri's urging, Miguel has accompanied me on the trip to Amazon oil country. He points to the sweeps of mowed-over rainforest on either side of the dirt road we are travelling. 'If plans for drilling Block 16 go ahead, it looks like our people will be spending many very dark nights.'

As we pull into the shabby fringes of the town very appropriately named Lago Agrio – Sour Lake – Miguel shakes his head and with an uncharacteristic flash of fury says, 'When the oil companies talk of bringing "progress" to the "Indians", this is the shit they have in mind for us. Look at this and tell me what you think of their promises.' To call Lago Agrio shit is being polite. Invariably described by tourist guidebooks as an 'oil boomtown', or as Ecuador's fastest growing city, Lago – the electro-mechanical nerve center of the Amazon oil industry – lewdly reveals itself as a cross between Dodge City and Calcutta.

Astounding is the ability of humans to conjure a full-blown slum in the midst of what was only twenty years ago virgin jungle. Open sewers, rooting pigs, piles of garbage on unpaved rutted streets so inhospitable that high-clearance pickup trucks are the local taxis, dilapidated housing, sooty tire-recapping stands, used auto part stores, general rot encouraged by the always humid climate, hookers displaying their dusky thighs in open doorways, $2-a-day oil workers knocking back their second sixpack by noon, and a prevailing mood of restlessness, tension and frustration as thick as the crude oil poured over the streets to keep the dust down. The smell of the crude is pungent, slightly nauseating and mixes poorly with the odor like singed hair that emanates from the blazing orange flames burning off gas from the oil pits in town as heavy metals, nitrogen, sulfur and carcinogenic carbons pour into the sky.

It's market day and in the muddy town plaza, mixed among the fruit and hardware sellers are a few Cofan indians dressed in their one-piece *kushmas* and their porcupine headbands hawking live chickens and handicrafts. From the nearby reserve of Dureno, their numbers have dwindled from 15,000 a few decades ago to less than 300 today – mostly a result of disease brought in by Texaco oil workers and by the eradication of their traditional wildlife stocks. 'We Shuars are still strong, as are the Quichua', says Miguel, nodding toward the Cofanes. 'We fight the oil companies so we don't end up like that.'

On the eastern edge of Lago we approach the Aguarico River – one of two main tributaries to the Amazon. In the creeks pouring into it, there is a tar-black, high-tide bath-ring staining the banks and shrubbery. Just across the road, Miguel leads me to a string of oil production pits. And like all such pits in the Amazon they are open and unlined. When it rains – as it does about nine months of the year – they simply overflow with their toxic brew of mercury, lead, cyanide and other poisonous additives. And the rest of the time, these lethal chemicals just seep through the ground and pollute the aquifers.

Every day of the year, an estimated 4 million gallons of venomous waters from drilling wells are dumped untreated into Amazon riverways, much of it right here in the Aguarico, and much of that originating upstream in the 'protected' Cuyabeno Wildlife Refuge, which has been plundered by oil exploitation. And over the last twenty years, 17 million gallons of crude petroleum have spilled – unrecovered – into the Amazon jungle just from leaks and breaks in the main pipeline. That's half again as much as the oil spilled by the *Exxon Valdez*. As we walk along the bare river shore, in sight of one of Texaco's main plants, Miguel says, 'They call these machines pumps. We call them vampires.'

A few minutes later we are back in the car and heading east to visit some Quichua relatives of Miguel's wife. Just where Lago rubs up against the joint Texaco-Petro-Ecuador facility we are stopped at a military checkpoint. Most of the populated Amazon is considered a military 'national security zone'.

'What company do you work for?' asks the teenage soldier, peering in my window. Miguel, again stewing in ire, answers for me. 'I am an Ecuadoran citizen. I am a Shuar. Why must I show you anything? This is a public road.' Anticipating the soldier's indifference, Miguel is already fishing out his ID. A look at my US passport, and we are waved through. Two more checkpoints in the next mile and then we are on the 'main highway' between Lago and Coca, fifty miles southeast. Our wheels hiss. Two to three times a month, the oil companies pour a thick film of black crude over the dusty thoroughfare.

Miguel's relatives live in the Quichua community of Sarayacu, ten miles east of Lago, just a few feet off the oil-slick road. They receive us with a bittersweet offering of yucca-based cider inside their two-room woodboard home, raised on stilts six feet off the ground. Like most of the local indigenous, they have seen their traditional forest sustenance disappear and have been slowly forced into the cash market economy, where they compete with equally poor 'colonists'.

Though there is a curling poster of Jesus on the wall and a calendar adorned with a bare-breasted beauty in a hammock, the woman of the household, Lucinda Gualinga, is a shaman – a believer in and master of the medicinal and spiritual powers of hundreds of jungle plants and animals. Speaking in Quichua, translated loosely by Miguel, she complains that the most sacred of animals – the river boas – have as much as vanished since two recent ruptures in the pipeline. 'The boas attract the rest of our animals and fish', Lucinda says. 'But there are no more. How could there be when the whole river was on fire?' Nor can the family bathe any more in the brook that runs just 200 feet from the crude-covered road since they started breaking out in skin rashes. And since a neighbor suddenly died five months ago, they are fearful of drinking their well water. 'What can we Indians do?' laments Lucinda. 'We complain about the oil but all the companies and the army want to do is crush us.'

At the nearby Carmelite Catholic Mission, health worker Monica Baez confirms the general malaise. 'It's terrible here', she says. 'Contamination of the air, the soil and the water. Coughs, bronchitis, rashes, anemias, headaches. And malnutrition. Among indigenous groups where that malady was recently unknown, there are now astronomical averages, like 70 to 80 percent malnutrition among the children.' Baez continues: 'And when people get sick there is no real medical attention. Seventy-seven thousand people in this area and one hospital with fourteen beds. In a fifty-mile radius outside the city there is one state clinic and a first aid post that the mission runs. And things get worse. After PetroEcuador was pressured into cleaning up some of these lands, they hired the people who lived on it. And they were paid to clean up the oil with their bare hands, with no protection at all. It's really criminal.'

One of the young priests, Raul Navas, complains of a different sort of pollution. As we sit in the Mission conference hall, a hand-lettered sign above him reads: 'Life Has Meaning Only When You Decide to Surrender It to Change History and Allow the People to Flourish.' Sipping on home-brewed chocolate as the brooding skies release a downpour, Navas says, 'There's just too many nonprofit ecology and anthropology groups passing out money around here. Not so many US groups, but lots of American money. And it doesn't go to build up the sort of indigenous organizations needed to make reform and resist further destruction of the Amazon. Instead it goes to individual projects run by these groups, which means chunks of money going to this or that community. It creates even more dependency. And it holds back real self-empowerment.' Navas suggests I go down the road to Coca, adjacent to so-called Block 16, where the CONOCO oil company has also had some recent luck in winning over individual indigenous communities to their drilling plans by promising civic development in exchange. 'But be careful', warns Navas. 'The last time a couple of reporters went down there asking questions about the ecology, the army arrested them as narco-traffickers.'

The priest's counsel was prescient. Less than thirty minutes toward Coca, I'm stopped at another military checkpoint. I deny being a reporter but my laptop in the backseat, Miguel in the front seat, and my flimsy story about being a tourist spook the soldiers who turn me back around toward Lago and tell me I had better first get a pass from the military command.

On the road back to Lago, the tropical rain walls us off in steady, gray sheets. The oil-doused roads turn treacherous as the unabsorbed water floats on their surface. Coming around a blind bend I see an aging truck, loaded down with cattle, hunkering in the middle of the road. I hit the brakes, but the fickle mix of crude oil and rainwater refuses to grant purchase to any of my four wheels. My Trooper's brakes lock up and the car skates and slides at a 45 degree angle over the impervious petroleum, coming to a rest only after smashing head-on into the truck.

Later that afternoon, once the car and truck have been towed away, Dr Donoso at Lago's Clinica Gonzalez applies a cast on my right arm and grimly jokes, 'Oil is what keeps us in business. It makes everyone sick, you know. And lots of car accidents on the roads. You're lucky you didn't get killed. You have no idea how many people each month crash or run off these roads and never come back. Thanks to the oil.'

As with most stories about Latin American politics, this one involves the United States. First, from Nevada to New Hampshire, the nation brims with internal combustion engines. Then, drilling opponents not only are confronted with a US oil company, not only is most of Block 16 to be sold to the US to pay off a foreign debt owed to American banks, but the Ecuadoran groups also have to navigate the roiling wake left behind by US environmental groups that have jumped headlong into the drilling issue.

An acrid gusher of contention ripped through the Ecuadoran environmental and Indian movements last year when the U.S-based Natural Resources Defense Council (NRDC) and its staff attorney, Bobby Kennedy, Jr, proposed that CONOCO be allowed to drill Block 16 in exchange for serious concessions. In closed talks with CONOCO, Kennedy and another NRDC attorney, convinced that more drilling was inevitable, suggested they might help lobby the rest of the US environmental movement to support the drilling project if in return the company would grant some $15 million in funding to Amazon Indian federations. When those private talks accidentally became public, nearly two dozen Ecuadoran environmental groups signed a public manifesto denouncing Kennedy and the NRDC as 'ecological imperialists'. Kennedy counterattacked by publicly condemning the Ecuadoran environmentalists as a 'tiny, urban elite' insensitive to the real needs of the Indians.

The controversy spread to the US, where the NRDC was also criticized by groups like Rainforest Action Network, Friends of the Earth and the Sierra Club Legal Defense Fund. NRDC's talks with CONOCO were halted. And last October CONOCO announced it was abandoning Ecuador for more profitable – and less controversial – oilfields in Russia. Now, other companies, led by Maxus Energy Corporation, have stepped right in to fill the void. And the bitterness over the issue of whether to negotiate still remains. This withdrawal of CONOCO is no victory', says Bobby Kennedy in an interview conducted at his Pace University office. 'This is exactly what we predicted would happen if an agreement wasn't reached with CONOCO. We have none of the leverage over Maxus that we had with CONOCO. Maxus couldn't care less about its public image. But with CONOCO they had a $90 million PR campaign to improve their image at stake, they had a gas station in every city that we could have boycotted if it had come to that. There are very few things to be hopeful about regarding the Amazon. CONOCO's willingness to compromise was one of those. Now it's gone.'

William C. Hutton, Maxus Corporation's general manager in Ecuador, responds that his company is 'totally committed to doing this job the right way and with the least amount of disruption.' He says that Maxus, one of America's largest independent oil companies, has adopted and will improve upon a 600-page environmental plan that was drawn up by CONOCO, which proposes the use of new, 'clean' technology linked with a company promise to keep new settlers out of the affected areas.

Most environmental activists in Ecuador have dismissed the company plans as either grossly insufficient at best, or completely unenforceable at worst. Along with a number of indigenous federations, the local environmental groups are pledging to continue an all-out campaign to halt drilling in the Amazon heartland. And many of those who criticized CONOCO – and Kennedy, for dealing with the oil company – believe that the withdrawal of CONOCO is proof positive that enough grassroots heat can be generated to melt down the will of any multinational that comes along. But Indian leader Leonardo Viteri is grim about the prospects: 'Our enemy has traditionally been a three-headed alliance of the oil companies and the army and evangelicals hired by them to pacify us. Now, there's a fourth head: some US environmental groups.'

Viteri holds that NRDC's strategy of milking concessions from individual oil companies begs the more central question of real indigenous self-empowerment. 'The real issue here is a global strategy aimed at securing indigenous rights over the land and resources we inhabit', says Viteri, a graduate of linguistic studies. 'The issue is not whether we negotiate or not. We indigenous people have to negotiate our daily existence. The question is negotiating *what* and with *whom*. We have nothing to talk to individual oil companies about. Rather we are opening talks directly with the Ecuadoran government on a broad agenda.'

That indigenous platform calls for exploring alternatives to an oil-based economy and instituting a per-barrel tax on any ongoing oil production to create a massive development fund for the Amazon's indigenous people. Or, as Amazon indigenous leader Valerio Grefa puts it, 'Oil drilling in Ecuador is not an environmental issue as the *gringos* think. It is fundamentally a political struggle. A struggle over economic power and the socialization of profits.' In short, a matter of social revolution of the sort difficult to imagine or countenance from the comfortable confines of Washington-based environmental lobbies.

'We have no alternative other than to redouble our resistance. Too often you Americans think of us as part of the Third World. But we are not', says Leonardo Viteri. 'When we live on our land, from our land, with our land, we live in a primal forest, in a primary, a First World for us. It's when our land is taken away, when it is contaminated and ruined, when our animals are scared away or die off, it is then that we are forced to live in the Third World, when we are forced to occupy the lowest rungs of the social ladder of the Third World. That's incentive enough to fuel our resistance.'

That sort of resistance to expanded drilling in Block 16, says Viteri, is likely to take on the characteristics of what has been called the Great Uprising of 1990. In July of that year more than a million Ecuadoran Indians, in a series of land disputes, spent a week of agitated protest, occupying farms, highways and city streets and bringing Ecuador to a virtual halt. 'Using that same sort of concrete resistance', warns Valerio Grefa, 'I guarantee you that no matter what the government says, there will be *no* drilling in Block 16 without our consent.'

But in private conversations, a number of Indian leaders and environmentalists caution that the words of Grefa and Viteri must not be taken so literally. The anti-drilling forces face a number of potentially crippling handicaps. For one, they say, the Great Uprising of 1990 fell far short of winning significant victories for the Indians. The uprising saw massive nonviolent civil disobedience by the Indians on a scale reminiscent of the American civil rights movement. But the indigenous were unable in one short week to even out 500 years of disadvantage. When the protests subsided, the Ecuadoran government retaliated with dozens of arrests, clamping the lid back on the countryside. The indigenous groups have an impressive ability to mobilize their constituency for short-term struggles but still sorely lack resources and experience in becoming serious political contenders.

Also, Ecuador's Federation of Amazon Indigenous – CONFINAE – has already flip-flopped more than once on the issue of negotiating with the operators of the Block 16 concession. CONFINAE leader Valerio Grefa, who today threatens a gotterdamerung against Maxus and who denounces the NRDC as agents of the oil companies, is the same leader who, last March, gave Bobby Kennedy a signed letter naming him as the Indians' official 'defense attorney' and authorized him to negotiate with CONOCO.

'Let's be real', says one Ecuadoran friend of mine, a militant environmentalist. 'These oil companies have a lot at stake here. So does our government. Oil export means half of our budget. It's naive to think drilling will be halted. And the indigenous know that. At the end of the day, you'll see all kinds of Indian groups making deals with the companies. It's only natural.'

Not only natural, says Bobby Kennedy. But desirable. 'The NRDC wants indigenous people to control their own resources and land', he says, agreeing with Viteri's proposition of self-rule in the Amazon. 'But the people who run Ecuador, backed by the army, are an economic autocracy. Now it seems there are a couple of ways of fighting them. You can go Viteri's way, the Cuban model, and go into the streets. I don't know how successful you'd be. A revolution. Granted, Ecuador needs one. But what kind? With guns? Or do you start by taking $15 million like we wanted to from CONOCO? And with that money the Indian groups can finance themselves, organize themselves better and make sure that from that point forward no oil company can do business again in Ecuador without first satisfying the needs and demands of the indigenous?'

Kennedy is clearly embroidering his characterization of Viteri, who is more inclined toward Macintoshes than to Mausers. But the question posed: pragmatic reform or radical revolution? is as valid today in Ecuador as anywhere in the Third World. In the meantime, Kennedy's NRDC – so badly burned by the CONOCO brouhaha – is keeping a low profile on the issue of further drilling in the Amazon. But as Maxus oils its bulldozers and sharpens its drills, other US groups are once again choosing up sides. Rainforest Action Network, Friends of the Earth and Greenpeace can be expected to join with militant Ecuadoran groups to try and block the new drilling.

But more powerful, more buttoned-down American groups such as the World Wildlife Fund and the Nature Conservancy – who purchased a $10 million debt-for-nature swap in Ecuador – have as much as openly endorsed oil drilling in Block 16. And it was the Nature Conservancy that, with oil company funding in 1989, drafted a management plan for Yasuní Park that allocated half of it for 'industrial use' – that is, mining and oil production.

The US State Department's Agency for International Development has also appeared on the scene. With funding of approximately $10 million for its Proyecto Subir and co-administered by the Nature Conservancy, CARE and a section of the New York Zoological Society, AID is developing a program to promote exploitation of 'sustainable biological resources' in the Yasuní National Park. And one of the project proposals, setting off alarms in the indigenous community, includes plans to foster 'social organizations' in the region – organizations that could wind up undercutting or competing with already-existing and politically more progressive groups.

This growing American presence inside the Ecuadoran environmental milieu leaves many local activists like CORDAVI's Marcela Enriquez unnerved. 'After the NRDC fiasco, maybe American environmentalists will learn some humility', she says. 'Their work should be in their own country. They should just leave us alone. How dare they come to preach to us when they come from a country that consumes 40 percent of the world's energy.' Her partner, Byron Real, adds: 'It's pretty clear to us that a lot of these American groups have decided not to oppose drilling in Block 16. They know that the next area to be drilled is the even more sensitive Block 22. These groups have already made up their minds to be what they call pragmatic. They are willing to trade Block 16 for 22. For them it's a comfortable decision to make from far away. For us it is a disaster.'

Disaster is probably the right word. The history of Ecuador shows that, after the briefs have been filed, the international telexes ignored, and the protests quelled, the oil pumps inevitably return to their ordained task, obediently and ceaselessly extracting the earth's life fluid until there simply is no more. The crude, meanwhile, is promptly shipped out and sold, interest obligations on the foreign debt are paid, and the debt still gets bigger and Ecuador still gets poorer. As for the indigenous, they do not, in fact, become extinct, no matter how voracious the pillaging of their homelands.

It's enough to walk out of the luxury hotels on Quito's tony Avenida Amazonas, or outside the gritty offices of Leonardo Viteri – actually, out to just about any intersection in Quito – to see that the indigenous, displaced from their traditional communities by Mack trucks, pumping stations and toxic production pits, indeed can persevere and make a new life in the capital. There they are, in magenta or teal blue, sometimes in an almost luminescent green, or a musty brown, often in store-bought petroluem-based polyester or rayon. Surviving. Squatting on the cracked sidewalk. Waving away bus fumes with hand-embroidered hankies. Selling Kleenex, caramels, candies, combs and nowadays even condoms to the hurried passers-by. Many of them, tourists. Many of the tourists, Americans. Many of them, undoubtedly, environmentalists.

Mother Jones
March/April 1992

10

CLOSE, BUT NO CIGAR

MIAMI AND HAVANA: JANUARY 1993. The *Granma*, the cabin cruiser that Fidel Castro floated in on from Mexico to launch his revolution against Fulgencio Batista in 1956, now sits anchored in an artificial sea inside a huge, climate-controlled glass case adjacent to the Museum of the Cuban Revolution. Next to it are planes and armored cars used to propel the socialist revolution to power on New Year's Day, thirty-four years ago. The embalmed *Granma*, the displayed armor, the pictures, documents and diagrams that fill the museum, the museum building itself – the baroque former Presidential Palace where a student commando group was decimated trying to assassinate Batista – all stand as symbols that celebrate, more than Communism itself, the island's martyred road to dignity and independence from the US.

That's perhaps why Alfredo, the 65-year-old black Cuban writer who toured the three museum floors with me, found himself more choked up than he would have liked to admit. A veteran Communist, he had just spent the better part of the day bitching about Fidel Castro, blaming him for Cuba's economic crisis. But once inside the hushed museum walls, Alfredo seemed transported, distracted from the rolling blackouts, the disappearance of gasoline, the breakdown of industry and the meager food rations. There was a rectitude, a purity, a nobility of purpose and cause that seemed to ooze from the displays and salve the pangs of momentary, daily despair.

As we finished up, I lingered at a souvenir counter next to the exit, taken by the exquisite series of 5-by-8-inch black-and-white candid photos of Che Guevara on sale. Noting my interest, Alfredo offered to buy me one of the portraits as a gesture toward our friendship. Asking the price, he was jolted by the answer. 'They are not for sale to you', the young woman behind the counter curtly informed him. 'Prices are only in dollars.' And Cubans cannot legally possess US currency. If you want to buy a picture of Che nowadays in Cuba you have to be a tourist, a foreign tourist.

Ninety miles across the ocean in Miami, Cubans there have always shopped in dollars. But some of them have recently been as rudely shocked as Alfredo was in Havana. The Museum of Cuban Art, founded by fiercely anti-Castro exiles, and now functioning out of a trendily rehabbed fire station on the periphery of Little Havana, always seemed like a bastion of secure anti-Communist culture in perhaps the most anti-Communist of all cities in the hemisphere. But recently, the good Cuban-American burghers who frequent the gallery were stunned to find that a new, much more liberal generation of exiles had won a majority on the museum board. Now, the walls of their refuge were frequently covered with the paintings not only by Cuban exiles but also by other local artists and by artists still living in Cuba, artists who had not denounced Fidel Castro. These Miami Cubans' dollars are negotiable in the museum. If they want to buy Communist art.

Are these the same Havana and Miami we have grown up with? Cuba's two biggest cities. Separated at the birth of the Revolution, they have apparently matured into a pair of grotesque middle-aged twins. Stamped with the same genetic codes, the two communities loomed in our collective consciousness as driven only by some primeval fratricidal urge. Through three and a half decades and over ninety miles of Caribbean froth we have seen Miami and Havana scorn each other as so possessed and corrupted by evil that salvation could come only through eradication. And a series of American administrations, egging on the fight, had turned Washington D.C. into the third leg of this Bermuda Triangle of hate, suspicion and treachery. Havana and Miami always meant to me: Revolution/Counterrevolution. Independence/Imperialist Intervention. Communism/Capitalism. Sovereignty/Submission. Dignity/Dependence. A blood enmity so thoroughly unremitting and obsessive that it once dragged the entire world to the brink of atomic immolation.

But these categories, as evidenced by the goings on at the two museums, today are about as useful as a Lenin lapel pin in Moscow. The world cannot change as much as it has in the last three years and simply leave the Cuba story deep-frozen in the Cold War past. Travelling between Miami and Havana nowadays you find two communities that no longer exist in simple confrontation with each other, but rather on what world-weary Italian politicians used to call 'converging parallels'. At the grassroots level, lifelong Havana socialists and Miami-based Bay of Pigs veterans are starting to agree on a vision of Cuba's destiny. An emerging consensus, or at least the potential for one, is starting to bridge the gaps of water, time and ideology.

In Miami, Little Havana's main thoroughfare, Calle Ocho, struggles to retain its facade of prerevolutionary Cuban-ness against the encroaching McDonald's and Burger Kings. Some of the old people listen to the unreconstructed anti-Castro vitriol pouring twenty-four hours a day from the battery of Spanish-language radio stations, but their children have grown into gringo professionals. Some even travel back and forth to that mythical homeland which their elders describe as something just a shade more brutal and horrific than the Seventh Circle. If they have any political interest at all it is more likely that of battling anti-Latino discrimination than it is overthrowing Fidel. Their grandkids, for that matter, watch MTV and couldn't tell Fidel Castro from Jerry Garcia. The shrill extremists are still the most powerful political voices in Miami but now have to compete with moderates who finally want to lift the embargo and seek reconciliation of friends and families, a nation.

In Havana, as well, the apathy of the young approaches that of their cousins across the straits. Many of the older generation of forty- and fifty-year-olds, those who benefitted most from the Revolution, now see Castro as the man most likely to bury it. Some of these revolutionaries, crossing the Rubicon of middle age, now find the world has been turned on its head. Their leftism leads them to conclude that today they may have more allies inside the halls of Miami's universities than they do inside the Cuban Communist Party. In both cities, more and more people increasingly listen to the same music, wear the same clothes and dream the same dreams.

The traditional debate about Cuba rings hollow. Declaring yourself simply 'for' or 'against' Cuba today means nothing, because the one historical fact that polarized Cuba's populace and much of the rest of the world, the Cuban Revolution, is already over. Communism doesn't have to be overthrown by the right or defended by the left because Communism in Cuba is dead. If the extreme right has its way and invades the island, the beachfront hotels it will be shooting up belong to Spanish capitalists. To the left, which talks about 'defending' the revolution – you have to ask just *who* or *what* it is that is being defended. Are we to defend the socialist revolutionaries who seethe against Castro's one-man rule, or the 'comrades' who throw rocks through their windows or stuff paper into the mouths of dissident poets?

No. What remains to be debated, in the immediate, is not if there should be a transition in Cuba but rather how to manage the inevitable wave of change that is already mounting. How to keep it from drowning Cuba in a sea of blood. And over the longer term, how to move Cuba into its future, preserving its independence and national dignity – how to prevent plunging Cuba into the abyss of a barbaric, Polish-style capitalism, how to avoid turning Cuba back into an American dependency. In these tasks, ordinary Cubans in both Miami and Havana are straining to find common ground.

What, then, still sustains the Cuba conflict beyond its historical shelf-life? What makes the straits of Florida feel like the world's last border between East and West? No matter that the East has disappeared. The answer resides in the three separate and hard-line bureaucracies in Miami, Washington and Havana that have been forged in the heat of this conflict, and now also find a convenient, if to the rest of us, disconcerting, convergence of their own. Looking toward the immediate future with fear, they know only how to draw on the instincts of the past.

In Miami, the anti-Castro elite, after decades of bluster in favor of militarily disassembling Communism has, to its horror, seen those regimes fall under their own weight. Not a single one was brought down by invading commando forces. With Bush out of the White House and the Communists out of the Kremlin, and with Castro still standing three years after The Fall, their nightmares are haunted by the notion of a peaceful, brokered transition in Cuba – one that would leave them on the sidelines. For the Miami Cuban hard-right, nothing is more reassuring than a snarling, intransigent Fidel Castro.

Likewise, unable to explain to his countrymen the collapse of the East as anything other than a sign of 'softness', Castro has cloaked himself in a mantle of orthodoxy, vowing either 'Socialism or Death'. With Cuba descending into economic oblivion and widespread discontent bubbling into public talk of the unthinkable – the *post–*Castro period – where would Fidel be without the American embargo to blame for all his economic ills and without the Miami right around so he can warn, *après moi, le déluge?* What better evidence of the symbiosis between Castro and the anti-Castro fanatics than the revelations last fall that the most militaristic of Miami's rightist groups – Alpha 66 – was led by a double agent. Not only was Francisco Avila Azcuy giving regular reports to the FBI, but he was simultaneously getting money from Havana to purchase weapons and boats. Nothing like a little – and harmless – anti-Castro raid from offshore now and then to bolster pro-Castro sentiment in the Cuban capital.

Finally, here in the US we have policymakers and politicians trying to shore up new voting blocs in the shifting political sands of the nineties. That's why Democrats like New Jersey Congressman Robert Torricelli cooked up his so-called Cuban Democracy Act last year that *tightened* the thirty-year-old embargo against the island. Then-candidates Clinton and Gore rushed to endorse the bill (signed by Bush last October) hoping to win over Florida's Cubans. Torricelli's law bans from US ports any foreign ship that has docked in Havana in the last six months, and prohibits US subsidiaries abroad from trading with Cuba. If a few thousand Havana kids would go hungry or sick as a result, what the hell? No one in US politics has ever lost any points by kicking Fidel Castro around. Pictures of Marines saving the lives of Somali babies fold a lot more smoothly into the national consciousness than would reports of an incoming administration upping the quota of pharmaceuticals allowed to flow into Havana hospitals. But history is an unforgiving teacher. If US policy continues to ignore the new realities and instead opts to keep stoking the furnaces of intransigence and frustration, Cuba might finally erupt into the blaze that too many in Washington have dreamed of. In that case, we may not be looking at just one more US foreign policy 'success', but also at the exploding cigar of Bill Clinton's presidency.

HAVANA: 'DIPLO-COMMUNISM'

One of the curators of the Havana zoo looks down at the pair of weather-worn ducks navigating the mucky surface of the pond and shakes his head in awe. 'There used to be four hundred of them a few years ago', he says. 'Now we are down to four. I call them the Ninja ducks. No one can catch them.' With all food in Cuba now sold by ration, and with the daily quota of bread down to one muffin-sized roll a day, with eggs limited to two per person per week, with meat restricted to one fish and three-fourths of a pound of soyburger per month, and with lines for these scarce products sometimes stretching into half-day waits, not only are zoo animals vanishing, but street cats now sell for 200 pesos each, a bit more than a black market chicken. A Cuban walking past a dressed turkey on display at a tourist-only restaurant rightly called it a 'fossil'.

Now entering its third year of what Castro calls the 'Special Period', in great degree because of the collapse of Cuba's socialist trading partners, the Cuban economy seems poised, like the zoo ducks, for extinction. Cuban government official Carlos Lage recently admitted that oil imports had dropped from 13 million tons in 1989 to barely 5 million in 1992. Other Cuban imports plummeted 75 percent in the same period. Gasoline rations – when available – are down to about a gallon a week, and the streets and roads are now dominated by a fleet of donated Chinese bicycles (and weighing in at a ponderous 57 pounds each, the Chinese were probably delighted to unload them on Cuba). At a prestigious medical institute last month, a day was spent in meetings to decide who deserved a few prized rolls of toilet paper. Scheduled power blackouts, originally set at three hours a day, have now upticked to eight. With filtration pumps idled, Cubans are boiling their tap water and adding their own chlorine. They also watch TV programs that teach them how to make their own candles, how to bake fruit rinds as meat substitutes, how to make their own toothpaste and deodorants, how to tend their own vegetable gardens, and – ominously – how to grow medicinal herbs. Even Cuba's fabled health care system lacks drugs and medicines, some of which – to the dismay of ordinary Cubans – are now for sale, only in tourist hotels, for US dollars.

For sale in the same hotels, garishly displayed on the lobby couches and aggressively soliciting clients, are hard-currency hookers – five years ago in Havana just a rumor. Got dollars? Then in the street you can also buy boxes of pilfered cigars, or anticholesterol tablets, or Colombian coke, or home-grown grass. Clothes, groceries, cakes, gasoline, cosmetics and basic consumer goods are also sold in dollars, legally only to foreigners, in unlimited amounts, in a series of state-run hard-currency stores stretched along Calle Primera.

And Cubans who as recently as a year ago were mortified at the thought of being surprised in the street with illegal dollars now pour into these shops (euphemistically called Diplomatic or Diplo-stores), the government not only winking its eye to the violation but now encouraging this parallel market as an escape valve. Not all Cubans, of course, can afford this privilege. Maybe 50,000 or so out of a population of 12 million, just those artists and writers who can sell some of their work abroad, or other Cubans whose visiting relatives have handed them a few hundred bucks. Or the Cubans who line up for a block in front of the government store they bitterly call La Hérnan Cortez. Inside a clerk relieves them forever of their personal tribute of gold and jewelry in exchange for dollar-valued certificates negotiable at the hard-currency stores. 'Imagine. I gave my whole youth for this revolution', says a 45-year-old Cuban journalist standing in line with me to buy food at the dollars-only Diplo-market. 'Hundreds of meetings, weeks of voluntary labor, who'd have thought it would end with me illegally buying eggs in US dollars? I guess this is the next phase of history, what you call Diplo-Communism.'

The proliferation of the dollar-based economy has rendered the Cuban peso worthless, thereby turning employment in Cuba into a formality. When a friend of mine went one morning to pick up his high monthly salary of 325 pesos as a book translator, from a publisher that had pressed no new book in fourteen months, he immediately handed the wad – worth only about $6 – over to me to take home as a souvenir. The US$100 he recently earned for some under-the-table freelancing was equivalent to nearly a year-and-a-half's salary. Another friend of mine just completed her doctorate in clinical psychology. But her material existence was guaranteed not by her forty-hour workweek as a therapist, for which she receives less than $2, but by the $200 she earned from selling home-baked Christmas cakes to foreign embassies. The Cubans who don't have access to dollars nevertheless pay dollar prices translated into pesos. Whatever you buy on the black market – and that's most everything except for the minimum food ration, rent, medicine and education, which to the credit of the Revolution remain essentially free – costs what it would in Miami. But the salary of a Cuban worker is about $4 a month. A doctor earns maybe $12. The net result is a nation of Communists who spend their day angling how to grab a hold of some American dollars.

'About the only people in Cuba who still believe this is socialism are European and American solidarity activists', says the book translator, whose father was a founder of the Cuban Communist Party. 'People's political attitudes are formed not by abstract ideology but by real-life experience. And here everyone's experience is that things are ever more unjust, ever more unequal, that the state is ever less willing to even things out, that we are already beginning to live a sort of post-Communist, savage capitalism.'

Just as things seemed to be touching bottom in Cuba this past year, the economy paralyzed and public confidence in the system evaporating, giving rise to conditions that in most other Latin American countries could lead to rebellion, Castro was given a new blast of political oxygen when George Bush signed the Torricelli bill on 23 October. Almost the entirety of the Cuban population reacted with disappointment and rage. Castro deftly capitalized on this sentiment that the US was trying to starve Cuba into political surrender. Further strengthening Castro's hand was an overwhelming vote against the Torricelli bill by the UN General Assembly, at a time when so many observers had written Cuba off as hopelessly isolated internationally. 'Now that the Soviet Union is gone', says my friend the translator, 'there is no government in the world as objectively pro-Castro as the US government.'

Indeed, on the heels of Torricelli's passage, Castro immediately cut the rations on food and gasoline, and government officials publicly threw cold water on budding popular optimism that president-elect Clinton, who had supported Torricelli, would seek detente. Simultaneously, Castro's government unleashed a wave of repression against Cuba's small but growing community of *left-wing* dissidents. In a besieged Cuba, Castro conveniently argued for the umpteenth time, there would be, there could be, no room for public differences.

Illustrative of how US policy perfectly complements Castro's own survival strategy was the disastrous trip made to Havana last month by George McGovern and former US diplomat Wayne Smith. Smith had been Jimmy Carter's envoy to Havana, and since he quit the foreign service in protest of Reagan policy he has been leading an often lonely crusade to normalize US relations with Cuba. Acting with no direct encouragement from Clinton, Smith took the initiative to meet with Castro in December 1992 to explore a post-Bush thaw. Smith was clearly looking for some thread of hope to take back to Clinton's people to argue for a more accommodating Cuba policy. Castro, who in the past has shown great respect for Smith, received him and McGovern in Havana on 10 December. And then Castro proceeded to hang them out to dry. 'Fidel sat them down and said, "We gave the Yankees Angola, we gave them Nicaragua, we gave them El Salvador, we gave them treaties on hijacking and narcotics trafficking",' a Cuban who was privy to the content of the meeting told me. "And we aren't going to give any more concessions", Fidel told them. "If Clinton wants change, let him make the first move. We are not lifting a finger."'

In case anyone missed Castro's point, at the very hour Smith and McGovern were powwowing with Fidel, a Communist Party–organized mob, working with state security agents, swarmed in front of the home of dissident Elizardo Sanchez, who was roughed up and eventually arrested. Few Cubans failed to notice that this incident was Castro's payback to the gringos. If the US did Castro the favor of passing the Torricelli bill, thereby justifying his refusal to open up Cuban society, then Fidel could return the favor to the American and exile hard-line by having Sanchez beaten up not only during Smith and McGovern's mission but by doing so on International Human Rights Day. That Elizardo Sanchez was a former Marxist professor who, now calling himself a Democratic Socialist, not only opposed Fidel but *also* opposed the Torricelli bill *and* the US embargo, so much the better for Fidel. Torricelli and his supporters needed Castro and vice-versa. Those who dared to assume the role of peacemaker, be it Smith, McGovern or Sanchez were not only superfluous, but dangerous. 'No one knows how to better manipulate American politics and politicians than does Fidel Castro Ruz', laments a Cuban journalist who is a current but disaffected Communist Party member. 'He sent Smith and McGovern home humiliated and empty-handed, made them look like fools in front of Clinton, and then tosses the Miami Cubans the red meat of a beaten up dissident. These aren't stupid mistakes. Fidel knows exactly what he is doing. He's saying, please Mr Clinton, don't lift the embargo.'

MIAMI: HALL OF MIRRORS

Cuban writer Jorge Daubar also opposes lifting the embargo. Daubar was first introduced to me two years ago at a rather genteel multinational meeting of mystery authors in the palm-shaded colonial courtyard of Old Havana's Cultural Center. Later that week, we shared New Year's toasts on the balcony of a retired major of the Ministry of Interior as we looked out over the moon-drenched bay of Havana. Now we share steak sandwiches and Diet Cokes at a Miami Beach restaurant, struggling to hear each other over the canned tracks of Paula Abdul.

Jorge has crossed the line. In more ways than one. Married to a Peruvian, Jorge was among the small percentage of Cubans who could legally emigrate with few problems. But his friends in Havana say they never heard him express a desire to leave. And while never a vocal supporter of Fidel Castro, the 51-year-old wheelchair-bound writer never was known as an active critic of the regime. He seemed to enjoy all the perks given the Cuban cultural elite. Daubar's friends on both sides of the Florida straits were surprised not only that he left Cuba, but even more so that since he arrived in Miami a year ago he has politically married himself to the most hard-line, ultra-right exile faction, the all-powerful Cuban-American National Foundation (CANF).

'I am, perhaps, the first "real" intellectual to join up with the Foundation', Jorge says with a sparkle of malevolent glee. Perhaps a bit hyperbolic, but not by much. The Foundation, as everyone calls it, has been the high-velocity political and lobbying vehicle of choice for the all-white exile business elite. Fixated on maintaining a constant state of hostility with the Cuban government, and seen by many as every bit as rigid and dogmatic as its archenemy, the Foundation historically has had little time for or truck with spiritually complicated and ideologically muddled artists and writers. Foundation leader Jorge Más Canosa, without question the most feared man in Cuba, has also attracted leagues of detractors in his home base of Miami. But Jorge Daubar has found common cause with Más Canosa's mandarins of commerce: an unflinching commitment to overthrow Fidel Castro. 'The Foundation is pragmatic and politically astute', Jorge tells me. 'And the Foundation isn't getting ready to support some kind of transition government for two years with the same old Communists. We are preparing to *be* the next government. You have to be real stupid to think you can dialogue with Fidel Castro. Either real stupid or so stupid you are actually an agent of Cuban State Security.' The rest of Daubar's discourse melds into the well-known cant of the Foundation: the more moderate Miami Cubans are dismissed as 'bandits', 'usurpers' or 'fakers'. The US government is considered an eternal ally safely in the pocket of the Foundation lobby. 'Republicans and Democrats', says Jorge, 'have lined up Indian file to support us.'

But one suspects that Jorge's affection for the Foundation transcends simple policy consensus. Starkly put, no one in Miami can deliver like Más Canosa and his Foundation. And for someone like Jorge Daubar, who has grown up in Communist Cuba, where writers are given state salaries along with the rest of the safety net given the general population, there has to be something very appealing about finding a rich and generous Godfather in the free market jungles of Miami. Indeed, before landing in Florida, Daubar spent several months in Peru working for a more moderate exile group, the Liberal Union, led by writer Carlos Alberto Montaner. But this grouping (with its pro-Yankee politics sometimes called the left-wing of the American Eagle, as opposed to the right-wing Cuban-American National Foundation) doesn't have anywhere near the numbers or resources of the CANF.

The influence and power of the Foundation, concentrated in southern Florida and Washington D.C., is nothing short of imperial. Special agreements with the US government allow Más Canosa to run his own private immigration service, so that select Cubans can be brought in from virtually anywhere in the world and painlessly slid through the US legal bureaucracy. Once ensconced in Florida, the newly arrived exile soon learns that the Foundation also acts as one-stop employment agency, housing authority, lobbying center and often intimidating and ruthless enforcer of right-wing political correctness. In Havana just as Fidel alone calls the shots, in Miami it's Jorge Más. And as in Cuba, in Miami if you want to get along you go along.

Jorge Daubar is a case in point. Within months of his landing in Miami and joining forces with the Foundation, this author, with one nonfiction book to his credit and with no hard-currency reserve, found himself with his own radio program on the short wave 'Voice of the Foundation', plenty of guaranteed writing jobs, promises to publish his old manuscripts and settlement in a comfortable middle-class home. It beats the condition of an average southern Florida Haitian boat person or a California-marooned Salvadoran writer by about ten thousand miles. And the only cost appears to be having to shift one's rhetoric twenty degrees rightward.

The wealthy businessmen who control the Foundation have always held political sway over the Florida exile community, but it wasn't until 1981, with direct assistance from Ronald Reagan's National Security Council, that the CANF was formally brought into existence. Just as Daubar says, these men who see themselves as the next leaders of post-Castro Cuba have built an influence empire stretching far beyond their immigration service and their private propaganda transmitter. They have schooled some 1,500 recruits in a sort of Foundation Peace Corps, the people they hope will be the managers of a free market Cuba. They have written a new constitution ready to be imposed on the ashes of socialism. They have drawn up real estate and property registers to help exiles in recovering expropriated homes, factories and farms. They hand out stipends, 'research grants', press junkets, favors, endorsements, recommendations and sundry courtesies.

But mostly the Foundation has played much the same role regarding Cuba as the American Israel Political Action Committee (AIPAC) has played in terms of the Middle East: ensuring that US foreign policy in that area responds primarily to the hard-line interests of each respective lobby, rather than to the conforms of real geopolitics and national interest. Not that the US government has exactly been held hostage by the CANF. Rather, the American government and the CANF have established an elaborate, mutually beneficial money-laundering scheme that runs something like this: over the years, the congressionally funded National Endowment for Democracy has given some $600,000 to the CANF, $100,000 in 1991 alone to finance a human rights project. But over the same last decade Foundation top officials and their families *gave back* almost $500,000 to congressional candidates or to the so-called Free Cuba PAC. That PAC, run by Foundation officials, has given more than $1 million in total to political campaigns, mostly to conservatives but also to a number of Democrats and an occasional liberal. Though George Bush and especially his son Jeb are favored friends of the Foundation, candidate Bill Clinton was also feted with an exile fundraiser in Miami at the onset of his campaign that netted him an estimated $125,000 and a picture next to Más Canosa for one night's worth of pandering to the Foundation lobby.

With Reagan and Bush in the White House and with a vote against Castro as the only congressional bet safer than a vote for Israel, especially in the last five years, the Foundation's bipartisan arm-wrestling could have succeeded just as well using only its left-hand pinky. Foundation hegemony in Washington political circles, reinforced by the Foundation's hiring away of a number of Republican administration officials, has assured that American policy, after Carter-era flirtations with a Havana detente, returned to a vintage deep freeze. The CANF has resisted any and every attempt to weaken the three-decade-old embargo on Cuba, or any of the anti-Cuban restrictions spelled out in the Trading with the Enemy Act.

A spectacular victory was won by the Foundation in 1985 when its vigorous lobbying overcame the objections of the American broadcast industry and the US government laid out tens of millions of taxpayer dollars to begin operation of Radio Martí, whose board and – consequently – much of its editorial policy is dominated by Más Canosa and Foundation appointees. In 1990 another Foundation triumph gave birth to Television Martí, another taxpayer sinkhole, which transmits a propaganda signal to Cuba that is seen *only* by the handful of Castro's technicians whose jamming operation obliterates the transmission.

Those Foundation victories were, however, only prelude to passage of the Torricelli bill, supported by both Republicans and Democrats. 'We have no worries about Bill Clinton or Al Gore. They know that even if Communism has failed, there are still plenty of Communists out there. Remember that Al Gore was a cosponsor of the Torricelli bill', I'm confidently told by Luis Zuniga, a top official of the Foundation. We meet in the three-story bunkerlike CANF offices in northwest Miami. Around us there are security gates, magnetic strip cards, ID badges, TV monitors and uniformed guards. Lots of guys in Ray-Bans, lots of cellular phones and walkie-talkies, bumper stickers and posters announcing 'I Don't Believe the Miami Herald'. The macho, militarist atmosphere immediately evokes similar interviews held in the offices of the Salvadoran neofascist ARENA party, of the Chilean Fatherland and Freedom Front, and – yes – inside much of the Cuban Communist Party and security bureaucracy. You get the feel that apart from whatever shooting it would take, these guys could make a rather seamless transition into the digs of Castro's political police and feel right at home. Just pull down the posters of Fidel and tack up the new ones of Más Canosa.

'US policy toward Cuba is long-term and not prone to sudden turns', Zuniga continues. 'I don't think Clinton will be fooled into changing a good policy.' But many of his advisors and appointees will nevertheless try, Zuniga worries. 'Liberalism in the US has often really meant socialism or even Communism', Zuniga assures me. 'Some of the people around Clinton see Castro as the embodiment of their dream of social justice.'

Who, I ask, does he have in mind?

Certainly, he says, George McGovern along with Wayne Smith, whose December peace trip to Havana sent the Foundation into apoplexy. Then he lists former Carter officials Robert Pastor and Secretary of State–designate Warren Christopher, who fifteen years ago committed the heinous crime of suggesting a 'normalization' of relations with Havana. 'And of course, Jesse Jackson', Zuniga adds. 'Not that these people are ill-willed. It's that they are naive, they are dupes. It's all right there in that book, if you want to understand them. You know the book, *The Masters of Deceit.*' The book written in the Pleistocene era of McCarthyite hysteria by J. Edgar Hoover, in which he lists the ten ways to identify a Communist (including people who pick up banana peels off the ground in which secret messages may be encoded). Here on the cusp of 1993 are our NED tax dollars at work.

Zuniga's major concern is that these American fellow-travelers will hammer away at Bill Clinton 'hoping to undermine our work' and 'convince Clinton to listen' to other Cuban exile voices, breaking the Foundation monopoly on speaking for Cuban exiles. And then in an eerie moment, Zuniga, as if tasting his own bile, forces himself to name these 'other Cubans' in exile who want to 'subvert' current policy: Ramon Cernuda, Carlos Alberto Montaner, Miguel Gonzalez-Pando. And, more to the point, he pronounces their names and characterizes these fellow anti-Castro Cuban exiles with the same disdain and scorn that Communist officials in Havana use to describe the same people. Zuniga even goes so far as to criticize the 'excessive' American press coverage given to dissident Elizardo Sanchez after his 10 December 1992 beating in Havana. Even if Sanchez has been sent to Cuban jails for as long as eight years and continues to be harassed and rearrested, Zuniga views Sanchez with nothing but suspicion. 'You see', Zuniga tells me with a serious grimace. 'There's a world of difference

CLOSE, BUT NO CIGAR

between what you call dissidents like Sanchez and oppositionists like us.'

I was tempted to answer that yes, I do see the difference. The dissidents like Elizardo Sanchez take their stand in Cuba and Zuniga and the Foundation take theirs with US government money from within the comforts of their Miami offices. But I remained silent, convinced the Zuniga would not much appreciate my observation.

HAVANA: BUSINESS IS *BISNEZ*

It's hardly just dissidents who are telling Havana's hottest new joke: in the year 2025, two explorers find a fifty-year-old map revealing a Caribbean island they have never heard of – Cuba. They travel to Mexico but find no one knows of any air service to this mysterious and forgotten island. Finally, from Haiti they find someone who takes them to Cuba by canoe. Arriving in Havana, the explorers find it overgrown and deserted, a tropical Planet of the Apes. Hacking their way with machetes to where the Plaza of the Revolution used to be, they find two Cubans, in loincloths, hunching over a pile of firewood. One of the Cubans is furiously striking two rocks together. But to no avail. In frustration he throws the stones to the ground and says to his friend: 'You know, *chico*, if they don't start distributing rocks that make a spark, then this government is finally gonna fall.'

In Cuba everyone wants change. And in Cuba everyone is scared to death of change. There are only two towering contemporary figures in Cuban politics, two poles between which Cubans see themselves caught in a decaying orbit: Fidel Castro, who looms ambivalently as your once generous grandfather-now-gone-bonkers. And Jorge Más Canosa, your Fagan-like evil uncle from Miami who wants to commit Fidel and adopt you, only to be better able to exploit you. 'Sure Fidel's got to go', says a Latin American writer, a long-time Havana resident. 'But I'm not joining the opposition. I look at myself as a revolutionary with terminal cancer. And like all terminal patients I hope for anything that will keep me alive a bit longer. Because I know that after Fidel Castro, things will get worse here for at least twenty years.'

Cubans, extraordinarily well-educated and politicized, know that a capitalist Cuba will not be Germany or even Czechoslovakia, but more like Haiti or the Dominican Republic. Many didn't like the old Soviet Union. More of them are horrified by the tailspin into barbarism that the new Russia has embarked upon. 'Forty-eight hours after Fidel is gone, we will lose everything', says the writer. 'We have hunger now, but that will become malnourishment. We have petty theft now, that will become armed robbery. We have workers who do nothing, that will become massive unemployment. We have corruption now, that will become our public ethic.'

Cubans of all stripes and categories will tell you the same. That's why Castro, and for that matter the Foundation, are reserving their greatest disdain for the small circle of dissidents in Cuba who still call themselves socialists. It's not only Elizardo Sanchez, but also much more prominent figures who have recently joined what's called the Democratic Socialist Current. Revolutionary Air Force General Alvaro Prendes, who shot down three US planes at the Bay of Pigs, and former planning official Vladimiro Roca – whose father was an intimate collaborator of Fidel's – have also entered the left-wing dissidence.

Much better known outside of Cuba than inside, the tenuous, tiny organizations these dissenters have established number their adherents only in the hundreds. They operate in a political space that is totally closed, where even well-informed citizens are likely to know only the names of a few cabinet ministers, because in Cuba there is only *one* leader. And with alarming frequency, the frontyards of these dissidents are becoming rallying points for the recently created Rapid Response Brigades, progovernment citizen squads in charge of harassing malcontents. 'But if you could imagine a political opening here that would allow these Democratic Socialists to run in elections', says a University of Havana political scientist, 'and if people could read their platform of opposing the embargo, opposing Más Canosa, and calling for a democratization of this revolution and some sort of economic opening, I guarantee you they'd sign up a million people the first week.'

In the meantime, Cubans, and it would hardly be an exaggeration to say all Cubans, express their dissidence not in politics but through economics. 'The black market here can be compared with God', recently wrote Cuban reporter Angel Tomás. 'You can't see it. But it's everywhere.' Unable to get the hard currency they need for staples, and with the peso worthless, Cubans massively appropriate whatever they need from their workplace. What they don't use, they sell. And in a grotesque way, this lumpen-capitalism becomes one more mainstay for the system. Any Cuban *bisnero,* any half-conscious Cuban businessman, knows that success is dependent on scarcity. Under full-blown capitalism, today's Cuban 'capitalists' know they would be tomorrow's porters, janitors and maids inside the intercontinental hotel of some multinational.

'Everybody's in on it', says twenty-year-old Franklin as he takes me for a walk down colonial Old Havana's Calle Obispo. The state-owned stores that line the street are shabby and bare beyond description, worse than if the CIA had been hired as consultants to design a cinematic Communist Backdrop. But no matter. The real *bisnez* here is on the street. Everyone's got a hustle. And easily spotted as a foreigner, if for no other reason than my clothes, I'm approached every few steps. The offers always begin the same way. Amigo? Are you Mexican? Venezuelan? A Spaniard? And then the menu of merchandise: Change money? Cohiba cigars? Rum? Handicrafts? Potency pills? 'You can fuck like *el caballo*', I'm promised, 'like a horse, like Fidel.'

Franklin chuckles at the petty scope of the offers. He's got a much better racket. After buying, for about US$500, the coveted post as manager and sole operator of a state butcher shop, Franklin receives 900 pounds of soyburger from the state every two weeks to be sold on the ration card to 1,200 people in his jurisdiction. 'The first thing I do is water it down, and because the soy absorbs like a sponge, I triple the volume', he says with a knowing wink. Just as the law demands, he sells 900 pounds at the official subsidized price of half a peso per three-quarter-pound ration. The other 1,800 pounds he sells to the *same* neighbors at a whopping 25 pesos a pound, about 60 US cents. His profit is incalculable by Cuban standards. 'But I only get to keep about 10 percent of what I make', he says. 'The rest goes to pay off the zone manager, the district sales manager, the inspectors and the local police.'

But with everyone in the neighborhood knowing what he does, I ask, isn't he afraid of being denounced by a Communist militant?

'I know all the Communists and all the informants in the neighborhood', Franklin answers. We are interrupted by two kids who want to sell me some Heinekin. Franklin shoos them away and continues. 'The Communists, the military, even the Rapid Response Brigades, are all good clients as long as you are just selling them food and clothes. For that reason they need me. It's just understood that with them you don't deal "heavier" shit, you know drugs, electronics, stereos.'

By now we have reached Franklin's house. I point to the apartment building across the way and ask him, in a hypothetical manner, of the dozen or so families that might live there, how many does he think are involved, not in just buying, but also in selling on the black market?

Hypothetical, my ass. Looking up and starting at the top floor Franklin reels off the list: 'In the penthouse are the two doctors. They sell their services, of course. Next to them is Franco and his wife, Communist Youth, they sell bike parts. Below them is Roberto, well, he sells about everything! Rogelio over there is a fisherman and sells his catch. Enrique on the second floor has a connection for car parts, mostly Ladas and Moskovitches. Salvador, he was one of Fidel's captains in the Rebel Army, well, he can get you gasoline. And that guy on the bottom floor was selling drugs. The cops came last week and there was a big shoot out and they bagged him. But he was free the next day. His dad is a big shot at a Varadero Beach tourist hotel.'

Before we part, Franklin gives me some advice on how I should pilot my solo walk back to the hotel among the sea of pestering *bisneros.* 'There's only one way to blow them off', he says. 'As soon as they ask you your nationality, tell them you're Russian. They know Russians don't have a fucking cent. That's why so many people here want to keep things just the way they are.' I tried out Franklin's theory on the stroll home. People fled from me like I had the plague.

MIAMI: THEIR DISSIDENTS AND OURS

María Cristina Herrera is no friend of Fidel Castro, having served in the anti-Communist underground of the early sixties. But she also knows that the life of a dissident Cuban in Miami can be as dangerous – often more dangerous – than that of a dissident in Havana. When I pull into her driveway in a tidy neighborhood in southwest Miami, the movement of my car triggers a battery of bright security floodlights. Four years ago a sophisticated remote control bomb went off at the end of this driveway, ripping off the garage door and destroying the car inside. The attack came after a meeting at her house on the eve of a conference on improving Cuban–American relations that Herrera had organized in her role as director of the nonprofit Institute for Cuban Studies. The bombing was preceded by a spate of personal attacks on her carried out by the half-dozen extreme right-wing exile radio stations that permeate Miami's AM frequencies – attacks that accused Herrera, among other things, of buying her home with funds from Fidel.

Today, Herrera shrugs at the attacks, accepting them as a routine part of her activist life. In any case, things are getting better, not worse. The moderate, even liberal, sectors of the Cuban exile community represented by Herrera are increasingly coming out of the closet, finding their voice, gaining political ground. Just as cracks open up in the decaying monolith of Cuban society despite Castro's efforts otherwise, there's also a blossoming of diversity in Miami, much to the horror of the Foundation and its supporters. Herrera tells me in her crowded home office, 'We have opened up turf that was rigidly controlled by the extreme right through its ideology and actions.'

Those rightist 'actions' Herrera refers to have become so much a fact of life in Miami that last summer the monitoring group Americas Watch, which generally concentrates on the dismal aspects of life in various Banana Republics, took the unusual step of issuing a report on human rights violations in an American city. Entitled 'Dangerous Dialogue: Attacks on Freedom of Expression in Miami's Cuban Exile Community', it lists twenty-nine pages of threats and violent attacks, including other bombings, against individual exiles and their institutions who have dared to stray from the rigid Cold War bellicosity of Más Canosa's

Foundation and propose more conciliatory policies toward their homeland. In some instances, local, state and federal officials under the political influence of rightist Cubans were complicit in the attacks. Other incidents, says the report, were encouraged by the exile radio stations.

This atmosphere of intimidation included the Foundation forming in 1990 an Information Commission that included two men who had been convicted in the 1976 Washington, D.C. bombing/murder of Chilean diplomat Orlando Letelier (although the convictions were later overturned, both men were later convicted of perjury charges). Professor Lisandro Perez, who helped turn back a bid by the Foundation to gain an academic foothold at Florida International University, says that the real enforcement tool of the hard right isn't dynamite but is 'an ethnic network which leaves everyone susceptible. They call you a Communist and you are through in this city. Lots of Cubans don't like the Foundation and will grumble in private, but wouldn't dare to say anything publicly. I can speak out because I have university tenure.'

Nevertheless, the expansion of Miami's liberal Cuban community continues. 'The fact alone that we have survived psychological terror, real physical terror, firings and blacklistings', says Herrera, 'is in itself a story of triumph.' Underlying the emergence, really in the last five years, of this alternative Miami voice, has been a gradual but radical reshaping of the makeup and disposition of the totality of the southern Florida Cuban-American community. Taken together, these changes give the lie to the standing stereotype, especially on the political left, of Miami Cubans as nothing but a half-million gun-toting whackos who spend their weekends taking target practice in the Everglades. American progressives will now have to come to terms with the disturbing fact that there is today more room in Miami to develop a left perspective on Cuba than there is in Cuba itself.

A half-dozen factors have contributed to this transformation. First was the influx of the more than 100,000 so-called 'Marielitos' in 1980 – a group younger, darker and poorer than previous Cuban immigrants. Having grown up under socialism, many came to Miami with a greater sense of social justice and far fewer economic opportunities than the white aristocrats who run the Foundation. Second, a generation of now fortysomething Cuban academics who grew up mostly in the States left Miami to finish their education and have now returned with more liberal views. Growing up alongside them was a younger breed of Cuban-American entrepreneurs, not embittered over the loss of property on the island, and more open and flexible than their parents. A more subtle, but nonetheless important factor has been the new generation of Cuban women, far more assertive than their mothers and willing to assume a more progressive personal and political attitude. More frequent contact between Cuban and exile artists, in part facilitated by Miami's Museum of Cuban Art, has also loosened the atmosphere of reciprocal suspicion. And finally, the collapse of the Cold War has, in the view of many Miami Cubans, rendered the hard-line approach to Cuba obsolete and counterproductive. Contributing to this questioning of the right has been the Foundation's own excesses. Many Miami Cubans, of all shades of political opinion, told me how embarrassed they had been by last year's shrill campaign by the Foundation against the *Miami Herald*, accusing it of being soft on Cuba; this when no other paper in the country affords so much space and so many jobs to those with anti-Castro views. 'Here we are in 1993 and the fact is that neither Reagan nor Bush could get rid of Castro. Neither has the strategy of the Foundation gotten any results', says Professor Perez. 'The older generation is just getting older and more and more people here [in Miami] are ready for a change in attitude.'

And the one Miami exile seemingly most willing to promote and maximize that change is fifty-year-old Francisco Aruca – a daring entrepreneur and political gadfly whose very existence Maria Cristina Herrera points to as the most reliable indication that there is a New Miami. Two years ago Aruca commenced a project that up to then had been strictly unthinkable. Using the capital he amasses from running the leading charter air service to Cuba, he purchased a five-hour-a-day block of time on a local 1,000-watt rent-a-radio, dubbed his slot Radio Progreso (the same name as Havana's most listened-to station), and figured that if Castro and the US weren't willing to bring a little glasnost into the divided communities' lives, he would. Predictably, his single-minded message of lowering tensions and seeking dialogue between the US and Cuba was met with an onslaught of abuse (several of his detractors told me Aruca was an 'agent of Cuban state security'), death threats, breaks-ins of the offices of his valiant on-air guests, and the inevitable bombing attacks. In the latest assault last year three men broke into the offices of his WOCN radio, beat and tied up one of the employees and vandalized the equipment.

But today, operating from within the station's new barbed-wire ringed fortress-like studios, Aruca has built up a large and popular following. His talk-radio format, with its built-in anonymity, provides Miami Cubans with about the only safe channel for unlimited debate and free expression within their own community. In that sense, Aruca's show, right down to the detail of a usually jaded management staff taking off time to crowd into the control room and watch him live on the air, reminds me of similar outposts of free speech I've seen struggling against the heavy repressive odds in places like El Salvador and Guatemala. I'd also seen the same sort of *frisson* in the offices of Havana's Radio Rebelde three years ago when, during a temporary domestic thaw, some young and innovative Havana journalists were putting their shoulders against the walls of the official envelope.

Of the five hours a day of airtime under his control, Aruca takes two for himself. For one hour he sifts through a pile of clippings and cuttings and spins out a pointed sixty-minute running commentary, always returning to the same point: intransigence and hostility from Washington and Miami only causes Castro to 'circle the wagons' – it's time, Aruca preaches, to realize that Cuba is not exactly hell, the US is far from heaven, and that many of the 'democratic' Latin American countries held up as alternatives to Cuba are much more like purgatory. His conclusion: lift the siege of Cuba and allow Cubans on the island to sort out their own problems without interference.

During the second hour of his show Aruca takes listener calls. I sat there for an hour and watched, with no little amazement, as call after call poured in, uncensored and unscreened, the majority expressing agreement with his views. Where there was disagreement there was polite and rational debate, not the hysterical screeching that characterizes the other Cuban radio shows. 'When we first started two years ago I'd say the calls were about seventy–thirty against me', he says in an interview after his show. 'Now the ratio is reversed.'

In 1978, with some encouragement from Jimmy Carter's White House, Aruca and María Cristina Herrera were among the original group of 'dialogueros', that small group of Miami exiles who, facing down threats, opened talks with Havana. Some progress was made. Travel for Miami Cubans became much easier. Some 3,000 political prisoners were released by Castro. And some diplomatic gaps were narrowed, but the whole process collapsed in part because of Castro's inability to shape a coherent exile policy and because of the turbulent events surrounding the 1980 Mariel mass exodus to Miami. The dialogue of the seventies, says Aruca, 'was strictly humanitarian. Looking for ways to re-unite divided families. Today the dialogue we search for is political. People are realizing that as bad as the economic situation is in Cuba there's going to be no explosion. Castro is not in danger of losing the support he needs to stay in power. To make progress on both sides we have to start talking.'

And Aruca has an optimistic theory, one shared by a number of moderate exiles. A hope, really, that notwithstanding the self-confidence of the Foundation that no US policy change is in the offing, a Clinton administration will mean a shift toward more openness. 'The Foundation is caught in a pickle between first and second', says Aruca with a giggly smile. 'They pissed off the conservative Republicans by giving some money to Clinton. And at the same time it will be ever more legitimate for Washington to start listening to those Cubans who differ with the Foundation.'

But I remind Aruca that it takes two to rumba and that Clinton was more than happy to hobnob with Más Canosa and the Foundation, take their money, support the Torricelli bill and in general take a more severe position on Cuba than George Bush.

'Precisely', smiles back Aruca, who as a member of the Democratic Business Council had served as one of Dukakis's Florida pointmen in 1988. 'But our optimistic view is that Clinton did what he had to do trying to win Florida and now he will slowly back away. And it's not just optimism. It flatly makes more sense for Democrats to make alliances with a different sector of Cuban-Americans than the Republicans did.' Aruca, and others, point to the 1992 congressional run of Democrat Magda Montiel Davis for a heavily Cuban southern Florida district represented by a pro-Foundation Republican. Openly campaigning on a platform of lifting the embargo against Cuba, Davis, who five years ago might have been rewarded with a midnight car bombing, instead reaped 34 percent of the vote. 'Cuba is no longer a foreign policy concern', says Aruca. 'It's strictly a domestic issue. So the role of liberal Cubans in prying Clinton open on this matter is crucial. I've told the Democrats: look, you can forget about winning 50 percent of the Cuban-American vote for the next five years, it's not going to happen. But in the meantime by echoing Bush on Cuba, by supporting the Torricelli bill, Clinton still won only 18 percent of our vote. I am sure, really positive, that if he had taken the opposite position, if he had spoken to the human needs of our community, of improving communications with Cuba, improving mail, permitting more medicine, freer travel, some trade and so on, he would have doubled that vote. If the new White House would call to it some Cuban businessmen other than those from the Foundation, it would also help the Democratic Party. Clinton has got to realize this.'

But will he? Aruca's not taking bets, but leans toward the affirmative, or at the least fervently desires a change. Many Cubans, he says still suffer from what around here is called the 'Plattista Mentality' – referring to the 1902 Platt Amendment, in which the US government reserved for itself the right to intervene in Cuban affairs. 'It's a bit circular. Washington might say because this is really a domestic issue now we'll make the change if we can see the constituency for it in Miami. But that constituency will appear to the degree Washington makes the change. In private many, many Cuban-American businessmen and others want engagement. But someone in Washington, hopefully the president, has to have the courage to flash us that green light.'

MIAMI: WHITHER CLINTON?

Television Martí, the US-funded station that transmits to Cuba from a giant gas-filled balloon over the Florida Keys, best symbolizes the absurdity of US policy on Cuba. At the cost of $20 million a year in taxpayer funds, its hundreds of employees pump out eight hours a night of highly professional, if propagandistic, programming. But in Cuba the only people who see the TV Martí images are the handful of state employees whose job it is to jam and obliterate the signal. Everyone in Washington, everyone at TV Martí, knows the signal pours every night into a void. Yet Bill Clinton promised that after his inauguration his administration would *increase* TV Martí's transmission to twenty-four hours a day.

This aberrational vow reflects the disturbing fact that American policy on Cuba serves not the interests of either country, but rather those of the powerful exile lobby, which completely controls TV Martí's content. 'Jorge Más Canosa knows very well that no one is watching', says a Miami critic of the station. 'But he also knows that the day the Cuban government falls, TV Martí will be his private, ready-to-go, off-the-shelf vehicle for personal political power.' In fact, as Cuba staggers, Más Canosa and the Foundation race to be first in line to take over the reins of power. There's the Foundation-drawn constitution, legal codes and property registers ready to be imposed, reversing the clock back to 1958. Working with the American PR firm MWW/Strategic Communications, the Foundation has published a 48-page proposal on the future of Cuba, in which the Foundation is cast as 'the only logical choice as leader in the establishment of the government and economy of the new Cuba.'

Pressuring Wall Street to underwrite a half-billion-dollar bond issue, which he predicts will fuel a post-Castro free market boom in Cuba, Más Canosa has pulled together a 'Blue-Ribbon Commission on the Economic Reconstruction of Cuba.' Enlisted to the cause already are Malcolm Forbes, Jr, who sits as Honorary Chair; US Senators Connie Mack and Bob Graham; a number of congressmen; Jeanne Kirkpatrick; former National Security Advisor William Clark; Hyatt Hotels; Royal Caribbean Cruise Lines; and Bellsouth.

The Foundation plans to be ready to step in immediately upon Castro's collapse and take over the island as if it were no more than a cash-strapped minor manufacturing firm. The Torricelli bill figures significantly in Foundation planning, because the new law prevents the US from economically aiding any Cuban transitional government not born of direct elections. So much for encouraging a peaceful, evolutionary changeover.

Nor has Fidel Castro taken any pains to ease the possibility of confrontation. His slogan of Socialism or Death! translated into the purge last fall of Cuba's number-three man, Carlos Aldana, who had been positioning himself as middleman for a transition. With Aldana's disappearance from the political scene, that leaves Castro as the only voice of the Cuban government.

The hope among those who want to avoid a midnight shoot-em-up be-

tween Castro and Más Canosa, of those who want to avoid the Cuba saga from
ending in a sea of blood, is to find a third way. This compromise strategy is
twofold. First, it aims at isolating the hard-liners found in the three legs of the
Cuba triangle: Castro in Havana, Más Canosa in Miami, and in Washington the
hawkish Democrats like Torricelli and Bob Graham. Second, this strategy of
convergence would unite reformers in Cuba, many of whom now work in the
government, liberals and moderates in Miami, and procompromise Washington
Democrats like Ted Kennedy, Christopher Dodd, McGovern and Wayne Smith.

The end product would be a brokered transition in Cuba, a peaceful changing of the guard, and one that would ameliorate not only the pernicious aspects
of the current regime, but would mitigate against the brutality of an unchecked
free market. 'I believe there is a revolutionary consensus still in Cuba. Not a
repressive notion but a nationalist one', says Lisandro Perez. 'Most Cubans agree
on a future strong role for the government, for the providing of social welfare.
A lot of people in Cuba are rightly worried about us in Miami coming in with
the Yankees, imposing a totalitarianism of the right, taking their houses away.
And the more the US is allied with the restorationist exiles who really do hold
that position, the farther it is from inducing the change that the Cuban people
want.'

But to reach the consensus that Perez and others envision, you need willing
interlocutors in the three key communities. And that's the rub. In Cuba, Castro,
for the moment, is allowing no compromise. In Washington, the compromise
position remains only a potential and so far Clinton has been leaning in the
wrong direction. Where voices of mediation and concession have arisen clearly
is in the liberal sectors of the Miami exile community. But those exiles who have
spoken up for dialogue and normalization of relations see themselves caught in
a nightmarish multifront crossfire: branded as 'CIA agents' by Castro, denounced as 'Communists' by Más Canosa, mostly ignored by Washington, and
written off, in ignorance, by US progressives as 'counterrevolutionaries'. And
yet, it seems, at least for those Americans who wish to help ease conditions for
Cuba, there is no better place to start than to begin seeking new allies in Miami.

The Clinton administration now must make its own choice. Take the easy
road, stay the course, clamp the embargo down tighter, and bat Fidel Castro
around for cheap political points. Such tactics will only pump up social pressure
in Cuba and when it finally blows, the Clintonistas can only hope the wind isn't
blowing in their direction. Or the administration can break the 35-year-old cycle
of counterproductive and ineffective Cuba policy and help peacefully reunite a
torn nation.

Ramón Cernuda, a Miami-based Cuban socialist publisher who has arisen as
the community's undisputed counterpoint to Más Canosa, argues that time is

running out quickly, that cataclysmic changes in Cuba are likely under Clinton's watch. And the US will bear great responsibility for how those changes play out. 'I can only hope that this new administration will pay more attention to dissidents in Cuba rather than exiles in Miami, that it will learn that US foreign policy on Cuba has to be made in Washington, not any longer in Miami', Cernuda says. 'The worst mistake Clinton could make would be to tie a liberalization of American policy to negotiations with Castro. No. US policy changes must be unilateral. Castro does not govern alone. There are plenty of reformers in the power structure, people who support Castro only because they see him as the last trench against the US. They are ready to listen to others but those others must give them something to reach out to. The changes we advocate will deflate Castro's discourse, leave him with nothing. You know Gorbachev told the US in 1989, if you want real change in Cuba, then lift your embargo.'

Wayne Smith, who has risked his political and academic prestige to forge a new Cuba policy, agrees with Cernuda but admits that things 'don't look real good at the moment. A new open attitude by the US would go a long way to help things. Cubans would no longer have to worry about the CIA and the NED and could let their guard down. The Clinton administration should say, clearly, that the Cold War is over, then lift the ban on food and medicines, shut down Television Martí, and go from there. See what the Cubans do next. We lose nothing. The Cubans win a chance at avoiding the worst.'

HAVANA: A LOST GENERATION?

Halfway between Ernest Hemingway's old digs at Havana's Ambos Mundos Hotel and the Bodeguita Del Medio bar, where Papa would suck up his syrupy sweet *mojitos,* squats Cuba's sixties-modern Ministry of Education. On the day before New Year's about 500 students were lined up outside the building to witness a speech by the education minister. The kids were maybe fourth-, fifth- and sixth-graders, decked out in their red-and-white and gold-and-white 'Young Pioneers' uniforms.

As the minister lectured them about revolutionary responsibility and imperialist intransigence, they looked at the ground, played with their curls or gazed absent-mindedly at the fluttering red flags the class leaders held high. But for all the revolutionary sloganeering the minister tried to lead them in, he missed the obvious. These kids had no need to parrot empty rhetoric. For looking at them you could *see* the best that this Revolution has produced. To anyone who has travelled the Third World, these Cuban schoolchildren immediately stand out as being extraordinarily healthy. Even now, with all of its economic woes, Cuba still shows off the best-fed, best-cared-for children in Latin America. Public school gatherings in any other Latin American nation would have evidenced disturbing signs of malnutrition, lack of clothing, filth, probably even drug use in the form of the spaced-out glare of ten-year-old glue sniffers. But these Cubans were still alert, clean, rosy and dignified.

This was hardly the first time that I had noticed this trait of Cuban school-children. When I came to Cuba, five, six, a dozen years ago, I saw the same thing. And when I also saw, during those visits, the abuses of a one-party state, the stupidity of a hermetically closed system, the idolatry of Fidel Castro, I didn't justify these faults. But I told myself, as did millions of Cubans, that there might be plenty wrong with the Revolution, that people were being asked to sacrifice a lot, but at least all this toil has guaranteed a future for these kids.

What devastated me on this current visit to Cuba is that for the first time I could no longer see that future. I felt I was looking at the last generation of Cubans who would be assured of food on the table, a place in school, and maybe not even this one past their puberty.

But then again, Cubans have shown a remarkable inventiveness. For the last thirty years they have figured out how to cannibalize car batteries, how to main-tain 1949 De Sotos using beercans for pistons, how to turn potatoes into hair dye, grapefruit into a meat substitute, how to stretch a couple of eggs and a pound of soy into three meals for three people, how to fashion toilet paper rolls into hair curlers, how to dress sharply in a country that has no clothing stores – ultimately, how to make a revolution under the nose of Uncle Sam and then figure out how to live through it for the next thirty years. And even those who didn't or couldn't, still found a way to craft seaworthy rafts and evade the Cuban Coast Guard and the Great Whites and paddle their way to Florida.

Maybe the Cubans' final test this century will be to invent a way to con-tinue the promise made to these kids. To reinvent yet one more Cuba, one with a future. Not a new Haiti.

Village Voice
26 January 1993

NOTE: In July 1993 the Cuban government legalized the possession and use of US dollars, thereby formalizing and accentuating growing class differences among Cubans.

11

RUSSIAN ROULETTE

After all, Don Corleone, we are not Communists.
Don Barzini, The Godfather, 1972

BAPTISM

MOSCOW, THURSDAY, 15 APRIL 1993. My first afternoon in Moscow and my guide, Gennady, pats his pocket for his tear gas gun. We're ten days away from the vote of national confidence in Boris Yeltsin, but a lot of Russians have other sorts of confidence ploys on their minds. The New Moscow is only one part democratic Athens, but nine parts El Dorado-turning-Dodge City. And Gennady and I are about to dismount in the middle of the rough-and-tumble Pushkin Square on a money-changing mission. From atop his twenty-foot pedestal, the great bronzed poet looks out forlorn, his hand over his tummy, suggesting a bad case of heartburn. And with due cause. His colleague, Maxim Gorki, has already seen his name removed from a stretch of this grand boulevard. The Pushkin statue, long the center of attention in this elegant corner of the city that houses *Izvestia,* has now found itself eclipsed by a more imposing, enticing monument of our times: the Golden Arches of McDonald's. Indeed, within the garish glow of the restaurant, 100 yards from the poet's statue, pulsates one of Moscow's most vibrant patches of street life, leaving the weather-tarnished Pushkin abandoned to the odd comparative lit professor passing through on sabbatical.

When Gennady's four-door Volga pulls up to park aside McDonald's, we are immediately sucked into a dizzying vortex of buy and sell. An aggressive team of twelve-year-old hustlers accosts our car before we get out, pounding on our windows, elbowing each other aside, shouting out offers of *Micdonalt Brikfest* –

the generic term for the entire fast-food menu. In their lavishly expensive leather baseball jackets, these kiddies are but the outer layer of a concentric ring of gangs – what Russians aptly call 'mafias' – that constitute the trunk of commercial life in Moscow. We count at least thirty of these freelance carhops around the square who, along with the dozen or so of their older, thuggish handlers (who stonily watch every move from behind dark glasses), have organized quite an ingenious and profitable express service for those customers not caring to queue up. Servicing the Lincoln Town Cars and Mercedes 560s that stop by, the kids take the food orders, add a juicy commission and then, skirting the block-long lines, pay off their contacts inside the golden kitchens. Within moments the Big Macs and fries come pouring through the rolled-down tinted windows of the waiting Big Spenders like so much wax-papered manna. And if these 'mafias' have so easily corrupted McDonald's, whose image-obsessed management deploys uniformed employees in Pushkin Square to sweep up hamburger remains within a 500-yard perimeter, you can imagine how they hold sway over any other poor schmuck who has decided to become an independent businessman.

Competing for the Pushkin Square consumers is a host of mustachioed Azeris, manning cardtables full of Dole pineapples, beer and cigarettes – though they are known to answer to their own native Baku syndicates. Beyond them, is a phalanx of Polaroid photographers specialized in posing you in front of the McDonald's so you can send a glossy print back to your envious rube cousins in Tashkent (using the right angle a sharp cameraman can work the four-foot-high papier mâché Mickey and Minnie Mouses out on the sidewalk into the same frame). Then, through the gauntlet of money changers, a bottle of beer in one hand, a cardboard sign in the other offering dollars and deutschemarks, and paying 5 percent *less* than the official rate.

And finally, on the corner, we reach our goal, the right place to change money. A line of so-called kiosks, newstand-size, stand-alone compartments, staffed by a single individual, sealed off from the outside world except for a small sliding window, butted up one against another like at a county fair. These pre-fabbed cubby holes are the eye-dropper dispensers of capitalist prosperity in Russia. The stands erupted out of nowhere like a bad rash last year and have since infected every major street corner in the city. Overnight, seven decades of world-infamous goods shortages came to an end. From now on Russians would lack for absolutely nothing – except money, of course. Muscovites are welcome to crowd up to the kiosk windows and ogle the bounty of imported commercial offal inside. A handful of these outlets are product-specific, blue and yellow Camel stands, white and pink for Baskin-Robbins. But most are a mongrel mix of Marlboros and Dunhills, Cokes and Fantas, Smirnoff and Stoli of course, Cricket lighters, Cuban cigars, brandy-filled Swiss chocolate bars, French orange

ON THE STREETS OF MOSCOW, BANANAS ARE THE
NEW STATUS SYMBOL: ONE BUNCH COSTS A DAY'S WAGE

juice, Christian Dior cologne, German ketchup and fountain pens, Austrian manicure sets, Polish kielbasa, Gillette shavers, bootleg videos and CDs, Barbie dolls, condoms and, at least in this part of town, lots of knobby nine-inch dildos displayed right next to Italian-made mix-masters.

And if you are among what Russian business magazines estimate – rather rosily – as the 2 percent of the population that can afford any of this, then you are welcome to step right up, knock on the glass, point to what you want, shove across the equivalent of three or four weeks' salary for an electrical engineer, watch the kiosk window open, and then cart away whatever little treasure you've bought.

And you'd better like what you've bought as well, even if it's defective or counterfeit – because, as the posted signs say: no returns, no refunds. Most of these kiosks also display a taped-up dollar bill in the window, meaning they will change money, at 5 percent *better* than the bank, thank you very much. And most also display Russian five ruble notes with a black 'X' over them, meaning, we don't accept that shit here anymore, at least not in small denominations. For in the New Russia, anything really Russian is considered second class. This is a whole country run by a team who believe they not only lost the Cold War but were always on the wrong side of it. And they now plan to spend the rest of eternity paying penitence, with interest.

Foreign cars sell at twice the international price and nearly half of them are Mercedes and BMWs. The rest seem to be high-end Volvos, virtually no one wishing to be seen in a cracker box Fiat or Toyota. The luxury autos, often with bodyguards bundled inside, jam the sidewalks outside the dollar-only Lancôme and Cardin boutiques, the retail outlets run by Reebok and Puma, the hard-currency Irish Arbat House grocery store, the $80-a-head power-lunch troughs, the half-dozen new Monte Carlo–style casinos inside the tourist hotels and, after midnight in front of the Red Zone, an elite disco replete with cages of dancing models built inside a former Red Army sports complex. Most of these buggies sprout phone antennas, and on the street, the older, bulkier cellular phones are more popular than the newer slimlines because they catch more of your eye. Russian yuppies wear their sunglasses without ever removing the little 'UV' or 'Ray-Ban' foil sticker over one lens, lest anyone not notice they are of foreign origin. Recent market surveys by Proctor and Gamble show that Russians, even those who speak only Russian, want consumer products labelled not bilingually, but only in English – at least those Russians among the 2 percent who are the only effective consumers.

The other 98 percent or so of the country has been assigned a different role in this new order – one remarkably reminiscent of what they did when they used to dwell in the Evil Empire. When their noses aren't pushed up against the kiosk glass they are to be kept to the grindstone. Because those who run this country have read Marx, if nothing else, and are now intent on carrying out what that old lion's head called the first stage of capitalist development – known rather rudely as Primitive Accumulation – the by-any-means-necessary phase when you pile up enough capital to eventually become legal ('"Kate', Michael promised, 'The Corleone family business will be totally legit within five years.'") The British did it, Marx bluntly pointed out, through piracy and by grinding the bones of the Hindus. The Russians have already lost their empire and aren't likely to build a new one very soon, so they'll have to make do grinding their own people.

Boris Yeltsin's economic shock treatment, called 'market reforms' in America and shaped by an entourage of US economic advisors headed by Harvard's ubiquitous Jeff Sachs, got it all off to a good start, plunging 90 percent of Russia below an already subterranean poverty level, cutting their living standard by two-thirds. Some million and a half Russians are already unemployed, and that figure is expected to triple within a year. Yet to keep afloat hundreds of bankrupt state industries, the government prints money round the clock, generating a savage inflation rate of 1,000 percent or more. Minimum salaries have eroded to $2 a week, high salaries barely three times more, while once tightly controlled prices have been 'liberated' to skyrocket. Pensions have become so paltry that pedestrian tunnels clog with raggedy *babushkas* selling Wrigely's gum, or, just as often, their own doorknobs and dinner plates to make do. The Moscow police say they are alarmed by a rash of disappearances of these same old ladies. After reading newspaper ads from new companies saying 'Elderly People, we will provide for all your needs in exchange for inheriting your apartments', the desperate sign away their newly privatized apartments, and are soon discretely bumped off and disposed of in trash dumpers. The vacant units are then resold for $35,000 to office-hungry foreign companies or to the high-rolling Godfathers of the various shakedown rackets and protection outfits that lace the capital. Young people don't make out much better. The fabled Pioneer camps that provided millions of Soviet children with near-free summer vacations in exchange for political indoctrination, says another report, are now being converted into private spas for the wealthy.

Not surprisingly, a recent poll by the probusiness Russian Institute of Applied Politics found Russians to be somewhat less enthusiastic than, says Dan Rather, about their new private sector. Only 15 percent of Russians have a positive opinion of domestic businessmen. Thirteen percent said they should all be jailed. One out of four Russians said they believed the country was 'ruled by the mafia'. A majority of Russians asked couldn't name any domestic businessmen. And more revealing, when asked who the wealthiest people in Russia are, 18 percent said Mikhail and Raisa Gorbachev, next came Boris Yeltsin with 10 percent, followed with 8 percent for former Moscow mayor Gavril Popov.

That Russians should confuse state power with wealth is no accident born of ignorance. The old Communist *nomenklatura* has chosen up sides in a tawdry bare-knuckles power struggle to legalize the privilege they have always held. Some of these politicians, no doubt, are authentic converts to democracy. But, all in all, what the American press has pumped up into a grandiose morality play over the fate of democracy is, at bottom, a race by the elite of the *ancien régime* to divvy up the loot once held in monopoly by the Communist state.

For this reason, among others, few Russians feel the need to rush to the polls next week to defend democracy. Two years ago, common Russians did stand with Yeltsin against the tanks because they saw in him a chance for their future, and in their animosity toward the old system they were hungry for any change. Even then, those actively engaged were but an tiny island surrounded by a sea of apathy. Now, on the eve of the national vote of confidence in Yeltsin's government, somewhere around half the population won't bother to vote. Close to half of those who do will vote against Yeltsin.

Even for an American, so accustomed to living in a country where serious political debate falls somewhere mid-list long after sports-talk, TV chit-chat, and musings on the weather, the bottomless indifference of the Russian people is indecipherable. It's not that they want to go back to Communism. There's a national consensus that the economy must be liberalized, and those who care to think about it all mostly agree that the ex-Communists in Yeltsin's executive branch are more reliable than the ex-Communists among his rivals in the legislative branch. But few dreamed the social cost would be so devastating.

So great now is the disjuncture between government affairs and personal life that the rupture seems permanent. And the feeling is mutual. One ominous trait the new capitalist order shares with its Communist predecessor is a disdain for what used to be called 'the masses', today politely referred to, and only when necessary, as 'the electorate'. Before arriving in Moscow, and in attempting to arrange a translator for myself, I spoke by phone with a long-time senior reporter for Radio Moscow who said she'd work for me. Gabriela, as I will call her, had long ago assimilated the mentality of the Soviet elite and had seamlessly made the transition from mouthpiece for the Communists to spokeswoman for what is today one of Europe's most zealously anti-Communist transmitters. I advised her that while in Moscow I'd like to mix my time meeting not only the official talking heads but also seeing as much ordinary life as possible. 'But why?' she asked in perfect, crisp English. 'I just don't understand.' I explained again and, then, a third time choosing simpler words. Rather haughtily, Gabriela cut me off. 'I understand your words perfectly well', she said curtly. 'I just don't understand why a visiting correspondent should want to waste time viewing ordinary life at a moment of such great national political importance.'

SIDESHOW

FRIDAY, 16 APRIL. On the streets of Moscow, the campaign around the coming referendum is almost invisible. There are no political banners and posters, only an occasional flurry of leaflets. And with news reports like those in this morning's papers, the whole electoral process rings similar to that of any other Brezhnev-era scramble for deckchairs atop Lenin's Mausoleum, only reinforcing the languorous mood of the electorate.

The local headlines report that, faithfully following a long Communist tradition of disgracing rivals by taking away their privileges, President Boris Yeltsin last night stripped his vice-president and archrival, Alexander Rutskoi, of his armor-plated Mercedes, seventeen of his twenty bodyguards and the use of a personal physician. 'Just like the old days', said a Russian colleague. 'Like when they'd erase you from an official photograph.'

A former military hero, Rutskoi was elected as Yeltsin's running mate in 1991. But a political chill soon set in between the two as Rutskoi became increasingly critical of the president's radical free-market policies. That tiff has now turned into a full-blown Cold War with the two men campaigning in opposite camps in advance of the referendum. But Yeltsin's petty sniping at the politically potent Rutskoi could backfire. The vice-president is the only other democratically elected figure in the country, a political leader in his own right, and a man who has recently been successfully mining the explosive vein of Russian nationalism. Rutskoi also stands as the only Russian politician, apart from Yeltsin, to poll significant amounts of public support and is a likely presidential candidate in any new election.

'This should teach you that Yeltsin is absolutely no more democratic than any of his rivals', says Sergei, a researcher trained in international economics. Recently a militant supporter of the president, Sergei has slumped into terminal disillusionment. We chat while lunching at the frightfully ostentatious Hotel Radisson Slavjanskaya. Strangely, or maybe not so, the foreign press has chosen this hotel, the one most remote from ordinary Russian experience, as their headquarters. This wildly expensive hotel – a simple buffet lunch and a Coke runs $40 – won't even take American cash. Only foreign credit cards, thereby excluding from its doors not only most Russians, but most of the Russian elite. 'Three main factions dominate the political landscape', Sergei continues over a $5 cappucino. 'On one extreme, Yeltsin and the radical free-marketeers; on the other, the nostalgic neo-Communists, who have entered a marriage of convenience with fascists and nationalists. And in between, Vice-President Rutskoi and the majority of the Congress of Peoples' Deputies, who mostly represent the factory managers and provincial bureaucracies. They also want to go to a market economy, but don't want to lose control over their enterprises. But remember, all three factions are branches off the same Communist tree, they all have the same political education and style, and they all harbor the same potential for authoritarian solutions.'

Indeed, no social revolution thrusting dissidents into power – as in Czechoslavakia or Poland – has occurred in Russia. Rather, one day the old *nomenklatura* just stood up and changed their lapel pins. 'If anything, Yeltsin has been *less* democratic than his rivals in the already undemocratic Congress', continues Sergei. 'Since the fall of 1991 Yeltsin has been a virtual dictator with special powers conferred on him by this same Congress that he now calls "communists" – the same Congress that stood with him against the tanks in 1991. This current crisis started last month when Yeltsin as much as tried to stage his own coup by trying to extend his special powers unilaterally. Today in Russia none of the leading political forces are really democratic, but at least some sort of tenuous balance had been reached by the different government branches. It's Yeltsin, not the Congress, that has threatened that balance. What Yeltsin really wants is what he politically grew up with: a rubber-stamp parliament. After the referendum, be careful. With a vote of confidence in his back pocket, and unable to implement his revolution democratically, Yeltsin could decide to call in the army and try to do it by force.'

THE RED-BROWN SEA

SATURDAY, 17 APRIL. The eve of the Russian Orthodox Easter. And the new Moscow City Government, which so far has brazenly pursued a policy of pitiless market materialism – having done nothing more than providing a single twelve-bed shelter as the capital's homeless count mounts to 100,000 – found God this week. Moscow Mayor Yury Luzhkov, widely accused in the press of personally profiting from a number of shady land deals and whose nickname is The Bribe, decreed three days ago that the city's poor be served charity meals in certain cafeterias – but only through Holy Week, which ends tomorrow. And just as the city officials once used huge banners stretched across the boulevards to command the population to 'Honor the Great October Revolution!' this week it has used the same sort of imposing red streamers to order them to 'Have a Happy Easter!'

Even the newly reconstituted Communist Party, now the single biggest party in the country with as many as a half-million members, announced it would hold back from any public demonstrations against Yeltsin during this holiday period, its general secretary issuing a statement saying, 'We hope the light of belief, hope and love will never be extinguished.'

But one group pointedly ignoring the pious observance is the National Salvation Front, which has declared today to be a 'Day of Struggle Against Boris Yeltsin'. Unusual amounts of gray-coated police and militia have fanned out through the city, as the Front leaders have organized a mass rally for this afternoon. Marshaling their forces outside the Kremlin walls, competing for space with roving, bell-ringing Hare Krishnas, the Front is a mainstay of that wholly surrealistic 'Red-Brown' alliance of neo-Communists and frankly fascist Nationalists. What they have in common is a conviction that Russia, or in the case of the Stalinists, the Soviet Union, has been sold down the river, that their national identity has been defiled by one Boris Yeltsin, who appears on their placards as the portrait supplanting George Washington on American dollar bills. Those caricatures bob through the growing crowd face-to-face with posters of the beaming Uncle Joe Stalin, an austere-looking Lenin, and a jumbled salad of prerevolutionary and Tsarist flags and pennants.

The Red-Brown foot soldiers run the gamut from scarved and hobbled *babushkas* who have seen their monthly pensions reduced to mere pocket change, through angry low-level *apparatchiks* nostalgic for party privileges, to members of the professional and working classes fearful of exploding crime rates and spiraling chaos in the streets, right down to peach-cheeked college students resentful that their future careers have already been bought out from under them by faceless foreigners. Their commanding general, a classic demagogic politician, founder of the splinter Working Russia Communist Party, Viktor Anpilov, a man who vows to reconstruct the economy as if guided by Stalin, and then rule the nation as if inspired by Pinochet.

'Ideological differences between us and our Communist allies are not important now', says twenty-year-old Volodya Semyanov, a leader in the fascist-minded Patriotic Youth Front and who wears the prerevolutionary insignia of the Baltic Fleet on his lapel. 'We are united to save our nation, to make a government that defends Russian interests, not American ones.' The appeal of the Red-Browns easily capitalizes on the population's sinking economic status, its growing alienation from mainstream politics, and the country's general slide into uncertainty. But it draws its followers into the most obscurantist sort of nationalism, laced with good old-fashioned Jew-hating.

As I watch this motley opposition march toward the rally site at 25 October Square, holding high the portrait of the dictator who built the gulags, there is, as expected, no applause from the swollen street crowds of Saturday shoppers. But neither are there any jeers or heckling.

'A year ago I would have laughed at these poor bastards with their Stalin posters and their Czarist and Nationalist flags, knowing they had no real support. Now I'm not sure', my guide Gennaday says. And then I hear from his lips the same joke that three other people have told me in two days. 'You know what Yeltsin's biggest accomplishment is, don't you? He did in one year what the Soviets couldn't do in seventy. He made Communism look good.'

DEATH-BED DEMOCRACY

MONDAY, 19 APRIL. A dark morning filled with drizzles and wet snow, but not as gloomy as the 8 a.m. news. Over the Orthodox Easter weekend, the English-language Open Radio reports, Russian Nationalists broke into a St Petersburg Jewish cemetery, turning over and despoiling forty headstones, tearing down fences and uprooting benches. In the breakaway Chechenya Republic southeast of Moscow President Dudayev, a former Soviet Air Force general who has not been punished by Yeltsin for unilaterally withdrawing from Russia, abolished his parliament and imposed a military curfew. In a separate item, 62 percent of young girls polled in one Moscow high school class say they want to become prostitutes.

Here I am sitting at a mid-day news conference, in a room full of Russian and foreign journalists, all of them, without the slightest sense of irony, writing down the results of the latest opinion poll on the referendum, one conducted exclusively among 341 of – yes – Moscow's Russian and foreign journalists! Um, make that 341 of Moscow's 'most seasoned journalists'.

The poll focused on the four questions Russians will be asked on Sunday: Do you trust the president? Do you support his economic and social policies? Do you want early presidential elections? Early legislative elections? The Conventional Press Wisdom on the final results: Yeltsin will win the vote, but lose the referendum. This because he will get more than 50 percent of the votes cast, but will not get a majority of *registered* voters, a condition of legitimacy attached to the process by the rival People's Congress. The parliamentary opposition will therefore win the referendum, but will come out the biggest loser because the largest majority is expected in favor of the question of holding new legislative elections. Yeltsin's hand will be strengthened because he will win the confidence vote, but he will be weakened because a majority will vote against his economic policies. Think you're confused? How about the Russian voters, who will be asked to mark not their preference of 'Yes' or 'No' on each question, but rather will have to draw an 'x' through the answer they *don't* want. And you wonder why Russians don't give a fuck about politics?

The man who oversaw the poll, sociologist Dr Nikolay Popov, is in reality a smart and respected political observer (after all, the absurd survey of reporters wasn't his idea – he was just paid to do it by the self-promoting International Press Center). 'Bottom line', Dr. Popov tells me later, 'the vote will NOT clarify the political situation. All of the players in the referendum will probably find something in its results to support their point of view.' No one will be forced to resign as a result of the plebiscite, and after some weeks or months of wrangling, new elections for Congress, or the presidency, or for both, or for neither, will be scheduled.

So, Dr Popov, what *do* the Russian people really think?

A slight majority want the market reforms to go ahead, he says, but overall feel they are negative.

Here we go again.

'You have to imagine a patient undergoing necessary surgery', Popov clarifies. 'Before the anesthesia takes hold, he may get angry at the doctor, curse him, even strike him. The doctor says, "You want me to stop?" And the patient whispers back, "No, please go ahead."'

So, then, the Russians really *want* a transition to the market? Popov pauses, refusing the bait. 'This is not East Germany, or Czechoslovakia. Over seventy years many generations were born into the socialist system and many Russians have acquired a full Soviet mentality. Russians may like the idea of a free market, but they also expect a whole number of state guarantees, supports and services. I think for a long time to come, people will want it both ways.'

Later, at a privately owned Russian restaurant over a modest dinner for two costing only three months' of a worker's salary, a Canadian colleague based here for the last year tells me of the stories she's working on: the implosion of all social welfare programs, the paramilitary training farm some neonazis run outside Moscow, the city's subculture of Ivy League American gangsters, the tens of thousands of domestic immigrants stranded in Siberia after their life savings were consumed by inflation, the KGB going into the corporate security business, and the Highway of Death between Moscow and Warsaw where smugglers and cops enact endless reruns of Road Warrior. 'I just love it here', she says. The only problem is that tonight we've talked till eleven and our driver has gone home. Not afraid to report on the war in Georgia, my friend is skittish about taking a street taxi at night. When she did so last month, the cabbie drove her to a corner where three of his friends jumped in waving pistols. After a short ride they took her purse and money, dumped her out of the car, and returned her press card, which was of no commercial value. Overhearing us trying to phone an elite radio taxi service, our waiter offers to drive us home. 'Three dollars', he says, holding up three fingers and smiling – and a bargain at twice the price.

THE AMERICANS ARE COMING

TUESDAY, 20 APRIL. It's the morning news in Moscow but High Noon in the Chechenya Republic, where the parliament has refused the order to disband and is now moving to impeach President Dudayev. Fighting continues between Armenians and Azeris. In the Republic of Georgia there are reports that moderate President Eduard Shevranadze is in danger of being overthrown by his defense minister.

Meanwhile, two 25-year-old Moscow-based Americans are planning a US-style campaign fundraiser for Boris Yeltsin this weekend. They are herding up a hundred grateful foreign businessmen and having them sup with Yeltsin's prime minister and Moscow's mayor in support of democratic reform, all at a per head tariff of US$1,000 – what an average Russian worker brings home in the course of eight and a half years. 'It is not a lot of money if you look at what is at stake', says organizer Jamison Firestone, who imports luxury cars into Russia. 'The entire heartbeat of the business community is based on reform.' Mat LeMaitre, a marketing representative for a posh local office and residential complex known as Park Place who serves as the event's co-organizer, says he's confident the dinner will be a success – he will draw on his experience working on the successful 1988 campaign to elect George Bush.

In the evening I return to the Radisson Slavjanskaya for one more American-sponsored pro-Yeltsin happening. One of the more mangy survivors of the Reaganite policy kennels, Allen Weinstein of the spookish Center for Democracy, has put together a Referendum Week political roundtable. Co-sponsor is the Moscow International Press Center and Club, whose American president is a paid lobbyist for Pepsi and 'several foreign oil companies', as he tells me while we sip Pepsi Lights at the center's hard-currency bar.

Several US network news honchos have shown up for the gabfest and are not disappointed by the impressive list of Yeltsin advisers and ranking officials turned out for us by the American lobbyists. Nor are they forced to revise any of their old standby scripts on account of anything they are hearing tonight. One panelist after another keeps referring to the parliamentary opposition as 'the Soviets'. Leading the chorus is Yeltsin's personal Pat Robertson, part-time Russian Orthodox priest, part-time People's Deputy Gleb Yakunin, who has shown up in his liturgical garb. The Constitutional Court, he says, has committed the 'crime' of not outlawing Communists – which only a few a years ago numbered

19 million people. His own church hierarchy is guilty, he says, of not denouncing everything and everybody ever compromised by Communism – apparently forgetting that his boss, Boris, was recently a member of the Politburo. This week's vote, Yakunin concludes, is simple: either Yeltsin or Communism.

NBC's Garrick Utley, sitting in front of me, keeps nodding his head as he listens to the simultaneous translation on his headphones. The Russian reporters, translators and fixers among us look at each other and laugh. Top Yeltsin adviser Sergei Stankeivitch, sitting next to Yakunin, blushes at his berobed comrade's stridency but says nothing.

FOLKS LIKE US

WEDNESDAY, 21 APRIL. 'To say this crisis is a conflict between Yeltsin the democrat and the reactionary Communists in the Congress is ridiculous, it is the sort of simplistic thinking I read in the *New York Times*', says Dr Max Bratersky as we chew boiled grey wieners that seem left over from when this building was the headquarters of the Communist Youth. Today it houses a Yeltsin-sponsored research institute where Max heads up its international department. The cafeteria lunch is bland, but my company is fascinating. In America, capitalist ideologues usually believe their own propaganda. But in Russia, many free-market advocates like Max, having been trained in Marxism, are a good deal more blunt about the whole matter. He is 100 percent committed to Yeltsin, but for reasons that have little to do with all the hooey handed us in high school comparative government classes.

'This is a fight over who will own the wealth', Max continues as we shift to a brownish vegetable puree of unknown origin. 'On the one side are the factory directors of the old system, who favor privatization, but slowly enough so that they wind up owning industry. Against them are others, from the very same class, but who are not personally directors but who are linked to Yeltsin.'

Next step in the Marxist method: what is the 'social base' of each contending group? 'Those of us who support Yeltsin are the intellectuals who are now able to market our skills more profitably; it is the New Russians, the New Rich, who are taking their share of the national wealth and don't want to give it back; the upper part of the army, who now get to steal a little, and not always just a little; a small part of the country's farmers, maybe a million of them including their families; and then, of course, the country's traffickers and speculators.'

As to Yeltsin's opposition? 'We are opposed by the unskilled workers', Max continues, 'which means most workers; the traditional members of state and collective farms, which are most of the farmers; by the low-ranking officers of the army, who are losing their houses and cars, and that's most of the officer corps; and finally by the factory managers and most of the *nomenklatura*.'

I proffer: 'You are opposed by most of the country?'

'Oh yes', says Max. 'By an *overwhelming* majority of the country. But we in the minority are more energetic, better organized, more clever, more resourceful, better financed and – so – we will win the vote, even if we have lost the country.' He punctuates his assertion by lighting up a pungent Italian cigarette and staring at me.

'Why do I support these reforms?', he asks, exhaling a gray cloud and anticipating my next question. 'I simply look at what my perspectives were in the old system, where I was a senior researcher at the very elite USA-Canada Institute but where I would forever be subordinate to party bosses. And I compare that to my situation today where, beginning in September, under this reformed system, I will be the director of Stanford University's overseas program in Moscow, I will be an associate professor on the Stanford faculty, I will have many opportunities, privileges. In short, I'm much better off now.'

'You will be, sure. But what about the country', I ask.

'This sounds cynical?' Max continues, looking at me like *I'm* the Communist. 'Yes, sure it is. I think maybe a third of the country will have something to gain under the new system. Two-thirds won't. Remember that this whole process was begun under Gorbachev, not from the bottom, but from an elite that had outgrown its own system and was feeling restrained. You should understand this as an American. In your country a cornerstone of your ethics is that each individual is responsible, only before himself and God, for making his own future. We have accepted that ethic. The other two-thirds of Russia, well, they cannot and will not.'

But that two-thirds might get a bit restless, I suggest to Max, and whip itself up into enough of a backlash to spoil it for y'all.

'You mean the so-called Red-Brown threat', he answers, totally nonplused. 'No. Listen, this transition is going to take a vast amount of time. Meanwhile, people are tired of this chaos and more and more of us agree that we need a government that can govern, one that will, by the way, shut down movements like the Red-Browns, an authoritarian democracy, something like Chile had ten years ago; this is not a bad solution.'

'You, as part of what they call here the democratic forces, are comfortable', I ask, 'with wanting a Pinochet?'

'Absolutely', Max answers. 'I'm talking about a government that can be elected democratically but will not be very democratic between elections. This is in good Russian tradition, it is something more and more the country needs and agrees upon, it is even something that can help us win over that other two-thirds who like having a strong father they know will be there to listen to their complaints. It is our only way.'

The most forthright political discussion I am ever likely to have in Moscow is over. An icy wind whips through Red Square, buffeting the sound stage being set up by Lenin's tomb in advance of the pro-Yeltsin rock concert set for this evening. A young man with a beard hands me a huge campaign leaflet from the pro-Yeltsin 'Democratic Choice' grouping. The flyer depicts a disgruntled Boris Yeltsin, with a cape and crown, bound by thick ropes to a velvet throne. His cabinet sits next to him, their hands and feet tied to strings held by the smirking leaders of the Russian parliament, who look down from a second-floor gallery. 'A president as powerless as the Queen of England, his advisers mere puppets, this is the product of a parliamentary republic', says the bold red print. 'But for a a strong nation, a country with an effective leader, and a stable currency', it further reads, 'we need a presidential republic!'

Radio Moscow's midnight newscast stirs me from near sleep announcing that the country's Constitutional Court has made an important ruling on the ground rules governing this week's referendum. On the one hand, the court has thrown out the parliament's insistence that the vote of confidence in Yeltsin require a 50 percent majority of all *potential* voters – rather than just those who turn out. This decision guarantees added moral weight to Yeltsin's expected majority. On the other hand, the court has upheld the provision that the fourth question on the ballot, asking for new elections for parliament, garner a majority of the registered electorate – making the possibility of such elections more remote.

LES MISERABLES

THURSDAY, 22 APRIL. The morning news: the Moscow Statistics Department reports today that basic subsistence requires a personal income of 9,000 rubles a month, more than twice the legal minimum salary. The mayor has issued a decree banning musicians from performing inside the Moscow subway system – thereby eliminating jobs for hundreds of young people. The city has announced it will now install light, electric and gas meters in every Moscow apartment, signalling an end to the near-free status of utilities that is left over from Communism. While Russian consumers prepare for the expected huge price hikes, foreign business is celebrating a report that the government is planning a two-year tax holiday for foreign companies that invest in Russia.

Today is also V. I. Lenin's 123d birthday and a much-awaited spring sun has lured his admirers out onto the cobblestones of Red Square, where the scaffolding from last night's pro-Yeltsin rock concert still lingers. Across from the ornate GUM Department store, now dominated by the hard-currency-only *Galeries Lafayette* – the people who malled Paris – a line forms in front of the black-and-rust-colored marble Lenin Mausoleum. I merge with the snaking, single file of Shanghai tourists – still Stalinist enough to wear the worst-cut suits you can imagine, but sufficiently capitalist to all be carrying new Japanese cameras. We are joined by Russian elementary school children brought here by their defiantly patriotic teachers, and by older Russians, some carrying scarlet satin banners with embroidered golden hammers and sickles, others carrying bouquets of blood-red carnations they will deposit at the monument door.

As we descend slowly into the austere crypt, there is an atmosphere of absolute solemnity, as if Lenin had died only last night. A squadron of steely eyed, uniformed militia and blue-hatted officers of the KGB, now renamed the Security Ministry, pat down anyone deemed suspicious. But this air of stony sobriety is readily shared by most of the visitors. While Joseph Stalin has become an object of official scorn, Lenin, the founder of the disappeared Soviet state, is still a figure of national reverence for many Russians, enough so that earlier talk of evicting him from his temple and burying him in the ground has been indefinitely tabled.

Through the cool, hushed, dim, granite-gray antechamber, we go past six-inch-thick steel doors, past more guards, down a flight of stairs, and finally into the blackened vault where, by placement and spot lighting, the waxen corpse of Lenin, along with his bed of stone sculpted with blazing red flags, seems to shimmer and float in mid air. And then, seconds later, back into the jarring sunlight, and we are walking the path aside the two dozen memorial niches slotted into the Kremlin wall, past Arthur McManus and Big Bill Haywood. Next comes the row of graves, marked by eight-foot busts, that constitute the Kremlin pantheon – the penultimate tomb that of Stalin, his pinkish granite face placidly and benignly staring back at the curious.

The tourists veer off to their waiting busses. But I follow the Russians on their Lenin Day pilgrimage into the cavernous square-block museum that bears the Soviet leader's name. Twenty-three exhibit rooms along three floors that chronologically document every minute aspect of the Bolshevik founder's life. And then, after viewing the gallery filled with memorabilia from Lenin's 1924 funeral, I come into the last area on the exhibition path, assuming I will view some sort of sum-up of Lenin's legacy.

And I am right, but only by accident. For this final corner of the National Lenin Museum has been leased out by the new government to precisely the New World for which the Bolshevik Revolution has been traded in: the M&M Model Agency. Garishly dolled-up Russian amazons in shrink-wrapped mini-skirts bustle to the ear-pounding shrieks of Madonna. A fashion runway occupies the center of the M&M facility, along one of its sides sits a display case offering for sale the usual debris dragged in from the street kiosks: cookies, cosmetics, purses, champagne, blue jeans and lots of Wella hair-care products. On the other side of the room, a rack full of pricey leather and suede clothes for sale. In an adjoining space, mothers help their daughters fill out job application forms. No one can explain to me what actually goes on inside M&M, except that it is some sort of one-stop boutique, beauty shop, 7-11 and what we may gingerly call, escort service. It's like the US government opening a massage parlor inside the Smithsonian.

Back outside on the museum steps: a jolting chimera eerier than Lenin's glimmering cadaver. About a dozen bedraggled septuagenarian pensioners, some with artificial legs, others with canes, another slowly waving a huge red-and-gold banner, all dressed in threadbare cotton overcoats and knit watchcaps. Among them a dwarf-sized *babushka* with gold teeth and bowed legs, her stockings fallen around her ankles, intently pumping an ancient green accordion, leading her comrades in an anguished dirge, lamenting the evaporation of their Soviet homeland. As other elderly ragpickers stop by to join them, and as an emotional, again mostly older, crowd gathers, this last incarnation of the Workers Guard wails out a grievous version of *Meadowlands,* the Red Army marching song. Its mournful phrasing is a begrudging admission that they have been defeated by a force they cannot understand, but one they know to be more powerful than all of God's White armies put together.

Seeing that I am taking notes, a chic passing pedestrian, one of those with a 'UV' sticker still on her sunglasses, points at the wizened clump and then rolls her index finger by her temple, telling me they are crazy; which is certainly true. Crazy they are, but *driven* crazy. More than aberrant nostalgia is at work here this morning. More than an apparition out of the notebooks of John Reed, this heart-breaking beggars' choir seems a scenario freshly scripted by Victor Hugo.

THE AMERICANS, AGAIN

FRIDAY, 23 APRIL. The news: As whatever campaigning there is for the referendum comes to an end, President Yeltsin's defense minister has been formally accused of embezzlement. The Russian attorney-general announces that his investigation has revealed that the minister and his senior aides benefitted from a land swindle in the process of relocating Russian soldiers coming home from abroad.

Before sunset the Front for National Salvation is back in the streets for a last-minute crusade against the government. Behind banners reading 'Zionism Will Not Triumph' and 'No Sell Out of Russia to the West', about 2,000 Front sympathizers break through heavy police lines at Mayakovsky Square. With the police deciding to pull back peacefully, the crowd noisily marches toward the parliament building – the world-reknowned White House where Russians gathered in August 1991 to oppose the hard-line coup. Once there, the throngs chant 'Yeltsin-Jew! Yeltsin-Jew!' and I am handed a newspaper adorned with swastikas.

You know it's an officially 'crucial' election, at least to those back at home, when not only CNN designs its own logo for the event, but also when veteran CBS pollster Warren Mitofsky shows up in town. And now that he's in Moscow. Mitofsky tells me he has established a wholly scientific and reliable national sample so that the exit polling he does on Sunday night will allow him to confidently call the outcome long before the Russian government does. This is one of the inexplicable quirks of the modern world. Because the Russians say the official vote count won't even start coming in for two days and will not be officially announced until 5 May. And I haven't met a single Russian who thinks it is in any way important that the vote comes in any earlier; they know that the crisis here runs much deeper than this week's poll, and that its resolution will stretch over a generation. But the Americans have made the decision that we should all know right away. But why? Perhaps so that one day a delusionary US presidential candidate can stand before his nominating convention and claim credit for consolidating democracy in Russia, just as a deluded George Bush boasted last summer that 'we' were the ones who had forced down the Berlin Wall.

WHEEL OF FORTUNE

SUNDAY, 25 APRIL. Voting day. By mid-morning it seems that voter turn-out will be higher than expected, at least in the big cities like Moscow. But Yelena and her husband, Volodya have no intention of voting today; instead, they are chopping up cabbage for a picnic in the woods. They are my hosts here in Moscow. Through a private Russian agency based in the US they have rented me a room in their family apartment just a few blocks from the KGB headquarters.

'I hate all politics, all politicians', says 35-year-old Yelena, 'I am indifferent', she says in halting but clear English. And she means it. She scorns Yeltsin as much as she does the Peoples' Congress. Yelena says the one good thing about the way Russia has changed is that she was able to have quit her official, dead-end job and now enjoys what she calls her 'total freedom' to privately tutor math, charge 75 cents an hour, and not report her income for tax purposes.

Neither she nor anyone in her family is a Communist, but she fears capitalism sufficiently so that her life is filled with a list of future uncertainties.

For the moment her field of vision permits her to deal with only the immediate economics of her family. Her precocious four-year-old daughter attends a Montessori school, 'the only kindergarten where the teachers don't call you by only your surname', says Yelena. But the monthly tuition is still subsidized, and Yelena can pay for it with what she makes in half a day. Her state-owned apartment, with two bedrooms and high ceilings – large by central Moscow standards – will soon become her private property. The cost of conversion is negligible. The bureaucratic red tape, a nightmare. And all of the contradictions of the present moment come to life in the saga of her apartment.

Communism made it possible to live for years in this flat, virtually rent-free. Even today, with inflation galloping at 25 percent a month, Yelena pays only 1,200 rubles a month for rent, utilities and telephone – an amount she earns in less than two hours. But it's more mundane problems that plague her sleep. 'I don't know much about capitalism yet', she says, nodding her head toward the bare overhead light bulb. 'But I don't think there's a single capitalist country in the world where electricity and telephone are free like they still are for me. Or where a good school still costs so little.' Will she earn enough, a year or two from now, she wonders, to pay her light bill *and* her child's school? 'They say that after the referendum, that after the people vote for reforms. They say the people will then be charged a hundred times more for electricity. Everyone knows it can't continue cheap like now when everything else costs so much.'

Her 68-year-old mother, a retired technical translator, comes in to join us. Granny immediately switches off the black-and-white television, killing the image of a Red Army officer in full dress, playing the equivalent of 'Wheel of Fortune'. 'Before we were poor', Granny says, 'but now we have to worry about feeding the children.' With that she serves me today's lunch: mashed potatoes and tea.

Volodya stops chopping long enough to sit next to me for the meal. When I ask why he's not voting, he makes a face as if he's tasting bile. He says that he earns 8,000 rubles a month – $9 – as a skilled plumber for the state railways. 'Ten years ago we lived much better. My bosses ten years ago were not nearly as rich as they are now. My bosses were Communists. Now they say they are capitalists. I say they are "commu-mutants" – chameleons.' What Russia needs, Voldya continues, is a 'strong hand', someone to get rid of the homeless, the beggars, the political squabbling, the speculators and traffickers. 'Stalin', Voldya says. 'We need another Stalin.'

'Typical Russian worker – a Stalinist', Yelena says, a bit embarrassed, hugging her husband from behind. She steers our lunchtime conversation to what we all think is potentially less controversial ground, my stay with their family. Home-stays are all the rage here in Moscow. And everyone's supposed to come out a winner. The foreign visitor gets around the bloated cost of hotels – often $300 or more for a night in a Holiday Inn–type room – and for a more reasonable $52 daily gets a private room, two home-cooked meals and a built-in Russian family. And the family, barred under Communism from entertaining foreigners, now not only gets to study Americans close up, but also gets to pocket a wad of those sought-after and nowadays all-powerful greenbacks. Yet one more example of the invisible hand of the marketplace stitching together supply and demand. Except, of course, it doesn't work that way.

Over tea, Yelena asks me how much I have paid to lodge with her. My answer shocks her, confirming her worldview that no matter who's on top, the Russian people will still be on the bottom. 'Russia is today one big circus', she says. 'And we Russians are spectators – paying spectators.' Of the $52 a night I have been charged, she says has been paid only $7. *And* not really in dollars, but in equivalent rubles, which are no good in most quality stores. *And* out of which she is expected to squeeze two meals a day for me. *And* if she were to purchase any of the basic amenities she says she would like to offer a house guest – good handsoap, toothpaste, shampoo, rich food – her meager profit would vanish. Her enterprising Russian compatriots in Arizona, meanwhile, keep 85 percent of the rental fee – for merely making a phone call to Moscow (for which I am charged separately).

'Welcome', Yelena says with a caustic twang. 'Welcome to the *new* Russia.'

Indeed, about the only visible change in Yelena's life since the fall of Communism is my presence – and with the anemic slice of the tourist pie she is doled out, I'm a bit of a disappointment too. Looking around her house, I see that she possesses none of the shiny *tchotchkes* that cram the kiosks and symbolize the dawning of the Good Life. In her home there is no Swift ham, no Glade, no Colgate, no Scope, Coke or Bics. In her bathroom, however, there is one small box of Russian-made powdered detergent, its colors a faded imitation of Tide. The instructions are written in Russian. Its name, as is the fad, is in English. Against a yellow background, orange letters spell out its chic, foreign name: M-Y-T-H.

VIVA YELTSIN!

MONDAY, 26 APRIL. Partial returns are drifting in from across the country's nine time zones and it seems a decisive victory. And the winner is . . . General Augusto Pinochet. Yes, it's Boris Yeltsin who has gotten the most votes. But it is the Chilean general who leads all personal popularity polls. And this is no personal interpretation of a foreign reporter. Pinochet is the name that keeps hauntingly coming up like a mad, sadistic Joker, no matter how I shuffle my conversations about Russia's future.

'With this mandate from the referendum, we can only pray now that Yeltsin will become a Pinochet', says Mischa, a Russian sociologist, an adviser to the president. We are drinking together at the Press Center, assembling election returns, sifting through the past week. 'There are two forces now in this country and the other side is not going to budge just because of the referendum result. Either we kill them', he says, referring to his rivals in the more conservative Congress, 'or they will kill us.' Though Mischa goes on to say that he uses the word 'kill' *mostly* figuratively. Because as others have told me this week, Pinochet is viewed here as a benign dictator, a guy who nudged out the Communists, didn't knock off that many people, went on to build a sparkling market economy, and then graciously bowed out. In fact, Pinochet's image is sterling enough that it should be noted that Mischa is the third Jewish 'democrat' this week that has not blanched in discussions with me to defend a general who was a avowed admirer of Hitler.

The fascination with the general stems from the obsession that Russian democrats now feel to be what they call 'normal'. By their logic, the Soviet Union was the most abnormal of places and, therefore, by extension, almost any country with a market economy is normal, desirable, regardless of its political system. It's a line of argument wonderfully similar to that used by the Stalinists in the past: personal freedom doesn't matter so long as the people's basic needs are met. Now personal freedom doesn't matter as long as business is allowed to operate freely. The free market itself has become the only measure of democracy. 'Singapore and South Korea didn't have to spend years debating economic market reforms: they just went ahead and implemented them. Those countries had a normal constitutional framework of the sort we need', says Viktor Borischiuk, a deputy director of the Canada-USA Institute.

When I note that both those countries had dictatorial, not constitutional regimes, Borischiuk brushes the criticism aside. 'Yes', he says, 'but they were normal dictatorships, ones that allowed private property, private enterprise, that built a social base for the market, that shaped a population willing to take economic risks.'

The debate over Russia's future, then, seems to be only one over what sort of dictatorship will emerge. With the Democrats so willing to embrace Pinochet, you can imagine the midnight fantasies of the 'antidemocratic' nationalists, Stalinists and fascists. What both sides agree upon is that Russia is headed only for more chaos, and he who can bring order is he who will rule.

But there is a third camp, I among them, who have come to believe that Russia has sunk into near permanent chaos, that beyond whatever its imagined merits or demerits the all-hallowed Market will never fully emerge in Russia, not even through dictatorship. Moving out of Communism, the Russians could have taken the old system and introduced profit motives, a regulated private and mixed sector to make a more reasonable transition. Instead, as the advanced capitalist world inevitably moves toward more state planning, even in the US where a new president speaks of state-managed 'industrial policy', Russia has lurched toward a nineteenth-century laissez-faire model with all the potential for one helluva backfire.

Long before market 'normalcy' these very incipient market forces could easily tear Russia apart. For how much longer will the nether regions of Russia, speaking different languages, sitting atop mounds of oil, gas, even diamonds, agree to pay taxes to, share the wealth with, and politically obey a distant central government mired in disorder?

Even the very industrial base of Russia, now in a moribund depression, threatens any future stability. In East Germany, which had a much higher technological base than Russia, 90 percent of the privatized factories, noncompetitive globally, have simply gone bankrupt, throwing millions into unified Germany's social welfare system. But here in Russia, tens of millions of workers in even more unproductive plants have so far been kept on state payrolls, fueling ferocious inflation. When those subsidies are cut – a prerequisite for any real market transformation – the country will be awash in unemployed, and with no money for welfare. So far there are only a million or so people out of work – a figure expected to quadruple in the next twelve months. But what will become of Russia when and if that figure rises to 8 or 10 million? The most common answer, the two words – other than Augusto Pinochet – most often repeated here: Social Explosion.

THE DAY AFTER

TUESDAY, 27 APRIL. Before leaving Moscow I go to visit an old friend, investigative journalist Artyom Borovik, editor of the monthly magazine *Top Secret*, and host of a TV show by the same name. One of the original cultural engines of glasnost, Borovik pushed the envelope of Soviet journalism in the mid eighties, writing passionately on everything that was taboo. Over the years we have met in different places in the world and argued long into the night, he on the right, I on the left. But today, on this last day of mine in Moscow, Artyom and I have reached a gloomy consensus.

'Under Communism', he says pointing out his fifteenth-story window over-looking the endless row of kiosks dotting Kalininsky Prospekt, 'the red banners promised the people a Communist paradise they never got. Now they promise them Colgate-Palmolive and Reeboks, and they won't get those either. Now I know that one day soon I will have to defend myself against hordes of furious people who will be out attacking anyone like me with a car, a good job, a little bit of money. Sure, yesterday I voted for Yeltsin – better the devil you know. But tomorrow I think I will be buying a rifle.'

Village Voice
May 4, 1993

NOTE: In October 1993 President Yeltsin closed down the Russian parliament after attacking its headquarters with troops and tanks. In subsequent national elections his political rivals were re-elected as a majority of the new parliament.

HERE

12

DUM-DA-DUM-DUM

The L.A. cops are idealists, almost fanatical in believing the rightness of their cause. They have a whole philosophy behind their tyranny. *Jim Morrison, 1969*

LOS ANGELES: MARCH 1991. The LAPD had been making nationwide prime time for decades before the Rodney King video exploded into the country's living rooms. *Dragnet, Adam 12, Starsky and Hutch, S.W.A.T.* and even the doddering *Columbo* were based on the same department, now run by Chief Daryl Gates. But as three baseball teams' worth of cops, twenty-one of them LAPD, swarmed in and systematically fractured King's cranium, ankles and arms, as they targeted his kidneys for dozens of blows from their two-foot-long solid aluminum Monadnock PR-24 batons, as they stomped and kicked him face down on the ground – while all the time the supervising officer took care not to break the two Taser wires that had each carried a 50,000-volt charge into King's body and were now dug into him like harpoons – millions of horrified viewers may have wondered whatever happened to those two nice, clean-cut young men in Sears-Roebuck suits, Sergeant Joe Friday and his sidekick, Officer Bill Gannon.

But for those of us who were raised and live in this city, at least for those among us who cared not to sleepwalk through the last thirty years, the Rodney King beating is not the aberration Chief Gates claims it is, no loopy, David Lynch–like spin-off of Jack Webb's old black-and-white TV series. No way. Indeed, the pictures of white LAPD cops taking batting practice on King's black body are, for us, nothing but the outtakes from *Dragnet*.

Long before anyone had heard of Rodney King, our houses shook and dogs barked as squadrons of French-made LAPD helicopter gunships buzzed our neighborhoods. Thousands of our residential rooftops were painted with huge white numbers so the choppers could coordinate with computer-equipped patrol cars on the ground. Infrared scopes mounted on the Aerospatiale helicopters could, after reading the heat signature of a single burning cigarette, guide the pilots to blind with 30-million-candlepower spotlights any lovers adventurous enough or tourists naive enough to attempt a midnight tryst on some of the most beautiful beaches in the world. Another wing of the LAPD air force, flying Bell Jet Ranger helicopters – just like the ones their counterparts fly in El Salvador – have been trained to swiftly ferry the elite SWAT troops into combat at any hot spot LZ in the metro sprawl.

Five floors below ground level in a hardened bunker, the world's most advanced police communication network – the ECCCS, employing NASA-developed absolute-secure digital transmissions – links the LAPD command structure with mushrooming databases that keep tabs on an ever-growing, ever-more-suspect, ever-less-white metro population. Those who engaged in opposition politics during the Reagan era, those who (like myself) wrote about those activities, and even City Council members whose job it was to oversee the LAPD have found their names illegally gathered and coded in the files of the now-disbanded Public Disorder Intelligence Division (PDID) – computerized information that was freely shared with ultraright East Coast political lobbies. As recently as last week, the few LAPD officers – all of them black – who had dared to publicly criticize Chief Daryl Gates were convinced that they were not only being followed by PDID's successor, the shadowy Anti-Terrorist Division, but that their cars were being vandalized by ATD operatives.

Our children regularly see LAPD officers in their classrooms as part of the so-called DARE antidrug program. There they learn of the ills of marijuana, coke and crack, often years before they've heard of the drugs themselves. As part of its 'war' on crime – or maybe its 'war' on drugs, or 'war' on gangs – LAPD units routinely barricade off whole residential blocks, always in minority communities, and set up checkpoints to search and question every motorist and pedestrian unlucky enough to wander into the newly designated 'narcotics enforcement area'.

While the media and the city administration ride the political horse of anti-gang hysteria, spurred by neighborhood house meetings addressed by police experts on 'narco-terrorism', the LAPD troop strength (and 'troops' is the word used by the police themselves) has grown nearly 30 percent in just the last five years. While city social services shrivel, the LAPD budget balloons.

Unlike the cops in many big American cities, the LAPD has yet to surrender, remaining as fixed and committed to its steely vision of law and order as were those two virtuous, blue-eyed rookies on *Adam 12*. This is a department that not only regularly beats the stuffing out of wise-ass car-chase suspects, it

'TO PROTECT AND SERVE'

also floods the county court's office with Latinos picked up for drinking beer on their own front porches (a violation of the city's open container statute). It's a force that, along with county and local police departments, not only has racked up hundreds of police shootings in the last two decades, but every year takes the time to write more than 5,000 jaywalking tickets in a city where the nearest crosswalk can be three blocks away. In a single day it can 'jack up' and sweep as many as 1,500 teenage 'hoodlums' into holding cells and still have the energy to bust a ring of dart throwers caught making $5 bets and apprehend suburban housewife scofflaws who are feeding the jackpot kitty in their morning bowling league.

We are talking the Mother of All Police Departments. Relatively free from corruption, strikingly efficient and aggressive compared with other metro forces, the LAPD uses the firepower of a midsized modern army to pry open the nooks and crannies of what it sees as a rotting civilization. But it's a police force that, at least until the King tape became the most popular of America's Grimmest Home Videos, existed independent of any civilian or political control and scrutiny. Whereas the city annually paid out $11,000 in damage suits against the LAPD twenty years ago, last year it shoveled over $11.3 million into the hands of brutalized citizens. Police misconduct lawyers report more than 600 calls a year arising from run-ins with the LAPD. This reputation is as far-flung as any cop show rerun: while living in Europe in the seventies, I can remember reading a stern warning in a French travel guide that went something like this: 'The LAPD should not be confused with the bobbies. Do not approach them on the street to ask for information or directions. Call upon them only in case of emergency.'

In a city that is increasingly cleaved between rich and poor, white and non-white, between Mercedes and '74 Chevies, between $30 million minimansions and $600-a-month roach-infested apartments, the white minority that continues to exercise a monopoly over political power (with a compliant black mayor in office) asks few questions of the 8,300 cops charged with upholding civilization. The faceless, nonwhite, increasingly foreign-born, ever-more desperate underclass, in the wake of Reaganomics and the white-led taxpayers' revolt of Proposition 13, has been more or less abandoned by every arm of the state, be it local, regional or national. Proposition 13 was a clear message that the only public service that would be freely offered to minority communities was a shit-kicking police department that would keep the lid on.

'The Rodney King beating is a watershed in the city's history', says a Los Angeles–area cop-turned-writer. 'But not the way people think. A watershed not in revealing police brutality, but a historic turning point in the city's having to face the one problem it never does: race.'

In normal times, the LAPD operates under a code of silence. Reporters are viewed askance, as a mutant species akin to ACLU lawyers. And since the Rodney King beating became public, a siege mentality among the LAPD has almost hermetically sealed them off from the press. But after an ironclad shield of anonymity was hammered out and guaranteed through mutual friendships, three veteran LAPD officers agreed to 'give their side of the story of what it means to be an L.A. cop'.

The three officers I spoke with are highly representative of the guts-and-glue of the LAPD. All born to working-class families in Los Angeles, all white, all army veterans, all with more than twenty years on the job, all in their early to mid forties, all members of an elite detail with citywide jurisdiction, they are the typical 'training officers' – the men who hone and shape incoming rookies, who in the privacy of the patrol car pass on the attitudes and rites from one generation of cops to the next, the men who will be there long after Gates leaves. For nearly three hours in the corner of a restaurant on the edge of downtown, for the first time since the Rodney King scandal unfolded, a group of LAPD officers spoke freely, for publication, with a reporter.

JACK: I feel sad about L.A. I feel we lost L.A.

GREG: We at least used to have the mystique of Hollywood. Now you go up to the boulevard and you got the whores, the female impersonators, every runaway in the world.

JACK: We've had an influx of tens of thousands of illegal aliens who contribute something to the economy, I guess, but also clog it up. Take North Hollywood. Five years ago it wasn't a bad place to live. Now there are twenty illegals on each corner waiting around for a job. This open border policy has got to go. We are getting all the world's rotten apples.

GREG: The hotel is full. Time to put out the No Vacancy sign. Too many people here. Too many of the wrong people.

DOUG: Yeah. You want to go downtown for a movie or play, OK. But getting there is the problem. I mean you're in the car, with your wife, and here are all these wetbacks everywhere, peeing all over the buildings, drinking beer, throwing shit all around. To me L.A. is a place where I come to do a job and then go home where I can be safe.

Doug, Greg and Jack, as is the case with almost the entire LAPD, live not only outside of the city, but outside of Los Angeles County – as far as a two-hour commute each way.

DOUG: I was raised like these two other guys here. Not from rich families. But you wanted something, you bought it, not stole it. The values we learned have turned to shit or are turning to shit because of the alien problem. They are going to ruin this city without a doubt. Economically, crimewise, every which way. Two out of three people we stop are aliens. Drive twenty miles through this city and stop people at random, you won't find too may who can even speak English.

The city the LAPD cruises has little to do with the bubble gum colors, snake-haired blondes on roller skates, and palm tree sensibilities of Steve Martin's *L.A. Story*. With the city limits spanning 450 square miles (only a seventh of the entire urbanized metro area) and crossed by over 500 miles of in-town freeway, the sunny, open public spaces of the past have been 'containerized' into covered malls, corporate refuges and upscale cultural enclaves. The cross-pollenation of races found in other big-city public transportation systems doesn't happen in Los Angeles: we have no such network.

In white Los Angeles there is an inbred fear of the crowd. Because the crowd, in a city where whites ceased to be a majority during the eighties, is colored. And if it's colored, the city logic continues, it is poor. And finally, if poor, it must be dangerous. Whites have abandoned the city's world-class parks as Latino families came in to hold piñata parties. Dockweiler Beach, the only stretch of sand in L.A. County that permits open-fire barbecues, has been ceded to blacks and Latinos. White teenagers who live a straight-line, ten-minute drive from the seashore will travel an extra forty minutes to bask in the color-free sands of Malibu and Zuma. The ten square blocks of restaurants and cinemas of Westwood 'Village' adjacent to the affluent UCLA campus, the only pocket of Los Angeles with significant night-time foot traffic, is now considered a 'rough' area because of the influx of black teens on the weekends.

Los Angeles, among 252 American cities analyzed by a recent University of Chicago study, was classified as 'hyper-segregated'. Segregation in this city is a function, however, not only of race and the centerless geography, but also of social class. A new apartment complex in the suburban San Fernando Valley, one with a waiting list for tenants, boasts that it is connected by an underground tunnel to the Sherman Oaks Galleria mall so 'you never have to leave your apartment'. From the airport tramstops to the art museum gardens, most of L.A.'s benches have been 'tramp-proofed', usually by making the seat round as a barrel, okay to sit on but impossible to lie on. Timed sprinkler systems scatter the city's 50,000 homeless from the few remaining public lawns as well as from the doorways of chi-chi commerce.

'Los Angeles as a matter of deliberate policy has fewer available public lavatories than any major North American city', writes social historian Mike Davis in his *City of Quartz*. 'On the advice of the LAPD, the Community Redevelopment Agency bulldozed the remaining public toilet in Skid Row. . . . The toiletless no-man's land east of Hill Street in Downtown is also barren of outside water sources for drinking or washing. A common sight these days are the homeless men – many of them young Salvadoran refugees – washing in and even drinking from the sewer effluent which flows down the concrete channel of the Los Angeles River.'

In the flinty eyes of the LAPD and the economically secure minority that cowers behind it, not only open space and – God forbid – crowds have become criminalized, but so have individual pedestrians and rogue motorists. If you're not tucked away in a fluorescent-lit office or security-gated condo complex, the cops want to know what you're doing out on the street.

The overwhelming majority of LAPD officers are white. Most are first- or second-generation immigrants from the South and Midwest. They look at the city they police today and they see it as a formidable, threatening, unpredictable foreign land. They shake their heads in disbelief – and often in open disgust – at a city in which 60 percent of the kindergarten classes has Spanish as its first language; where the largest single racial group among UCLA freshmen are Asians; and where the most common name given to a male child born last year was José.

MARC COOPER: What do you feel when you work in the South Central section of the city, where the population is mostly black and Latino?

JACK: Fear and excitement. Life down there is very cheap. People are dying there while we are sitting here talking. One police division out of eighteen in the city has more murders per year than all of England. Life's cheap. So there's a good chance there you'll get in a gunfight, see some violence.

GREG: It's really us against them. Not against blacks, really. But there is a lot of crime down there. You look at the guy on the corner and you know he's not working, he's waiting to rip off a purse. You got the dope dealers there in their nice cars.

JACK: The feeling we get from down there is what anybody else gets. Except we wear the badge. What you feel against you is hate. They hate us.

DOUG: The people committing the crimes hate us. And the good people don't understand us either. They don't understand what real life is about. They sit back and watch those [Rodney King beating] tapes and say, 'Isn't that just awful.' But is it really?

JACK: I'm not a sociologist, but the problem down there is no family structure. You see children having children with no fucking idea who the father is. In the black communities all the kids have different last names. All the mothers have six, eight kids and no fucking idea where they are. And they couldn't give a damn because they are too busy pumping out another kid. Picking up the government check. Every Cadillac and Mercedes you stop in the south end of town has food stamps in the glove box. They're on welfare and we're out here driving Volkswagens while they're driving Bentleys. I mean I saw a

ROLL OVER, CHE GUEVARA

*policeman dying in a car wreck once in the south end of town. Every resident and neigh-
bor was out there while the paramedics were trying to give him CPR. But when he ex-
pired at the scene, the entire crowd cheered, clapped, whistled when they put the blanket
over his head. This makes you cynical, bitter, makes you see life for what it is. Makes you
see you are seen as the enemy down there. Makes you see maybe we really are an occupying force. When you clap when someone dies, to me that's not even a human being. You
see the parents doing it, the kids, and watching and it makes you sick, pisses you off.*

The South Central ghetto that runs the twenty miles from the civic center
through Watts and Compton to dead-end at Los Angeles's gritty postindustrial
harbor has little, visually, in common with Harlem, Bed-Stuy or even Boston's
Roxbury. There's plenty of gang graffiti on the walls and fences, but behind
those barriers are fairly well-kept rows of single-family homes, with green
lawns and trimmed hedges, far from the tenebrous tenements of the East
Coast.

True, South Central spreads itself out on a plain of dense metropolitan
flatlands in a city where residential prestige is associated with canyons, hillsides
and beachfronts. But there are palms and gardens here, and even a few parks.
One neighborhood, packed with postwar apartments backed by swimming
pools set among banana trees and ferns, was lush enough to have been called
'the Jungle'. But to the older L.A. police officers who grew up in the near-rural,
all-white suburbs of the city, and to the recruits from Kansas lured to the force
by $40,000 salaries, South Central is an exotic, harrowing, terrifying land inhab-
ited by unruly natives.

Today the cops still call that street of apartments 'the Jungle', but not for its
now-tattered tropical landscape. The Jungle today is the capital of the West
Coast crack traffic. 'It's "the Jungle",' as one cop told the *L.A. Times,* 'because
that's where the jungle bunnies live.' Or, as the police wisecracked over their
radios on the night of the Rodney King beating, 'Gorillas in the Mist'.

The economic devastation of this community, its badge of segregation
from mainstream Los Angeles, manifests itself in the so-called commercial district. Its main artery, Central Avenue, which in the forties cradled a raucous
music scene – till the LAPD cracked down on multiracial night clubs – and in the
sixties housed the headquarters of the Black Panthers – till the LAPD inaugurated its SWAT team by dynamiting off the Panthers' roof in a 1969 shoot-up –
is today a seemingly endless road to nowhere. The stores that aren't boarded up
are imprisoned behind iron bars. Used appliance stores, dingy pawn shops, and,
most of all, liquor marts – increasingly owned by Koreans – dominate.

Latinos have recently moved into what was a solidly black domain, attract-
ing a few *panaderias* and *carnicerias*, but here there are none of the supermarkets,

department stores or strip malls that clutter and entice the rest of the city. Even gas stations are scarce. The handful of businesses that have truly valuable merchandise on the premises – auto parts stores and used car lots – are protected not only with bars, but also with the same coils of lethal razor wire used by Guatemalan oligarchs around the perimeter of their estates.

Almost half the black families that live in the ghetto flatlands fall below the poverty line. On a per capita basis, less government money has been spent on social services and job training in this part of the city than on the affluent, white Westside. Mayor Tom Bradley has suffocated spending programs for youth recreation, allocating in 1987 only $30,000 for recreational equipment for 150 centers that supposedly serve tens of thousands of inner-city kids. Youth unemployment hovers near 50 percent.

Against this background, along with the migration of well-paying manufacturing jobs to Mexico and Asia thanks to the 'trickle-down' economic policies of conservative city, state and national administrations, L.A.'s youth gang culture has grown into one of the most resilient in the Western Hemisphere. Estimates on youth gang membership in L.A. County range from a low of 10,000 to ten times that amount – the most common figure being 70,000. What is certain is that an average of two gang-related murders a day take place in L.A. County.

The Cain Street Crips favor aquamarine Dodgers caps. The Watts Grape Street Crips are into Lakers purple. The 118th Street East Coast Crips wax nostalgic in their Yankees hats. The Lime Avenue Bloods show off Celtics green. The gang they have as common enemy wears dark blue: the select units of the LAPD division known as CRASH (Community Resources Against Street Hoodlums). After a Japanese-American woman (L.A.'s 'most acceptable minority') was mistakenly killed by gunshots from a black gang in the predominantly white Westwood area in late 1988, cries for a crackdown on gangs issued forth from that neighborhood's liberal white city councilman.

Within weeks the LAPD, led by its CRASH division and under the banner of Operation Hammer, mounted full-scale retaliatory raids on the black community. In April 1988, 1,000 extra cops were sent into South Central, and in a single night they rounded up 1,453 black and Latino teenagers. Since then a state of siege has persisted in South Central, where each night – and often during the day – any teenager on the street is fair game for an LAPD roust, 'jack-up', or bust. An astonishing total of more than 50,000 youths have been detained in Operation Hammer's ongoing maneuvers. And, much like the tactics I've seen used by General Pinochet's militarized police as they rampage through politically unreliable shantytowns in Chile, as much as 90 percent of the victims of Operation Hammer are released without charge – having been arrested in the first place as an act of sheer intimidation.

'The black community is under siege from fall-out of racism, gangs, drugs and violence', says a forty-year-old black man I'll call William, an aide to an elected black official. 'I need a protector. But if I'm walking down the street and see some gangbangers on the one side and an LAPD car on the other, I'm not really sure which group I'm more afraid of. But actually, I feel more threatened by the police. The gangs see me as a tall, powerfully built foe. To the cops, I'm one more nigger.'

William, dressed in a three-piece suit, walks me through the Crenshaw Mall, the only full-scale enclosed mall in urban black America. Refurbished in the mid eighties with city funds handed over by one of Mayor Bradley's white campaign contributors, the mall has an entire substation of the LAPD built into it. Even that was not enough to attract national retail chains, and today the shopping center is nearly empty.

'The LAPD now exercises authority to stop any black person in this community and subject them to any threat with total impunity', William continues. 'I mostly get stopped in white neighborhoods, twice last year. Let me tell you, I have been hassled by cops so many times that when I get stopped now, I shuffle, I shuck and jive! Those dudes are asshole motherfuckers. They want you to give them a reason to kill you. I may be six-foot, five inches and 240 pounds, but when I get pulled over by the LAPD it is all "Yes-suh, no-suh, how high you want me to jump-suh?"'

In the wake of the Watts riots and the black power movement, today's generation of black youth has assimilated rebellion. 'It's an attitude that comes smack up against the torqued-down opportunities of Reaganomics', William argues. 'It means we are now engaged in a day-to-day confrontation with the power structure. A confrontation we don't have the power to win.' Black youth, he says, 'will no longer do stoop labor. It wants the same opportunities that other immigrant populations that have been here seven, eight or nine generations have. Black folks no longer want to do what white folks want them to do to get ahead. We are not going to get up any more at 6 a.m. and put on a uniform for McDonald's. So how else do our youth achieve a sense of power without submitting to the rule of white society, other than by becoming outlaws? And that's where we meet the police.'

JACK: Rodney King? Some dirty son of a bitch that was supposed to get two years and instead got six months. This whole thing shows you why people say it's Us Against Them. Suddenly, there's an opening to take shots at the police and now everyone and his brother is a fucking expert on the police. No one gives a shit about the police officers. Everyone in America is against them! Bury them! They're gone, dead, fucked! But everyone knows Rodney King. Why don't the newspapers run the criminal records of the two guys who were riding with him? Lengthy records, I'm sure. No one knows the name of Russ Custer, a cop blown away by an illegal alien. But they know Rodney King. That's what makes it Us Against Them. I hate to even say Rodney King's name.

GREG: We don't condone what happened out there, overkill. . .

JACK: It was a tragedy.

GREG: Definite overkill.

DOUG: From what I've seen on this job I would venture to say that King and his buddies that night did some crime and we just haven't found the victim yet. No doubt in my mind those guys weren't driving around just to be driving around at three o'clock in the morning. They were looking for a crime to do or coming back from one.

JACK: Too bad there's no audio portion on that tape. It's not as simple as it looks on tape.

DOUG: I think King wasn't doing what he was being told to do. They teach us to make people do what you tell them. If they don't, you escalate. Like they took the choke-hold away from us because a few people died. If we had the choke-hold what you saw would have never happened.

JACK: That was the most humane way to put a guy out. You choke'em out. Once you don't have that, your only option is to beat'em. Maybe they beat him too long. According to the film, it looks like they did. But if he's not complying with orders and he might have a gun or knife in his waistband or something, hey, you know. ...

COOPER: What do you think was running through the minds of the Foothill division cops who chased and beat King?

JACK: You chase a guy at high speeds in the night like that, it's like someone has a gun to your head and says, 'I'm gonna kill you.' Then he presses the trigger and it's empty. You're still going to beat the shit out of him anyway because he scared you to death. Like Saddam Hussein scared the shit out of us with chemical weapons and even though it turned out he didn't use the gas, we still made him pay the price. Same with Rodney King. You got to chase him through red lights not knowing if you are going to crash and then he gets out of the car dancing and strutting, not acting normal. And you say, yep, PCP. This is what went through the officers' heads. I can't condone what they did, but I know what I would have felt after the chase myself. Sad part of it is some of those young cops are going to go to jail.

Fifty miles northwest of LAPD's downtown Parker Center slumbers the glorified desert truckstop of Castaic. Home to Sergeant Stacey Koon, the supervising officer at the scene of the King beating and one of the four cops indicted on felony charges because of it. Many other LAPD officers live out here as well as in even more remote hamlets up the road toward Bakersfield. The mailing list of LAPD personnel is kept secret for security reasons, but an estimated 90 percent or more of the force lives outside the city they are paid to police.

But in L.A. there are no equivalents of Queens or Yonkers. Rather, a one- or two-hour drive away, in the desert or mountains – not in suburbs nor even in what we have come to call 'bedroom communities' but in that peculiarly Southern California–type cantonment known as a 'housing developments' – lives most of the LAPD. Spiritless, soulless, prefabricated neighborhoods with no history, not even an immediate identity beyond the huge signs that announce: '3 Bedrooms – 2 Baths – Security Gate – $119,000!'

Along a dusty half-mile stretch of access road along Interstate 5, the entirety of the Castaic business community sits as if at one big National Franchise Expo: a McDonald's, a 7-Eleven, a Del Taco, a Fosters Freeze, and two chain motels. A single strip mall is the only reminder of urban life, and it's an hour away down the highway. At its center is a CB supply store with a faded Confederate Stars and Bars hanging over the doorway.

And who cares? Not much chance of any blacks living here. Or Latinos. Or Jews for that matter. On the hill above the mall are three residential developments, all Spielbergian tract homes on loan from the E.T. set, all identical, all the same sandstone color, most with a garage that serves as Saturday workshop. There's an extraordinary number with small boats in the driveways (I counted thirteen in a quarter mile).

This is cop utopia. No minorities, no gangs, no crime (except for an occasional trucker's dust-up at the Country-Girl Saloon), 'a great place to raise kids', as they say. A perfectly ordered uniformity and predictability. A whole town of compliance, if you will. Safely distant from the dystopia of the daily beat – peopled by deviants, perverts, criminals and aliens – desert towns like Castaic are a perfect incubator for the LAPD's closed police culture.

'The problem with the LAPD is they recruit from the outside. All cops hate the city. But when you come from the outside in the first place, you never stop hating it. Who can be surprised, then, that these guys all live as far away as they can?' says former NYPD narcotics officer Bob Leuci, the celebrated 'Prince of the City'.

Another ex-NYPD officer, Jim Fyfe, now a professor at American University and a national expert on law enforcement agencies, calls the LAPD a 'closed society' of 'rigid men of steel . . . a local variant of the FBI, with all of the same good and bad points. The LAPD is a national model for modern urban police departments, an aggressive, legalistic policing that allows the individual officer little personal discretion in the field. He merely follows an impersonal policy. That's why you can't talk your way out of a jam with the LAPD.

'Most LAPD cops wouldn't engage in the kind of beating you saw on the King tape', Fyfe continues. 'Neither would they turn in a fellow cop. It's a fraternity in which no one can get through their career without breaking some law or another. So everyone is compromised. Combine that with an atmosphere of Us Against Them and you get the mentality of a whole society apart, of a police department not of the city but above it.'

A certain dehumanization of the civilian, the potential enemy, festers inside the police culture. As American GIs went off to fight successive wars against 'Gerries, Japs, Slopeheads, Gooks, and Ragheads', the LAPD's 'soldiers' have carried on their war against 'assholes'. You can see the first glimmers of it in the old reruns of Sergeant Friday who, decades ago, was already quick to demonstrate his Just-the-Facts-Ma'am impatience with his all-white interviewees; and though they were all either innocent victims of crime or witnesses to it, Sergeant Friday would grimace and strain to barely tolerate their jabbering tomfoolery. They were, after all, just civilians. Or, in the officially unofficial locker-room lexicon of the boys in blue, mere 'assholes'.

'Burglars and rapists aren't necessarily "assholes" in the eye of the LAPD', says Fyfe. 'An asshole is a person who does not accept whatever the police officer's definition is of any situation. Cops expect everyone, including a stopped motorist, to be subservient. Any challenge – or the mortal sin of talking back – and you become an "asshole". And "assholes" are to be re-educated so they don't mouth off again. The real cases of brutality come in the cases of "assholes". Cops don't beat up burglars. Last week I had a talk with a 25-year veteran of the LAPD who says he knows of no car chase that didn't end with the cops beating up the motorist once he was caught.'

DOUG: *Yeah, in Houston they call'em 'turds'. In New York I think it's 'shitbird'. Here we call them 'assholes'.*

JACK: *A good officer can weed out an asshole from the common citizen, say a white guy is working in a black area. If he's treated nice by a black person he'll come on back to him overly nice, because it's so rare you get treated nice down there.*

GREG: *We treat people the way they treat us. Frankly there aren't a whole lot of cops who feel much compassion anymore for some guy just because he's in a shitty situation. You just say, 'Hey, another asshole.'*

DOUG: *That's why like 98 percent of the guys live outside the city. Not just that housing is cheaper and that you want your kids out of the L.A. schools where there's so much violence. You don't want to go to the grocery store and be in the checkout line standing next to the same asshole you arrested the night before. You just want to get in your car and get away from the shit you've seen all day, from the city where everyone thinks we are the assholes!*

GREG: *I remember a class at the academy some twenty-odd years ago where the instructor says, 'Within a few years you guys, your only friends are gonna be cops.' Everyone laughs and says, 'Bullshit.' But you know, he was right.*

JACK: *The businessmen don't like you, the poor Hispanic doesn't like you, the blacks don't like you. So you retreat into a cave full of policemen, where you are understood. Where you can sit around and say, 'Hey, I saw an asshole on the corner doing such and such', and everyone knows what you're talking about.*

DOUG: *That's right. When a guy walks into the bar you know he's an asshole, you just know it. And there are all the other assholes buying him a drink. It's a lot easier just to hang out with cops.*

JACK: *Yeah, but a lot of the overall togetherness on the job has disintegrated since I came on to the job. It's the problem with female cops, with the lowering of standards for minorities. I don't want to sound like a bigot, but when you lower the standards it's the black cop who suffers because people think he's got the job only because he's black. This has divided the department more than anything.*

DOUG: *You walk through the station nowadays, you don't say anything about females, about blacks, about whites.*

JACK: *We're not even allowed to talk about women. We can't even have a Playboy calendar on our desk. No jokes. No nothing. When I came on the job there were Polish jokes for the Polish cops, black jokes for the black cops, and everyone was still your buddy. That was the best part of the job. And you'd die for those other guys.*

GREG: *It's not just L.A. It's the whole country. Now we have got to hire women, women who can't pass the physical tests.*

DOUG: *I resent the women.*

JACK: *Me too. And he who pays in the long run is the citizen. Because you got a female [in a police] car and it's a nonworking car. Money down the drain. There's been more shootings now by female officers because they are plain scared and can't handle the suspect any other way except to blow him away. Some guy you'd ordinarily get down with a nightstick, and now he's dead just because he got drunk. Not to say this about Hispanics, but you know Saturday nights are a ritual for them. They like to have parties and receptions and you know when the cops come you better get ready for a fight, nine times out of ten. When you work East L.A. that's just part of the game. One of those guys walks up drunk to a five-foot female, she's just gonna shoot because she knows there's no way to restrain him.*

Newcomers to L.A. tend to equate the Westside of the city with the 'white' part of the metropolis. Though it's a cliché, being white in Los Angeles is every bit as much a state of mind as it is a place of residence. There are, indeed, a few all-white neighborhoods, and they are for the most part (but not exclusively) on the west side. But the explosive growth of the city and the influx of immigrants from all social classes has hit like a blockbusting train. The San Fernando Valley, for example, a 75 percent white refuge ten years ago, today is 42 percent minority.

As Angelenos of color, therefore, overflow the traditional boundaries of the ghettos and seep into historically white enclaves, the Anglo population has been circling its wagons in ever smaller, ever more checkerboard pockets of racial homogeneity. The white middle class, and more accurately, the middle class of all colors, hangs on to its identity – and to its property values – by subdividing, remapping, chopping, and splicing together wholly imaginary 'communities'. Their tools: simple two-by-five-foot blue-and-white 'town' signs provided by the city Department of Transportation.

Allow this example: When too many Salvadorans and Mexicans moved into the Los Angeles neighborhood known as Canoga Park, the better-off, mostly white homeowners on the western fringe of the area petitioned their area council member to allow them to secede and form a new 'community' called West Hills. With one phone call from the council member's office, a new – and better – community was born when a half-dozen of the Department of Transportation signs were posted around the newly delineated perimeter. Now, since everyone involved still lives in the city of Los Angeles, nothing had really changed – except that 'West Hills' property values doubled overnight.

That's People Power, L.A.-style. White, affluent, militantly organized homeowners. And while, depending on their location, they might vote Democratic, and while on the Westside they are markedly 'liberal', they are, nevertheless, pungently redolent of White Citizens Councils. These groups form the basis of support for the LAPD.

When I visit the president, who I will call 'Rick', of a Wilshire-area homeowners' association I will dub 'Park Square', I pull up to a preciously manicured but simple California bungalow, price-tagged at $700,000. Two Salvadoran gardeners fine-tune the oleander, careful not to scratch the phone-equipped super Beemer parked on the street. (On-street parking in this community is permitted only during the day by order of the homeowners' association. 'With overnight parking banned, any car on the street at night can be spotted as suspicious by the private patrol or police', Rick's roommate, Frank, tells me later.) On the lawn, as is the case down the block, a blue triangular sign from a private security agency warns of 'armed response'. The interior of Rick's home is sheer Santa Fe splendor, from the Navajo rugs hung under the sky-lit walls to the Western hanky slung round the neck of his lethargic 85-pound mutt named Butch.

'We have a positive attitude, positive relationship with the LAPD', says Rick. 'We invite them to meetings and they tell us how to mark your valuables and stuff. You never really hear anything negative about LAPD here. People realize they have a tough job to do, though it seems now the only way to turn around their image is to have Chief Gates go.'

His roommate Frank, a realtor, agrees. 'Gates is an arrogant asshole. That's what most people around here think. This is a neighborhood that is about 85 percent liberal. But at the same time, look, you couldn't pay me all the money in the world to do the job they do. This is a tough city. I myself, for example, never have a reason to go to poor neighborhoods. Why would I go to Watts, to Compton? There are no restaurants there, no museums. I mean, I've lived in L.A. nine years but I've only gone through those neighborhoods on the freeway on the way to Palm Springs or somewhere. Why would I go to Watts, except to have my hubcaps stolen? We do go to the Coliseum (in South Central L.A.) to watch the Raiders games, but when we do we take Rick's car. It's cheaper, in case it gets ripped off.'

'That's what L.A. is like. Geographically segregated', Frank continues. 'In my own business you see it. What drives the real estate market is how safe a neighborhood is supposed to be. And my customers associate safety with distance from black neighborhoods. It's not race per se. Like if a black has the money to move into your neighborhood, no problem. The catch is, you don't want to be near a whole neighborhood of poor.'

JACK: Chief Gates is a good administrator, but let's just say he ain't no Norman Schwarzkopf out there leading the LAPD troops. The upper echelon of LAPD has never had better troops in the street, but they live different lives than us. They don't even know our names.

GREG: They could bring another chief in tomorrow and to most guys it would just mean hearing a new name.

COOPER: So no big deal if Gates goes in the next few weeks?

JACK: I didn't say that! That would be very demoralizing. He goes and we get an NYPD here. To us, New York cops just show up for their paycheck and don't give a shit. All bullshitting aside, here in L.A. we go after criminals. And Gates did come up through the ranks, just like us, so in that way we do respect him.

DOUG: The main thing about Gates is that he's not Tom Bradley. Say what you want about Gates, but he's an honest man and Bradley isn't.

GREG: I think Bradley's dishonest. He took money from banks and claimed he didn't know what it was for. Come on! And he's going to investigate us? Now we got the FBI investigating 243 cops. I'm insulted. The asshole in the street – here we are back to assholes! – he's got more rights than we do. We can go up to the asshole and say, 'Hey, we want to talk to you' and they can say, 'Hey, fuck you.' He's got that right. But now they tell us the FBI can walk right into my house, in front of my wife, and interview me and if I refuse, I can lose my job. It's just not right.

As one local editorialist put it, the beating of Rodney King is seen by many in Los Angeles as acceptable 'collateral damage' in the LAPD's much-needed war against crime. 'The one service council members can provide their constituents is beefed-up police patrols in their neighborhoods', one City Council aide told me. 'To get that you have to be on good terms with the LAPD. For that you support chief Gates.'

As far as the white liberals are concerned, police abuse has never been a sexy issue. 'The Westside agenda has not spent nearly enough time on any domestic issue', says a key political organizer inside the entertainment industry. 'People here are privileged, and they are not touched by the LAPD. They talk a lot about Nicaragua, South Africa and apartheid, but not racism here at home.'

'The Westside attitude tells you a lot about the essence of white Los Angeles', says a black adviser to a local state senator. 'They like having a moderately liberal, relatively powerless black mayor who gives the city a face of dignity. But they also want a redneck, get-tough police chief who will kick butt. Not either/or, mind you. They want both!'

GREG: You want to fix this city? I say you start out with carpet bombing, level some buildings, plow all this shit under and start all over again.

JACK: Christ, you'd drop a bomb on a community?

DOUG: Oh yeah, there'd be some innocent people, but not that many. There's just some areas of L.A. that can't be saved. And you are restricted by so many laws. Let me give a for-instance. Say twenty years ago, every night I would put a lot of people in jail for not having their green cards. A lot of people.

GREG: Yeah, we all did, it was a felony.

JACK: Take'em right to immigration and right back on the bus to Mexico.

DOUG: Then we get a letter from some commander saying we can't do that any more. Now see what we got.

JACK: Actually anything that gets close to the answer would make this place look damn near like Nazi Germany. I don't think we are ever going to get there and I'm not sure I'd want to see it. But if you want to start with solutions, then I think birth control is a big part of the answer. The Catholic Church tells everyone to have babies and then these babies, when they are sixteen, start sniffing paint. Now I'm not talking about all the Mexicans. I'm talking about families of six kids that live on $8,000 a year and everyone is out there stealing stereos. It's a social problem. But our job is to arrest them. Anything you say along these lines is going to be construed as racism. I'm not talking racism. But I am talking about the black women having 80 percent illegitimate babies. In the black community you got Bill Cosby as the big role model. But what I see every day looks more like Sanford and Son. You say that in the newspaper, they say you are a bigot. You can't say anymore, 'Let's close the border down, let's take the army down to the border', do whatever you have to stop them, because if you do, they say it's racism.

As never before in recent history, political skirmish lines in this city are being drawn up along racial lines. In the suburbs of the San Fernando Valley, Councilman Hal Bernson says calls to his office are running nine to one in favor of Gates. On the other hand, at a meeting of black leaders in South Central last weekend, pro-Gates Councilman Nate Holden was shouted down by calls of 'Uncle Tom'.

The day before, an unusually large crowd for politically lethargic Los Angeles – more than 5,000 people, mostly black – marched to police headquarters demanding Gates's removal. Characteristically, Mayor Bradley now says he will not get involved in the legal struggle to sack Gates. But a growing list of other local, state and national black officials plan to keep the heat on both the mayor and the police chief. Fearing that a single public, violent incident between police and blacks could touch off major disturbances à la Watts 1965, the various investigative commissions will now be scrambling to contain and defuse the minority community's anger, which, more than a month after the King beating, only seems to mount.

These elite commissions of city and corporate power brokers will no doubt discover and report back with feigned horror that the LAPD has, in fact, established patterns of racial discrimination and abuse. A few cops will go to jail – maybe. And a more liberal Police Commission will act on the investigators' recommendations for departmental reform. But at least one expert observer, police researcher John Van Maanen of MIT, warns that out of such enlightened civic-mindedness, the LAPD may become an even greater threat to the civil liberties of the city it patrols.

'Without question, any emphasis on more training, more professionalism, is the wrong one', Professor Van Maanen says. 'The police would like us to think that selection of individual officers and flaws in training are what produces the Rodney King incident. But the real problem lies in the police culture itself. The kind of cops we'd like to see on the street either soon quit the force or very swiftly become socialized into the peer-supported macho brotherhood, a sort of anthropological tribalism that has become quite rare in the late twentieth century. More training, more professionalism, really means police will become more insular, that more money will be spent to let cops spend more time with other cops in the academy, that cops will become even more detached from the community.

'It would be much better for us to look at how to make the police, in a sense, less professional', Van Maanen continues. 'Make them become and remain part of the community they work in. Otherwise we just contribute to the sort of "professional" detachment that directly contributes to the Rodney King sort of incidents.'

JACK: When I grew up in this city there was a guy named Nick the Cop, who lived in the neighborhood. He knew everyone of us. Do something wrong and Nick would come up and slap you, send you home and call your folks the next day. We shit our pants whenever we saw Nick the Cop coming. But we respected him. He was a tough Mexican officer who worked by himself and if he needed to know something, he'd talk to you real nice. If you didn't tell, he'd get sterner. There were kids who stole cars and surrendered to Nick the next day because they figured he'd find out anyway. Things like that. But things like that are things of the past.

Village Voice
16 April 1991

13

CLINTONSOMETHING

MANCHESTER, ATLANTA, ORLANDO: FEBRUARY 1992. The morning after the New Hampshire primary the mood on the Bill Clinton campaign jet is exultant. Things are smelling *very* presidential. Our group of reporters listed on the flight manifest has swollen overnight as Clinton's strong second place showing is confirmed. The newly dispatched detachment of ten Secret Service agents punctuate the Importance Of It All. The gale-strength positive spin churning from the Arkansas governor's chorus of aides and flacks seems potent enough to lift the very wings of our chartered MD-80. The gust is at least forceful enough to convince you that the early morning rain at Manchester Airport is God's special way of baptizing Billy Clinton as having been officially reborn as Democratic presidential front-runner.

As the jet engines rev, the ruddy-faced, sturdy-framed candidate stands prominently in the aisle making last minute calls on a cellular phone. And Clinton beams and boasts and jokes. His campaign balloon survived the pricks and tears of the thorny Genny Flowers scandal, it dodged the typhoon that raged around his draft status and now it is set on a course due south. Back to Clinton's home territory, back to his natural base. After surviving New Hampshire, the Clinton strategy has gelled. Go whole hog into the delegate-rich southern primaries, winning most and probably all of the seven regional contests to take place in the next two weeks. Along the way, pick up what you can in Maine, South Dakota, Colorado and Idaho. And then carry the momentum into Illinois on 17 March to put the clinch on the Democratic nomination. 'For us, the South is do or die, make or break', a top campaign advisor told me. 'Thankfully, it's our home field.'

With these thoughts in mind, no doubt, Clinton concludes his pre-takeoff phone call with a good-natured, jocular promise, 'Gotta go now, buddy', he says to whomever is on the other side of the line. 'Time to get all them redneck votes!

Three hours later, under the glass roof of Atlanta's huge CNN Center, Clinton kicks off his southern drive at a meticulously staged campaign rally. An exquisite specimen of late twentieth century American politics, the gathering plays out like a dramatic re-creation, a computer-modelled simulation, of what used to be good old hometown politicking. Wholesale media politics disguised as retail.

In the middle of the mall's food court a hastily erected dais cradles a perfectly racially balanced group of seventy-five local party and elected officials. Behind them, a towering backdrop of an American flag. To their left, a strawhatted Dixieland band cranks out 'Happy Days Are Here Again'. Around them, about 500 Clinton supporters chant 'We Want Bill' and wave their mass-distributed 'Comeback Kid' posters. And in a tactic that would warm the hearts of any Mexico City wardheeler, most of these 'supporters', it turns out, are local high school kids with no detectable political preference, delighted to have been bussed in to stand and cheer as temporary reprieve from geometry class. But no matter. The real intended audience of the event are the fifty or so reporters and dozen TV cameras afforded a special roped-off section just to the right of the stage (a perfect profile camera angle).

And what commences, for our consumption, is what around here is called *vis'tin' with frien's and neighbors*. Master of Ceremonies and Georgia Governor Zell Miller lays on the southern schmaltz as thick as the pink fat around a plate of hog jowls. 'Welcome home! Here in Georgia we know how to honor one of our own!' Miller bellows. And then looking straight at the TV cameras, Miller tears into Clinton rival Paul Tsongas like a modern-day Bull Connor at an ACLU garden party: 'I know a thing or two about southern politics. And let me tell you something: The Democratic Party is no more going to nominate an anti–death penalty, anti-middle-class politician as our candidate for president than Barbara and George Bush will be inviting Pat Buchanan over for Sunday supper!'

That gets the high school kids clapping and hooting. Hell, this rally is turning out to be as much fun as *Terminator 2*. Hasta La Vista, Paul. Southern style. And Miller comes back with more. 'I think it's time to tell it like it is. And the truth is Paul Tsongas would lead the party we love right back down that well-worn path of defeat!' Seems like at any moment, Miller will be rolling out a hanging tree – one fit special for Tsongas. And making sure his audience understands that the controversy around Bill Clinton's Vietnam position will not be allowed to play poorly in the south, the governor continued: 'This old Marine Corps sergeant is proud to call Bill Clinton one of our own'! Miller booms. 'Not only does he support the death penalty, he isn't afraid to carry it out!' Miller says, reminding the crowd of Clinton's refusal to stay the execution last month of a severely brain-damaged convicted killer. And as to fears that our inner cities are percolating new killers and rapists, Governor Miller promises that 'Bill Clinton will build more boot camps throughout this country than any other politician!'

Now the mike passes to candidate Clinton. And while he doesn't miss the chance to open with how good it feels, after leaving Yankee territory, to now 'be the only candidate here without an accent', Clinton positions himself, at least compared to Governor Miller as very much the kinder, gentler of the two Good Ole' Boys. He decries America as 'rudderless . . . leaderless' and as being in a 'ten-year decline'. Directly contradicting Miller's tone, Clinton bemoans an 'American people more divided than ever . . . race against race . . . class against class . . . and region against region.'

The next day, during a campaign stop in the city of Albany, Georgia, our press entourage tries to pin Clinton on the stark contrast between his words and Zell Miller's. Clinton concedes that Governor Miller's blood-call for the death penalty and his parochial attack on Paul Tsongas were 'tough stuff' and that he, Clinton, had not even heard Miller's intro from where he was standing. But neither does Clinton proffer any criticism of his Georgia ally. 'My supporters all over the country yesterday were edgy', Clinton says. 'But I want to keep the campaign on the issues. And I have never campaigned on the death penalty and never will.' But then a minute later he goes on to tell us that he believes Paul Tsongas's position on capital punishment (something the former Massachusetts senator supports in 'crimes against society') is a 'fudge'. One wire reporter later jokes on the press plane: 'I'm thinking of writing a lead that says, "Bill Clinton accused his rival Paul Tsongas today of fudging on the death penalty, while Clinton fudged on the issue of campaigning on the death penalty."'

But a wire report like that would hardly be what we call New News. Clinton's politics are and always have been the politics of fudge. 'I want to go beyond the politics of left and right, liberal and conservative', Clinton vowed at the Atlanta rally. What he really means, however, is not going beyond both positions, but *holding* both simultaneously. Let Zell Miller appeal to the rednecks and Bubbas and I'll woo the doctors and lawyers – while all the time maintaining plausible deniabilty – seemed to be Clinton's preferred approach. What is more vintage Clinton than that same speech in Atlanta where he promised to build a shipload of boot camps. But not just any old boot camp, mind you. Rather, *community-based* boot camps. By November, who knows, they might even become 'ecologically sound' boot camps.

Hence, my ambivalence about how far Clinton has come. I felt it intensely on the night of the New Hampshire primaries. In spite of my discomfort with Clinton's politics, I found myself pulling for him as the voting results came in. And I was genuinely pleased when he scored as well as he did, coming in the wake of the Gennifer Flowers scandal and the revelation of his letter to his ROTC commander. It felt like a victory, and a much-needed victory after more than a decade of cascading defeats and retreats. A victory because, finally (if maybe only temporarily), a politician of my own sixties generation had beaten back one more assault of moral McCarthyism.

Like the generation of political activists from the thirties, who had to suffer silence or pay the consequences during the fifties witch-hunts, my generation of politicians have had to be as agile as pinballs dodging the questions of sex, drugs and Vietnam. In Clinton's case, the Flowers episode miraculously wilted along-side George Bush's recession. And now, after New Hampshire, it appeared that for the first time my generation could offer up a viable presidential candidate who had clearly spoken out against the stupidity and immorality of the war in Vietnam (Bob Kerrey, who was even better positioned to take that stand, instead campaigned shamelessly on his military record, boasting that 'his patriotism can't be questioned').

I don't know what kind of reaction Ted Koppel thought he'd get out of the hoi polloi from reading Clitnon's 1969 letter to the ROTC over ABC's airwaves, but it invoked in me – and a number of my friends – a new-found respect for Bill Clinton. A careful reading of that letter reveals what is undoubtedly sincere and well-thought-out opposition to the war in Vietnam.

But there's also the foreshadowing of the politician who would come to be known a decade letter as Slick Willie. 'Unction and real charm do battle almost sentence by sentence' [in the ROTC letter], Michael Kinsley rightly observed. Yes, Clinton was without question honestly and admirably concerned about the future of his nation. Almost as much as he was worried about Numero Uno. Indeed, if the Clinton letter nudged me at all closer to supporting him, it would have to be on the basis of pure nostalgia.

Most striking about the ROTC letter is not how radical Bill Clinton was in the sixties (in fact, the position he stakes out sits squarely in the most gentle-manly faction of the antiwar movement), but how radical his political transfor-mation has become. Even with its hedging about 'political viability', the ROTC letter is no less than eloquent and moving. But Clinton's 1992 'defense' of the letter (talk about 'fudging'!) cheapens his own history. By not standing stead-fastly by his words and saying 'Damn it, I was right then and I'd say the same thing now', he turned a young man's stand of moral clarity into a cloudy pool of ambiguity and situational ethics. By retrospectively conditioning what was perhaps his most pristine moment, Clinton threatens to submerge himself in the mire of Vietnam, a full twenty years after its conclusion. If you trust the voters to forgive you for having finagled the draft and opposed a genocidal war as a young man, then why not trust them to support you for remaining a man of principle and pledging that, as president, you'd never again embroil the United States in a deluded overseas military adventure?

Clinton owed no apologies, but he offered them in any case. Implicit in Clinton's public explanation of the ROTC letter was that he was guilty, not of some political felony, but of a passing fever of youthful impudence. Closer to my sentiments are those of Andrew Ward, who slammed Clinton in a *Washington Post* editorial: 'As for myself, I don't feel guilty for having ridden out the war while other boys died in Vietnam. I feel desolate but not guilty. Guilt I reserve for the sons of bitches who sent them there to die.'

To even speculate that Clinton might have taken a position like that in 1992, I admit, is to test the imagination. There was never a chance that today's Bill Clinton would say those words. Not the man who kicked off the first televised Democratic debate last December by posturing precisely as one of those 'sons of bitches', by zealously reminding the viewers that he was the 'only candidate up here' on the stage that had unreservedly supported Desert Storm (a boast that he has since quietly and prudently stricken from his stumping).

Indeed, after listening to Clinton for three days and three nights on the campaign trail, it's clear that he is not a candidate who is trying to shape and mold his message in ways that make him 'electable' by the American people. Instead, Clinton is a candidate who first found what he is convinced is *the* electable message, and then built his campaign backward from and around that formula. By the time Clinton entered this year's race, he had studiously pored over and assimilated the tomes of Conventional Wisdom stacking up in the aftermath of the Democratic defeats of 1980, 1984 and 1988.

Penned primarily by the elite of the inside-the-beltway first string political correspondents – most notably Thomas Edsall and E. J. Dionne – these analyses argued that Democrats had lost five of the last six elections because the party had become identified as the toady of 'special interests': blacks, 'welfare queens', criminals, bra-burners, hairy-legged lesbians, AIDS patients and wheelchair-bound defenders of the Spotted Owl (that is, everyone in the country who doesn't look like a *Washington Post* correspondent or a member of that other special-interest group that holds power: the corporate elite).

The only remedy available to Democrats: move to the center (as if they had been to the left under Jimmy Carter) and put forth a candidate conservative enough to win back the suburban middle class and the more down-scale Reagan Democrats who had bolted the party in reactionary horror. Enter Bill Clinton.

Clinton's stump speech, then, his monotonous intoning of the 'forgotten middle class', of 'more rights but more responsibility', is lifted – almost word for word – from the concluding chapter of E. J. Dionne's newly published *Why Americans Hate Politics*. In his call to build a 'new center', Dionne lays out the grid of Clinton's campaign. 'A central theme of a politics that will restore popular confidence must be: Reward the work performed by the vast American middle', Dionne writes. 'The great American middle felt cheated by our policies for most of the last thirty years. . . . In liberalism it saw a creed that demeaned its values; in conservatism it saw a doctrine that shortchanged its interests. To reengage members of this broad middle, liberals must show more respect for their values, and conservatives must pay more heed to their interests.' All of which amounts to pretty bad news for those of us delusional enough to have found the traditional American margins of liberal versus conservative too restraining. In the nineties, we are now told, we have to grow up and bring the sidelines in even closer.

And that is Bill Clinton's special talent. His appeal. His 'electability'. I don't see, really, why you have to go read all of E. J. Dionne's mostly dreary book to understand this candidacy. It's really the old tradition of being everything to everybody. And Clinton, whose political trajectory is marked by what pundits call his skill at building consensus and defusing conflict, is master of this sort of 'circle-squaring'.

Clinton's call for workfare instead of welfare sends thrills up the backs of the Archie Bunkers. But then he goes on to placate his more tweedy, liberal constituencies, stressing that this 'welfare reform' will also expand educational and health benefits for the poor. Watching Clinton speak to a plaza-full of not-so-well-to-do pensioners in Winter Haven, Florida was to witness this political dipsy-doodle at its most sophisticated level. Clinton was sounding dangerously close to some sort of left-wing populist – thrashing and trashing the Bush administration's economic and social policies as instruments that strip away the dignity of the American people. He had connected with his audience of ever-more precarious and frightened retirees – and he knew it. 'We have to put aside the policies of the eighties which affected all our lives', he said, his strained voice starting to crack. And then mimicking Jesse Jackson's blow'em-away speech from the 1988 convention, Clinton held his audience rapt when he thundered, 'We have to tell the truth to the American people. Most poor people in this country are Americans who work for a living. The real untold heroes in this country are the Americans who get up everyday, go to work, work forty hours often at a job they can't bear, going home to a house not worth living in, raising those kids the best way they can, bringing home wages below the poverty level.' His proposal for a national earned-income credit that would guarantee minimum income for all Americans brought a storm of ovations.

Then Clinton moved on to the issue of crime. And here came the curve balls. We have too many people in prison – but not enough cops, he argued. And instead of locking up first-time offenders in jail we had to build a vast network – yes, of 'community-based boot camps' – that would offer not only discipline, but education, guidance and love. Bigger applause now. And watching that elderly, all-white crowd of Florida retirees, you have to ask: which part of that proposition were they applauding? The part about nurturing and educating, or the thought of having all those inner-city kids locked up in disciplined camps? I'd guess it was both notions that stirred the crowd. And therein resides the genius of Bill Clinton.

'Bill Clinton is our Gorbachev', says one of the candidate's most liberal campaign aides. 'He knows what he has to say to get elected, but you have to trust his basic instincts. Even when he joined up with the DLC (the conservative Democratic Leadership Conference) he did so to move it toward more liberal positions.'

That Clinton is not only acceptable to liberals, but is himself a 'progressive' candidate is a notion shared by an impressive national network of sixties and seventies activists who themselves come from progressive, even radical backgrounds. Clinton is supported by Ruth Messinger, who not only is Manhattan Borough President but also a member of Democratic Socialists of America. His media adviser, Frank Greer, ran Fred Harris's populist campaign of 1980. His pollster, Stanley Greenberg, worked with progressive democrats on South African and Nicaraguan issues (while Clinton was dishing out Arkansas state medals to contra leaders). His general counsel is David Ifshin, former president of the National Student Association, who in a different life twenty years ago shared a *pension* with me in Allende's Chile before travelling off with Phil Ochs to get arrested in Uruguay.

And then there's that odd group of what you might call Former Student Body Presidents of the Sixties Against the War that constitute a sort of Clinton brain trust. Robert Reich, former Dartmouth student body president, and Ira Magaziner, who presided over the students of Brown, are among Clitnon's closest economic theorists. And then there's Derek Shearer, former Yale student body president, former pal of Tom Hayden, co-author of the book *Economic Democracy* and ideological guiding light of the so-called People's Republic of Santa Monica – the 'radical' municipal government that flourished in the Los Angeles suburb in the early eighties (Shearer was and is married to the former Santa Monica mayor, Ruth Goldway). Indeed, Shearer, who co-chairs the Los Angeles Clinton campaign (along with long-time party hack and legal rep of the oil conglomerates, Mickey Kantor), is responsible for recruiting a long list of progressives into the Clinton fold.

But under the influence of Dionne, who Shearer cited several times in a thirty-minute interview, the whole notion of progressivism has taken a crash diet. 'I support Clinton because he is a progressive', Shearer told me. 'And it's time we grew up and realized we are all too old for symbolic candidacies. We have to redefine the meaning of what it means to be progressive, in a less ideological way.'

'Clinton believes that government involvement can actively change people's lives for the better. And so do I. As to all the single-issue groups out there, the women's groups, the minority groups and so on, they have to realize that if Clinton gets elected it is their only chance of having a seat at the table. Then they are going to have to come in and argue for what they want. They may not get everything, but they will have a voice and will have to learn to use it in negotiation.'

And left-of-center support for Clinton is bound to build if he maintains his momentum toward the party nomination. 'We're looking at a turning point in American politics', says Anne Lewis, former Democratic Party consultant to Jesse Jackson. 'And the liberal wing of our party is responding, thank God. The old dividing line in the party was really around military and foreign policy issues. That's where you saw the difference between Scoop Jackson and Sam Nunn on the one hand and other Democrats on the other. But with the Cold War over, it's a mistake to assume the same old divisions. So as a liberal, what is it that I can see in Bill Clinton's record as a governor that I would object to? Very little actually.'

Actually, Governor Clinton has got a deplorable environmental record, an even worse record on labor and some pretty ugly tax policies. But there are some bright spots. No other politician in Arkansas history, and few other governors in the south, have as enviable a record as Clinton on racial issues. As state attorney general he appointed three black deputies during his 1976–78 tenure. As governor he named blacks to run the department of finance and administration, the state agency of development and finance and the state health department. Numerous blacks have been appointed to state boards and commissions – more than all his predecessors combined.

Jesse Jackson, and others in the traditional liberal wing of the party, will try to keep the pressure on Clinton and keep the Democratic center of gravity from veering too far to the right. But in this battle for the soul of the party, the progressives face an uphill struggle. The momentum is clearly with those who favor concessions to that minority who already votes – especially the Reagan Democrats – rather than an 'inclusive' strategy that empowers the disenfranchised.

This tendency visibly surfaced, and paved the way for Clinton, last fall when Democrat Harris Wofford staged his dramatic defeat of Bush crony Dick Thornburg in the Pennsylvania senatorial race. At the time, not a few professional windbags pointed to a resurgence of Democratic 'populism' because Wofford had stressed the health-care issue.

But Wofford, far from roiling the masses against the wealthy, ran a campaign that just as easily could have been headed by Pat Buchanan. Willie Horton was resuscitated, this time, by counterposing the 'rights' of criminals with the denial of the 'middle class' rights to health care. The other leitmotif of the Wofford drive was laced with xenophobia, defending domestic jobs against those exported to poorer countries. What Wofford did in Pennsylvania, Clinton aspires to on a national scale. And the Democratic machinery, with some trepidation (around 'electability' and not ideology) is coalescing around him.

Only Clinton can defeat Clinton in the southern primaries this month. Tsongas stands little chance. Clinton has the money, the organization, the endorsements, the backing of the Southern Democratic establishment. 'It's true that Clinton's toughest nut here is his military record', Georgia Senate Majority Whip Wayne Garner told me. 'But Tsongas just doesn't play here. I've been a legislator for twelve years now, and I know I speak for most of my colleagues when I tell you we are just not going to run again on a national ticket headed by one of these northeastern politicians. Tsongas, and everyone of those other guys, is seen as just out of touch with our people.'

And if Clinton does as well in the south as his allies predict, then he might just be unstoppable nationwide. His candidacy may or may not be able to unseat Bush, but it would definitely mark a whole new era of Democratic redefinition. Some might consider it to be the Democratic Renaissance; others the Democratic Demise.

At the Church Street Station Mall in Orlando, Florida, the Clinton campaign is in the midst of an afternoon rally. This time around the crowd seems more genuine than the bussed-in folks in Atlanta. But the event still remains ersatz politics. The same stage with smiling local pols, the same sort of press area strategically located for purposes of television and the same stump speech from Clinton.

Though by now, late in the day and running on near empty, Clinton seems to be faltering. His speech is choppier than usual. He tries to pump up the tone, but he can tell it is still unsatisfying. He's not really speaking to his live audience who isn't really listening; there is no real engagement. His 'message' is but a stringing together of what will no doubt become this decade's nostrums – conjured and married to evoke the desired visceral responses from a mostly passive, TV-viewing public, passed off to the rest of the world as the 'American electorate'. For a moment, Clinton's speech seems to meld with and then be enveloped by the cacophony and jumble of the open air mall around us, his stage just one more stand among the earring sellers and T-Shirt vendors. Absent is any, even half-hearted attempt to – excuse me – build a democratic movement or even a capital 'D' Democratic Party movement. The idea here is strictly to get 50 percent plus 1 of the votes that are to be cast.

A West German tourist at my side asks me if all American political rallies are like this – a circus without substance. When I answer yes, he smiles and says that some of his neighbors from East Germany have told him that's what politics were like under the Communist administration. Probably an exaggeration, I tell him, given that such an empty process had so little credibility in Germany, while here half the people still vote. And just then, Clinton gets my attention with a dramatic pause in his spiel. 'Why am I running? Why do I want your vote for president?' he asks rhetorically. And then answers: 'I'm running because I have always looked upon public service, I have always looked upon elected office as a way to change people's lives for the better.' And that fleetingly touches something inside me. I'm sure that Clinton is telling the truth. The boy who wrote that letter to the ROTC in 1969 unequivocally ran for office a few years later believing that he would change our world for the better.

After all, my generation, Bill Clinton's generation, was among the most radical to come along in this American century. In 1969 Clinton, writing to the ROTC, aligned himself with the most pragmatic among us. Most of us just wanted to burn down the ROTC buildings. Some of us did. But even the more cautious Clintons were our comrades. We thought the world was ours. We had learned from our French counterparts the year before that our task was simply: Be realistic – demand the impossible!

And here, two decades later, Bill Clinton is before me talking once again about changing people's lives for the better. But now even the possible seems to be impossible. Now it's accepting what is. Now it's capital punishment, boot camps, workfare and more responsibilities which – I believe – are all the things we rebelled against together twenty years ago. But I'm not convinced that my generation's aspirations are best expressed or represented by these Clinton-something politics. Not all of us were Rhodes scholars, or student body presidents, not all of us drive Porsches or even Volvo stationwagons, not all of us are ready to declare a ceasefire. Most of our generation, in fact, doesn't come near meeting Bill Clinton's means test for being part of his 'middle class'. Most of this generation makes less than $30,000 a year, many are the names that swell welfare and relief rolls upon whom Clinton would like to impose more responsibilities. They can't even dream of the social mobility which seems to motivate Clinton's campaign staff much more than any behind-the-scenes jabbering about changing the world.

I'll admit that history might absolve Clinton and his supporters. Maybe he is ahead of the curve and sagely foresees the limits of oppositional politics in 1992 America. It's true that Democratic politicians to Clinton's left in recent years and in this current campaign have failed to win a large following. Maybe it's the fault of the message, maybe of the messengers. Maybe Clinton will be our Gorbachev – or at least Andropov – and finally open the doors of national power to my generation. Maybe Derek Shearer is right and it's time to grow up. But I look at the hollow rally around me, I listen to the end of Clinton's speech, and I can't help but think there's got to be more to it than this. Or at least there ought to be.

Village Voice
3 March 1992

14

BY THE LIGHT OF A THOUSAND FIRES

For there are those who live in darkness,
And those who live in light,
Those in brightness you see,
Those in darkness, out of sight.
Bertolt Brecht

LOS ANGELES: APRIL 1992. Panama, Iraq, now Los Angeles. True, as one Marine put it, 'It's not as cut and dried here as in Desert Storm – you don't know who your enemy is.' But the 10,000 troops, shipped in mostly after the upheaval of the last week was over, found plenty to do. Machine gun-toting detachments of the National Guard sealed off the basketball courts and bike and skate paths of Venice Beach. Platoons of soldiers secured their positions under the burned-out palm trees of the Civic Center. Some forty-five miles from the epicenter of the disturbances, desert-camouflaged armor stood sentinel over a string of shopping malls as white suburbanites went binge-buying, stocking up on food, treats and videos before the dusk-to-dawn curfew fell again. At the boutique markets – the Gelson's and Pavilions – polished Jags and buffed-out Range Rovers shared parking space with Humvees and APCs as the patrons weathered two-hour checkout lines. Soldiers also kept the freeways open as those who could afford it raced away, booking every $350-a-night resort room on the white-sands beaches of Santa Barbara, Laguna and Dana Point over their cellular phones.

Meanwhile, another thousand Marines roared into the heart of L.A.'s black ghetto, past still-smoldering fires and blocks of collapsed buildings, cautiously eyeing another set of anxious citizens lined up three and four abreast. This was no frenzy for food, or gasoline, or videotapes, though. All that was long gone, looted, incinerated. These South Central residents endured hours under the smoke-filtered sun from the moment the curfew lifted, deep into the afternoon, to pick up their welfare and Social Security checks from a paralyzed post office – in the vain hope that, if you got there early enough, there might be time to head north for supplies and beat it back before nightfall.

South Central certainly did not greet the soldiers with confetti and yellow ribbons. But, given the Hobson's choice of being policed either by the black-uniformed LAPD, with its 'super sniper squads' and battering rams under the command of Chief Daryl F. Gates, or by the winter soldiers temporarily dispatched by Mayor Tom Bradley and Governor Pete Wilson, well . . . there was hardly a contest.

After all, it was Chief Gates and his free-swinging clubbers who got L.A. into this mess in the first place. The not-guilty verdict in the Rodney King case not only launched the phosphorous flare signaling that it is completely legal to beat the stuffing out of black men, and that justice is a word reserved for whites only, but also ignited twenty-seven years of boundless fury and frustration bottled up since the last uprising.

In the fourteen months following the Rodney King beating, the liberal power structure appeased a furious city with elite commissions, reports and appointments. Promises were made that reconciliation and reform would eclipse Gates's tarnished star. But all the official harrumphing was blotted out in an instant by the chorus of yelps from ecstatic cops celebrating the vindication of their fellows, by the screeching sirens of fire trucks, police cars and ambulances, by the crash of collapsing buildings, the sobs of those who lost their livelihoods and loved ones and ultimately by the crowing of a smiling, swaggering, epaulet-decked Daryl Gates who, when everything was said and done, was still chief of police. And still with no fixed retirement date.

By early Sunday morning, the tally was 10,000 businesses laid waste, 58 corpses at the morgue, 9,500 people arrested and a price tag approaching a billion dollars. A small, multiracial detail of civilians, meantime, armed with brooms and dustpans and led by actor Eddie Olmos was busy sweeping the streets. With the official media and bewildered political leaders latching onto this operation as 'just what the city needed' and 'the beginning of the healing process', reality was disappearing from the spotlight, threatening to turn this exercise of civic goodwill into one more ritual of collective denial.

What looks to the television cameras like so many mounds of rubble is, in reality, a mosaic of anger over decades of LAPD brutality, of agony over a court system that sends a black man to jail for shooting a dog while freeing a Korean shopkeeper who shot a black teenager, of frustration over an economy that no longer provides a real living, of discontent with a welfare system that punishes. The growing heap being carted to the city dump contains the recognition by

THE REVOLUTION *WILL* BE TELEVISED

blacks, Latinos and disenfranchised whites that they are not merely discriminated against, but abandoned, written off as 'losers'. 'The people who were responding with such violence today are not people for whom the problem is just Daryl Gates', said one black activist. 'The problem is the notion that some people count and some don't.'

Among the shards of shattered glass are the mirrors that reflect an ethos common to both the smoking ruins of South Central and the affluent brokerage firms and corporate offices of the Westside. An ethos of a society whose schools are financed by a lottery, whose faded prosperity is based on overcharging the taxpayer for toilet seats and hammers for planes that can't fly, whose elected officials leveraged the next three generations on bad real estate deals, whose icons are Michael Milken and Lee Iaccoca and whose public morality is 'I've got mine, you dumb nigger, now go get yours.' Well, they did. And in the light cast by a thousand fires, for anyone who cared not to overlook it, you could perceive a momentary, flickering glasnost, ghetto-style – a society revealed to be built upon timbers dry as the mesquite that pocks the hills of L.A., a country whose rotten carcass, like the torched and looted structures of Los Angeles, could now only be propped up by the muscle of the one institution that the Demopublicans still have the will to fully fund: the Pentagon.

'The Rodney King trial? NOT GUILTY? Forget that! We don't get no justice.' Willie, a 22-year-old black male, originally from Fresno but raised in Kansas City, said as the L.A. riots began to subside. A security guard at a supermarket who now resides in Hollywood, Willie was dressed in the new UCLA sweatshirt he had looted from a neighborhood store.

If we don't got no rights, and nobody gives a damn about us, hey, why not riot? Ain't nobody watching us. I'm going to do what I want to do. I'm going to loot all these white man's stores. They don't care about us. Why should we care? I'm just taking back what's mine, what's ours, for free. I just walked in and grabbed what I could and put it on and walked out. It felt good to me. It took some of that pressure off of me. Like, yeah, we're doing this to the white folks, yeah, we're doing this to the Koreans. I said, when they come in and see their store burned down or broken in, they'll see how we feel. That's justice. The only part I don't like is we did our own community. Shouldn't have done that. Should have gone to Beverly Hills, Simi Valley, Rodeo Drive.'

It wasn't a matter of 'I got something for free.' Look, I paid forty-eight dollars for these pants. It ain't no problem. It was a matter of, 'I'm taking from the white man. How do you like us now?' That's what it was. I'm taking from y'all now. How do you like us now? You can't do nothing about it. Y'all helpless. Y'all thought we were useless, y'all had to keep us behind closed doors. But it wasn't true. They thought we would just shut up and just sit down and watch y'all treat us like little dogs. It wasn't true. We just said,

'Forget that.' We got to show them that we just as much human, we want equal rights, we want this just as much as y'all got it.

At the height of the looting and rioting, it was difficult to escape the conclusion that the turmoil most benefited one man: Chief Daryl Gates. In the week before the Rodney King verdict, Gates – alone among city officials and public leaders – predicted widespread violence should officers Timothy Wind, Laurence Powell, Theodore Briseno and Stacey Koon walk free. The chief triumphantly declared that he had set aside a million dollars to pay overtime for putting down an uprising. But when the uprising began, Daryl Gates appeared to be in hiding.

The shock wave that emanated from the Simi Valley Courthouse became deadly at approximately 5 p.m. Wednesday. At the intersection of Florence and Normandie avenues, practically dead-center in South Central L.A., what began as bottle- and rock-throwing soon turned to the looting of a liquor store and a small neighborhood market by perhaps two dozen people. As television news helicopters arrived, the situation turned ugly. Live, unedited, on every station along the dial, a macabre, public reenactment of the Rodney King beating was broadcast. This time, however, it was whites being pummeled by a crowd of blacks – just as Gates had warned. White drivers who pulled into the fateful intersection were dragged from their cars by the angry mob. For an hour or more, the audience of electronic onlookers watched passing motorists being clobbered with fists and rocks. One after another, the merciless beatings progressed, as the hovering newscasters repeated, 'This is all being watched at the police command center. These images are all being monitored by the police. They know this is happening.' Back at the anchor desks, the talking heads confidently intoned at first, 'I'm sure the police are on the way.' Later, that became a panicky wail: 'Where are the police? Where are the police? Why don't they arrive?'

By the time the last victim, ill-fated truck driver Reginald Denny, rolled his eighteen-wheeler smack into the middle of the deadly mayhem, TV news crews were practically frantic. Pleading for a police presence, they narrated an attempted murder. One man yanked Denny from his cab, two others kicked and stomped him as he lay helpless on the asphalt. Finally, a third man grabbed an oxygenator from another victim's truck and crashed it down upon Denny's skull. While he lay on the ground, another man came up to him and slowly went through his pockets, fleeing with Denny's wallet. It was a pitiful, wrenching picture, and the whole city was watching. The lens of the video camera confirmed that this grisly, real-time drama was officially a crisis.

Chief Daryl Gates, the one man in a position to halt what up to then appeared to be an isolated incident, ironically, was on his way to a fundraiser in opposition to Proposition F – the June charter amendment that was written after the King beating to reform the LAPD. 'There are going to be situations where people are without assistance', Gates said, as he was leaving the cushy Brentwood fundraiser. 'That's just the facts of life.'

Inexplicably, Daryl Gates's own augury was now reality. The man who said he'd never let it happen in his town, who had budgeted a million dollars in anticipation of a general insurrection, declared no tactical alert, issued no orders to block off the streets leading to and from Normandie and Florence, offered no police escorts to ambulances and fire trucks. The garrulous chief, usually given to incendiary remarks and decisive action, was silent. 'Daryl Gates was in a position to allow the black community to go up in flames', an aide to black State Senator Diane Watson said. 'And he did.'

Even after Governor Wilson granted Mayor Bradley's request for National Guard militia, Gates took a day and a half to deploy the first 500 citizen-soldiers out of a complement of 6,000. Police Commission Vice-President Jesse Brewer, once the city's highest ranking black officer as deputy chief, observed that Gates may have slowed the entry of the Guard because 'the chief likes to feel he can handle everything by himself, without any help from anybody.'

It was vintage Daryl Gates. What other police department would allow its cops to beat an innocent man to within an inch of his life, leaving him emotionally riven and allegedly brain-damaged, and fourteen months later sit idly by as twoscore other innocents were nearly beaten to death? Gates's message was loud and clear: Now you see what it is like when you don't want an effective police department, a force that cracks heads. The boss of L.A.'s Police Protective League quickly seconded Gates, wagging his finger at complacent liberals, saying that this is what you get when you have a police department that is 'understaffed and undermanned'.

'Daryl Gates is delighted', Senator Watson's aide continued. 'It could not have worked out better. He got the vindication he has claimed he and his cops deserved.' Gates's inflammatory omissions were hardly improvised. From the very moment Channel 5 news aired amateur photographer George Holliday's video of the assault on Rodney King, Gates has successfully stared down Mayor Bradley and his liberal allies. The chief's seeming omnipotence stems not only from his limitless arrogance but from the policy of appeasement pursued by the Bradley coalition of downtown businessmen, black community leaders and Westside liberals – the key supporters of the Christopher Commission reforms. Like a Latin American colonel to whom democratically elected leaders are always kowtowing, Gates can usually count on his opponents to temporize and backpedal for fear that they may arouse the pro-police constituency to action.

Hemmed in by antiquated local ordinances insulating Gates behind civil service protections, the Bradley establishment has been unwilling to tap into the anger of its natural constituency, the black and Latino communities. Like their national counterparts in the Democratic Party, Bradley and his handpicked police commissioners, as well as his allies on the City Council, prefer to appease conservative swing voters in the San Fernando Valley rather than mobilize the mass of unregistered and potentially volatile voters at the bottom of L.A.'s food chain.

'We didn't want to offend Daryl Gates', Meyer Westrich, a key Bradley adviser and author of the police reforms appearing on the June ballot, said in the wake of the riots. 'We felt we had to tiptoe around.'

The conciliatory stance, designed to nudge Gates aside, was a shambles from its inception. In March of last year, at Bradley's insistence and with the blessings of the City Attorney, the Police Commission suspended Gates. Within days, the City Council – angered by the commission's new-found independence – overruled them, with five of Gates's erstwhile liberal opponents providing the swing votes to *reinstate* the chief. It was a flip-flopping fiasco, only to be compounded later, in July, when Gates made a written promise to leave the department by April 1992. By late summer, the Christopher Commission gave the official stamp to the public's dismal rating of the LAPD as a brutal, racist, autocratic, occupying force. Still, Gates persevered, despite his promise to resign. And, once again, the City Council, the mayor and the Police Commission acquiesced, insisting that Gates would be gone by April, when a new police chief would be on board and the reform initiative would be before voters.

And so the charade went, right up to the eve of the riots. One week before chaos brought the months-long waffling to a cold, sobering halt, Police Commission President Stanley Sheinbaum and Chief Gates got into a shouting match. Gates announced he was making promotions and changes among the top echelon at Parker Center – a direct slap in the face of chief-designate Willie Williams, the black police commissioner of Philadelphia. Sheinbaum – the gruff, seventyish, left-liberal rainmaker, financier of *Ramparts* magazine and former head of the ACLU Foundation – was unequivocal. Gates would make no such appointments.

By Tuesday, twenty-four hours before L.A. went up in flames, the Bradley minions wimped out one last time. Gates could make his staffing changes – thereby prolonging his paramilitary legacy – so long as the commission 'oversaw' the new appointments. Once again, the chief snickered as his opponents backed down. 'Had the City Council swing votes put Gates out the door last year', Westrich concluded, 'I don't think this city would have reacted with this level of anger.'

When they pulled out that white trucker and beat him, I laughed, it was funny to me. Say he didn't do nothing? Well, Rodney King didn't do nothin' either. Really, later on I might start regretting it. But right now, the way my anger is, let's beat 'em all up. Let's beat up all the white people. On Third Street, this chick I know busted the window. And the white man come up and he wanted to play hero, he wanted to play macho man. He come out there and she dropped the bat. He picked up the bat and started swinging at her. I'm like, running. And I look, and I say, 'What the fuck . . .' I ran back there, there was another black, so he ran back there. But we couldn't get too close because he had that bat swinging. I swear to God, if he would have dropped that bat, I would have killed his ass. I would have killed him. I would have busted his head open. He would have been right there bleeding. I wouldn't care.

Couldn't care less about them people cleaning up. I don't care. I'm cracking jokes on them, 'You're cleaning up all that mess that we did? Oh. That's nice of y'all.' (Laughs). They're giving out donuts and stuff. Alright. Cool. They reward us for tearing it up. Cool. (Laughs) I don't think they're fools. They are just nice, kind-hearted people. But it's white people, though. They are trying to say, 'See, we don't feel bad, we're cleaning up.' You see black people down there cleaning up too. But I'm saying, those are the ones that are more up there, they've got something.

They were right to say, 'Don't do that.' But I didn't want to listen to them at the time. At the time, when you think about it, when people say, man, when they said, talking to you not to do it, it's in there, in your own mind. But, you know how you've got that good man, saying you're right. And you've got the Devil saying, 'And, fuck that shit. See that new coat over there, man, get that shit.' You're going to run over there and get it.

I didn't feel bad at all. Right now they're crying over there, the people that own those stores. I want to laugh. Why are you crying? That's fake. You just want donations. Just take your loss, like Latasha Harlins. We didn't cry when the Korean (shop owner) killed that girl. We felt bad, damn, why'd they kill her? Damn. We just took it as a loss, turned our cheeks. But then the Rodney King case, they said, 'Not guilty', and we said, 'Nah-nah, we can't turn the other cheek on this one', cause we don't have no more cheeks, we keep turning.

Me myself, I get frustrated. When this shit hit, when they said the verdict, Wednesday, I went to work, can't no white man talk to me. Can't nobody talk to me. I'm like, 'What are you doin'?' I was working that day. But, really, I wasn't working that day. Really I was there, but I wasn't doin' nothin'. Homeless people, I'm supposed to keep the homeless out of the parking lot. I kept certain homeless people out, such as (whispering) white people (smiling). White homeless people pack up, you gotta go. Get outta my parking lot. Black ones, "spare change, spare change", you can do this all night if you want to. I don't usually do that, that was getting out my frustration. Built up, anger.

That day all the white people walk up to me and talk about it. 'Hi. I don't know

why they did that. I'm so against that.' They kiss my ass because they feel I might say,
'Come on boy, let's go loot this place right here.' I got a partner, we went to this restau-
rant. He said all he wants is an orange juice and donut. So this Korean woman gave him
extras. 'Have a nice day, have a nice day.' He said, 'Man, all I want is one orange juice.'
It was free because they were afraid. Man, fuck them. Whites were friendly because they
were afraid. Honestly, truthfully, you know they go back home saying, 'Niggers, they
destroying they own selves, forget them.'

Was I afraid when the cops came? No. Because the cops couldn't do nothing. Most
people just turned around and looked at them, say, 'Fuck the cops. You ain't no justice.
Fuck y'all.' As we were saying 'Fuck the cops', we were breaking windows. 'Fuck you,
pccchhh' (he mimics the sound of glass breaking and swings his hands). 'You're not no
justice.' It was a party on the street, that's what it was, a party.

Last week's convulsion snapped the confines of the 1965 Watts riots, spilling
out of the traditional borders of the black ghetto, edging northward and west-
ward, into Downtown and Hollywood, crushing Koreatown in its wake, threatening the outskirts of Beverly Hills and leapfrogging the Santa Monica
Mountains into the Spanish-speaking areas of the once all-white San Fernando
Valley.

Like a computer-generated map pinwheeling off the screen and coming to
life on the streets, the geographical outlines of the violence accurately redrew
the boundaries of underclass Los Angeles. While the torched-out shopping dis-
tricts on Hollywood Boulevard still draw camera-laden tourists from Osaka and
Oshkosh, the tattered wooden-frame homes up and along the residential side
streets were long ago ceded to the burgeoning numbers of casually employed
Latinos who populate city street corners selling oranges, peanuts or a few hours
of their physical labor to passing motorists. Looking at the TV charts of looting
and arson incidents, there must have been some thousands of white people who
finally realized that in this hypersegregated town, it is they who now live in a
ghetto – a white ghetto – surrounded by a Third World city.

The urge to loot was all but universal here, in the real city. Multiracial
crowds, young and old, entire families, sometimes three generations strong,
swarmed up and down the city's commercial thoroughfares, moving as quickly
from store to store as power shears buzzing the wool off sheep. Shopping carts
collided with station wagons in a race to load up as much as possible. In one
spectacular operation, one motorist in Hollywood rammed open the doors of a
pawn shop, backed up ten yards and then rammed in again to open the doors
wide for his accomplices and friends.

At other times it was bloody and grim, punctuated by gunfire, curdling
shrieks and acrid smoke. In the next moment, maybe just down the block, it

would be a carnival, a block party of conspicuous and gratuitous consumption, forever memorialized on whirring videocameras, some of them liberated just moments before. 'I came all the way from Santa Ana to get me some free stuff', said a fortyish Chicano and then, turning directly to reporters, the cameras rolling, he boasted, 'Mom, we didn't get the shoes you wanted, but we sure got a lot of good stuff.'

While the columns of smoke towered into the skies and the human and property casualty tolls mounted, it became clear that this was a rebellion not only against the white establishment, but also against its black component. Indeed, the very fruits of the Watts riot of 1965 were not immune from last week's flames. After Watts, the city's disenfranchised were told that their redemption resided in electing to office a progressive generation of politicians that could pass on concrete benefits to the grass roots. The 1973 election of Tom Bradley, supported by a coalition of white liberals and supposedly progressive business interests, seemingly vindicated the rioters of 1965. Yet after two decades of liberal administration headed by a black mayor, Los Angeles's African American community now lags farther behind other minority groups and sees its already tenuous economic standing being further eroded. In short, the Bradley Revolution of 1973 has become, by 1992, the Los Angeles Establishment.

In those first hellacious hours, as the first fires were sprouting, Mayor Bradley and the city's black leadership huddled with a roiling crowd of 2,500 in the preeminent First A.M.E. Church. When Bradley took the pulpit and pleaded for peace, he was met with a cascade of booing from the mostly middle-class audience. One angered woman rose to her feet and, staring at a momentarily speechless mayor, yelled, 'What are you going to do? What are you going to do?'

A few moments later another irate young black woman, ignoring the roster of clergy and politicians waiting their turn to speak, charged undeterred toward the podium. The crowd, inspired by her boldness, chanted, 'Let her speak!'

'We can't rely on these people up here to act', the woman thundered as she motioned to the politicians behind her. 'I believe they have our best interests at heart, but we cannot rely upon them. . . . You know what you need to do.'

That first night's meeting collapsed into chaos and outrage. Bradley and several other black politicians and clergy were left literally talking to themselves as the agitated audience moved into the street and melted into the whirlwind of violence sweeping around them. The car of liberal councilman Zev Yaroslavsky – one of Chief Gates's earliest critics – went up in flames. So did the office of young black councilman Mark Ridley-Thomas, a former executive director of the Southern Christian Leadership Conference of Greater Los Angeles and one of the original leaders – going back some thirteen years – of a militant but unsuccessful campaign to place the LAPD under a civilian review board. By the morning light other symbols of black advance had been reduced to ashes. The Crenshaw shopping district, heart of L.A.'s black middle class and the only significant commercial district in South Central, had burned to the ground.

A yawning abyss had opened between the new urban poor (not to mention the growing underclass) and an aging black leadership that was forged in struggle some thirty years ago. 'People were in no mood to hear anyone tell them to be calm, "Don't do this",' said the SCLC's Joe Hicks. 'There is an incredible lack of respect for black elected officials. They are considered symbols of the white power system. They are impotent and unable to deliver the goods for blacks. They get absolutely no respect. No matter which black official spoke on Wednesday night at the First A.M.E., they were taunted and booed. With all of the flip-flops over the last year from the mayor's office and from the city, people just felt locked out of the political process. They have little respect for the institutions in their own community and little respect for others' and their own lives.'

As the violence spun out of control and took on increasing tones of self-destruction, yet another meeting at the First A.M.E. Church was called for the next morning – a closed-door conclave of the fifty top black leaders in the city. Another failure. 'That second meeting demonstrated that people just plain didn't know what to do', a young activist who attended the meeting said, 'It showed that the traditional leadership are comfortable with certain formulas and don't know how to go beyond them. No one was prepared to legitimate the rage being acted out on the streets. They feared that legitimizing the rage would legitimize the violent actions. Some of us tried to argue for a course of action that would take that rage and rechannel it into massive, and peaceful, civil disobedience. But they didn't want to hear that either. The impulse was to keep the peace, to postpone any action. To put out the line that the people out there rioting do not represent the rest of us. I felt that saying that was to play into the hands of the racists.'

And many of those racist hands were tightly gripped around the city's media microphones. With the black leadership refusing to legitimize if not condone the social explosion for the most part, the electronic media took over spin control. This was, after all, ratings sweeps week, where the scheduled reports on pregnant lesbian nuns, on sexy Mexican soap opera stars and white men who will only sleep with black women were rudely preempted by the searing flash of reality. The sleazy, titillating sweepstakes scripts prepared months in advance were burned to ashes. But no problem, the unfolding urban violence was immediately and deftly repackaged, reshaped and made suitable for maximum ratings impact.

Given open-ended airtime, the TV 'news' departments turned the uprising into one continuous, 24-hour-a-day drive-by shooting, all Live from Copter Five.

The chauffeur-driven, million-dollar-a-year local TV news anchors, whose only contact with South Central is from inside their locked cars en route to Palm Springs, were now wringing their hands about the 'innocent victims' of the violence, cowering with their families in those 'nice, little, well-kept houses', as Channel 7's Ann Martin put it. 'This is the sort of thing that happens in other places, not in our town', Martin added. 'But now just look.'

'Creeps' is how her partner Paul Moyers described those defying police in the streets. 'Hooligans', ruled Channel 2. 'Thugs, criminals and gangbangers', said Channel 4. 'Look out for the Crips and Bloods gangs' was the drumbeat on Channel 5.

Then a new round of anchors. 'How much of this is fueled by anger? And how much is fueled by alcohol?' inquired another great mind. Some street reporters saw their best stories in interviewing the window smashers live, but only if they were polite. Any 'incendiary' language, any obscenity, any real passion or anger for that matter was squelched and extinguished with the hurried flick of a director's switch. 'You're going to have to control your language if you're going to be on television', Channel 7 reporter Art Rascon scolded an angry young man who had just blurted out 'fuck' a number of times on camera. By the second day of violence, Channel 7 field reporter Linda Mour was sitting on the news set being interviewed live about her experience reporting on looters. 'Did you get the impression that a lot of those people were illegal aliens?' asked anchor Harold Greene.

'Yes', a clairvoyant Mour flatly replied.

Mayor Bradley? He's an Oreo cookie. That white man got him wrapped around his finger. Everything they do: 'Tom Bradley, I want you to do it that way.' 'Yes sir.' City Council, they the big people, all white men that tell the mayor, they're running him, and he can't do nothing but say, 'Okay, I'll do it that way.' Fuck, he's the mayor. He can't fire Chief Daryl Gates. That tells you something right there.

Martin Luther King, that's the first thing they say, 'Wait a minute, y'all destroying Martin Luther King's truth.' I'm telling you right now, fuck Martin Luther King, he's a sell-out too. If you read your history book it will show that he's always talked to Lyndon Johnson, always talking to him, in his back room, in his office. He sold out. He's the one that wanted to march. But not Malcolm X. Stand up for my brother Malcolm X. He represents – just like the shit you seen there. And that's what he would have done, he would have recommended violence. If we can't do it talkin', then do it with violence.

I work full-time, five dollars and seventy-five cents, slave labor. I can't keep working for the white man. I can't keep working for five dollars and seventy-five cents. I can't come up on five dollars and seventy-five cents. That's what makes a man mad. That is what makes a black man start selling drugs. They want the same things as the white

*man. They want the same Mercedes, they want a big mansion, they want a helicopter.
They want everything the white man gets. We want the same things they let everyone
get. In others words, we want to be equal. We want to live in Beverly Hills.'*

As the median skin hue darkened in Los Angeles in the seventies, developers
bulldozed stand after stand of California live oak, pushing the white suburban
envelope to the very edge of the county line and beyond through the Santa
Susana Pass. Succeeding lumps of flesh-colored townhomes (all with identical
faux-Mexican tile roofs) festered into the metastasizing melanoma known today
as Simi Valley. A hundred thousand souls, drawn by 'good schools' (read all-
white) and relatively low housing costs, have set up camp just across the Los
Angeles County line, separated from South Central and the Rodney Kings of
this world by two mountain ranges and sixty miles of freeway. Before the high-
publicity police trial of the last six weeks, Simi's only claim to notoriety was
serving as home to the Ronald Reagan Presidential Library.

It was a stroke of genius, then, when the LAPD defense lawyers managed
to change the venue of the police-beating trial to this somnolent 'burb. What a
laugh they must have had together when Judge Stanley Weisberg acceded to
their request, agreeing that adverse, saturation media in Los Angeles had made
a fair trial there impossible. No matter that Simi was part of the same L.A.
media market. Judge Weisberg, legal sources say, found the one-hour daily commute from his Beverly Hills home the most attractive and convenient of the
options available.

Several hundred LAPD officers live in Simi. Then there's the untold number
of L.A. County and Ventura County deputy sheriffs out there, coaching Little
League and fixing Sunday barbecues. Like some sort of local Huey Long, presid-
ing over and micromanaging the entire Conejo Valley, which includes Simi and
the neighboring town of Moorpark (whose mayor was forced to resign in 1987
after using the word 'nigger' twice in a newspaper interview), is State Senator Ed
Davis, Daryl Gates's immediate predecessor as police chief (who will always be
fondly remembered by local columnists as the man who suggested that any captured airplane hijacker should be tried on the spot and then hanged 'at the airport').

Simi Valley places what you might call a premium on order. When local
teenagers, bored out of their skulls in a town whose entertainment pinnacle is
cruising the Dairy Queen, took to skateboarding around the barren paths of City
Hall, an ordinance was hastily drafted to outlaw the activity. When the kids
moved their hangout to the parking lot of a 7-Eleven, the owners installed loudspeakers that began spewing classical music as a sort of audio-adolescent repel-
lent.

At the Kountry Folks coffee shop, nestled among the auto malls on Easy Street, the Sunday-morning breakfast crowd quietly ate their sausage and eggs and glumly stared at the TV monitor hastily installed behind the counter. The images of burned-out strip malls and smoking supermarket skeletons fluttered as haunting reminders of the city they left behind and of why, a few nights before, at the height of the violent paroxysm, the California Highway Patrol had restricted access into Simi Valley to properly identified residents. After the morning meal, life in Simi will resume its patterns of reassuring normalcy. Some chores around the house, maybe waxing the car, watching the Dodgers or the Raiders, some shopping at the discount outlet, or maybe some powerboating around the barren-shored, artificial lakes carved into the nearby desert floor.

Whatever the leisure activity, it's doubtful that the pictures of destruction carried out as retribution for their neighbors' performance on a Superior Court jury will recede. More likely, they will linger and burn into a crust of fear, mistrust and often a quite open hatred of blacks, a flagrant racism as profound as the unabashed anger and incendiary resentment that torched L.A.'s poorest neighborhoods last week.

When Watts exploded in 1965, pundits and investigators rushed in and, after a careful study, concluded that while race and poverty were indeed endemic, the actual violent outburst was the work of a 'criminal fringe'. A redneck-run LAPD was left unreformed, and its diseased essence brought forth the Daryl Gates of today. Why would anyone conjecture that, this time around, the analyses will be any more generous?

The fateful decision made by the Simi Valley jury is destined to be more than an asterisk when the history of this period is written. The sensibilities that underlie that verdict will surface again, in the months to come, when the 'solutions' to last week's uprising are proffered. The tsk-tsking over the destruction of South L.A. has led many to delude themselves that something good must come of this, that such a wrenching *cri de coeur* from the L.A. underclass just cannot go unheeded.

But these are the nineties, not the sixties. Whatever half-hearted reform that came in the wake of Watts was part of a national War on Poverty, vastly different from today's War on the Poor. That message was unabashedly transmitted this weekend when Mayor Bradley named utility *Übermensch* Peter Ueberroth as head of the commission to Rebuild Los Angeles. This Prophet of Profit immediately warned there would be 'no handouts' and that it would be not the state or federal government, God Forbid, but the private sector that would reconstruct the ghetto. But it is that same private sector that has, under Bradley's stewardship, systematically retreated from, abandoned and ultimately strangled South Central Los Angeles. In 1992, twelve years into the Reagan Revolution, are we to believe these entrepreneurs will experience a moral conversion? All this while Republican governor Pete Wilson, who had the audacity this past week to quote Martin Luther King and Thurgood Marshall, will return next week to his preferred political cause, a ballot initiative aimed at a 25 percent cut in welfare.

The immediate future of Los Angeles is more likely to be determined by the mean, myopic, empty spirit of places like Simi Valley than by the fleeting compassion symbolized by this week's multiracial cleanup of the riot zone. 'The riot in the inner city will probably be followed by a second, even more devastating 'riot' in the suburbs', historian Mike Davis wrote as the rage over the Simi Valley verdict burst around him. 'The suburbanites won't burn Korean liquor stores or stone Parker Center. They will simply tighten the fiscal vise around the central city – where they will never again venture – and let it bleed. They will organize death-penalty parties and victory parades for the LAPD and the National Guard (Operation Urban Storm?). And Daryl F. Gates's book will top best-seller lists in [the white suburbs of] West Hills and South Pasadena.'

Perhaps Davis's grim vision has been shaded by the death and destruction that marked this week. But while the Watts outburst of 1965 seemed to some a dress rehearsal for revolution, its 1992 encore was but a rumbling, tectonic shift, an adjustment along the seemingly bottomless fault line of day-to-day despair. Once the wrenching was over, it was back to business as usual. Sergeant Stacey Koon, acquitted for supervising the beating of Rodney King, was finishing his memoirs, had got himself an agent and was now negotiating a movie deal.

What better indicator that Los Angeles was back to normal?

Village Voice
12 May 1992

NOTE: This article was co-written with Greg Goldin

15

EARTH CIRCUS

RIO DE JANEIRO: JUNE 1992. The one or two million Brazilians who stitch together a life in this city's notorious hillside *favela* slums are among those on the planet most affected by the trashing of the earth. But if any significant number of them care to visit the remote site of the UNCED Earth Summit this week and listen to George Bush decide their own children's future, they'll have more than the 45-minute, $25 taxi ride to overcome. There's the formidable question of the Brazilian army tanks and halftracks keeping watch not only over the streets at the foot of the *favelas*, but also the military steel and armor arrayed along the entire twenty-mile stretch to the Riocentro Convention Center – all part of the 35,000-man security force deployed in the city. Once at the UN site they'll be confronted with an armed security perimeter at once pretorian and irrational – so much so that even some properly credentialed reporters have had to argue at the gates for two hours before gaining entry.

Not that there are any Brazilian slum dwellers, nor any other sort of Brazilian outside of diplomats, journalists and professional ecologists, who would have any reason or desire to attend the Earth Summit, the first world gathering whose stated goal is to save the planet. The residents of Rio, perhaps better than anyone, know that the much ballyhooed Eco '92 is turning out to be little more than history's most expensive photo-op for a hundred of the world's heads of state.

For weeks before the Summit opened, the city's prostitutes and transvestites were swept away from their beachfront haunts, the ornate fountains fenced off to keep the beggars from doing their laundry and the ubiquitous gangs of street kids who camp out on subway grates – three of whom are killed each day in Brazil by merchant-backed murder squads – shipped off to God-knows-where. Meanwhile $123 million in Brazilian government funds that could have been used, say, for children's welfare, was spent building a new superhighway direct from the airport to the UN Conference center. Other millions went to painting, planting trees and widening sidewalks.

But for all the prepping, preening and posing, whether it be by the Brazilian trash collectors or by the Bush-Quayle spin team, the snapshot that emerges from Rio is of a world doomed to remain grotesquely frozen in two: where American kids spend their nights in the bluish glow of eco-correct Nintendo games while two-thirds of the Third World still burns wood for all its energy. Where private clinics in the Anglo world treat the scarf-and-barf 'victims' of bulemia while in India the quest for 900 calories a day is usually futile. And, finally, of a UN Earth Summit so dominated by the privileged that the vacuous blasts of hot air updrafting from the conference are bound to raise global warming more than its flaccid treaties will reduce it.

George Bush's sandbagging of any effective treaty to reduce global CO_2 buildup and his open sabotaging of a biodiversity agreement already approved by ninety-eight other countries has understandably drawn the obsessive glare of the American media. But it has simultaneously served to obscure the core truth that the official US attitude, deplorable though it is, is nothing but the extreme expression of the Earth Summit's *overall* message: This World Is For Sale. Yammer all you want about the global village, or the global this or the global that. But the only real topic on the UNCED agenda is the *global market*.

Twenty years after the first UN meeting on the environment, held in Stockholm, this Rio Summit marks the triumph and celebration of the strain of soft, conciliatory, corporate environmentalism known as the Third Wave. A wave now poised as a veritable tsunami threatening to wash away any recognition by the rich countries that the greatest threat to the environment comes not from the densely populated Southern poor but from the rapacious overconsumption of the North.

When George Bush addresses this world body this week, he may indeed draw a few catcalls and hisses on the specifics. But his central thesis, that unfettered free trade is the only hope for a prosperous, healthy world and that there must be no environmental barriers to that world trade, will be enthusiastically applauded by the lighter skinned delegates who control the funding levers of UNCED and the World Bank. The UNCED General Secretary Maurice Strong has already endorsed that idea.

The relentless pressure exerted primarily by the US during the two year series of pre-Summit negotiating sessions insured that the UNCED action plan to be approved here this week, and known as Agenda 21, will clearly 'reflect an unbalanced approach biased in favor of liberalized trade at the cost of environmental protection,' according to a scrupulously detailed study by six major US

environmental groups. According to that same report, the US and Canada succeeded in deleting from the Agenda 21 draft some nineteen paragraphs on consumption and lifestyle, especially those that proposed a UN monitoring system
for those trends.

The totality of Agenda 21 is also silent on any need by governments and the
UN itself to monitor or control transnational corporations (TNCs). Indeed, the
corporate business sector is treated throughout Agenda 21 as individual entities
with 'rights' to be protected, as self-regulating engines of worldwide 'sustainable
development'.

'If you have globalization of TNCs, you need globalization of their regulation. But Agenda 21 ignores this issue', says Barbara Bramble, Director of International Programs for the National Wildlife Federation, one of the most
conservative American environmental groups monitoring the Summit. 'Better
to call the UN program Agenda 20, because it addresses the needs of the last
century, not the coming one', Bramble continues. 'It refuses to tackle the hard
questions – debt and trade. No way the Third World is going to get sustainable
development with trade left as it is.'

The Summit's Agenda 21, previously hyped as a possible Universal Earth
Charter, now reads like a wish list for military-industrial lobbyists. The global
climate treaty maintains fossil fuel dependency and eliminates any call for compulsory target reductions in CO_2 levels. The Agenda makes no reference to the
need to regulate the burgeoning biotech industry. It has abandoned the original
UN resolution seeking an emergency plan to save the earth's forests while it
simultaneously ignores the land and cultural rights of indigenous peoples. Also
overlooked is the issue of military-related nuclear contamination. Nor is there a
call for a permanent ban on the dumping at sea of radioactive waste.

Agenda 21 also fails to recognize that there are no safe storage or disposal
solutions for nuclear waste. Likewise, the UN Agenda refuses to call for a ban on
the international shipment and dumping of toxic materials, thereby relieving the
wealthier countries of having to solve their own waste problems. Perhaps most
revealing is, just as the Cold War collapses, the staggering UNCED silence on
disarmament. War damages the environment, says Agenda 21. Therefore, all
future conflagrations, it says, should strictly comply with 'international law' governing war.

'The UNCED is no longer a forum on the environment, on greenhouse gas
or on scientific data, but rather a conference on commerce', says Martin Khor, a
Malaysian economist for the Third World Network, among the most respected
of southern hemisphere environmental groups. 'You see some rivalry among
the northern countries each looking for trade advantages. Bush, for example,
watered down the CO_2 treaty precisely because he knew the Japanese and the

Europeans would more efficiently and quickly reach any mandatory targets. But mostly the Earth Summit is where the North unites to defend itself against the South, to hold on to intellectual property rights, to restrict transfer of technology, to tell us it's OK if the US cuts down its forests but that we shouldn't. Truth is, no Third World country can really engage in sustainable development under these trade conditions without being overthrown. If I, as a Third World leader, say OK, I want to stop cutting my forests, I want to reduce my rubber exports and instead I want to grow food for my own people, well I'll be accused by the North of sabotaging the world economic system, of creating a price hike in timber and rubber, of restricting economic freedom. How long before your country starts financing guerrillas against me?'

The probusiness tilt of the Earth Summit is no accident. The direct level of influence by private enterprise upon the UN has reached a pinnacle during the process leading to and culminating in the Earth Summit. Earlier this year, UN General Secretary Boutros Boutros-Ghali, following recommendations made by the right-wing Heritage Foundation, closed down the UN Centre on Transnational Corporations – frequently a critical voice on business affairs.

In the meantime, two years ago, Earth Summit leader Maurice Strong appointed Swiss billionaire Stephen Schmidheiny as his 'principal advisor for business and industry'. A member of the board of ABB, a manufacturer of nuclear reactors, Schmidheiny pulled together forty-eight other like-minded executives into the so-called Business Council for Sustainable Development (BCSD). Employing the services of PR powerhouse Burson-Marsteller, the BCSD presents itself as enlightened entrepreneurs now ready to lead us into a green revolution even though its members list includes heads of some of the dirtiest corporations in the world. (Burson-Marsteller, according to the Greenpeace 'Greenwash' study, has a long history of repackaging environmental criminals as earth-friendly. After the Valdez and Bhopal disasters, Exxon and Union Carbide were image-doctored by BM. The same agency also helped bail out Babcock-Wilcox after the Three Mile Island meltdown, as well as aiding A.H. Robins after its Dalkon Shield IUD was found to be dangerous. Currently, Burson-Marsteller is also acting as PR consultant to UNCED. Pro bono.)

Among the BCSD's mainstays are DuPont, which still denies that its lead gasoline additive is harmful and which also holds the title as the world's largest producer of ozone-eating CFCs; Royal Dutch Shell, the world's largest oil company; the Mitsubishi Corporation, whose interests range from chemicals to nuclear technology to timber; and the Dow Corporation, which first made its concern for ecology and humanity publicly known when it provided napalm for the Vietnam War. Without any risk of overstatement, apart from the handful of powerful government delegations, the BCSD has become one of the most influential players at the Earth Summit, methodically shaping the drafting of Agenda 21, guaranteeing maximum support of free trade and minimum regulation, retaining US-style patent rights for tight private control of technology and information and, in passing, consistently winning the warm public praise of UNCED General Secretary Maurice Strong. Strong also solicited and received corporate donations to UNCED's Ecofund '92 – to finance conference support activities. Coca Cola, Xerox, Minnesota Mining and Manufacturing and oil mammoth ARCO all ponied up a minimum of $100,000 each and, in return, now have the right to use the official Earth Summit logo for their own advertising and marketing purposes. 'This is a repeat of Earth Day', says Greenpeace official Ken Bruno. 'Millions of people get mobilized, but nothing happens. The whole show gets watered down and controlled by the corporate backers.'

With as many as 30,000 environmentalists converging in Rio, you'd imagine a chorus of strong, articulate voices of protest yelling out against the failed promise of UNCED and offering a counterprogram. With 5,000 journalists in town on the prowl for a good story, it's an historic, not-to-be-missed opportunity. And those voices of principled dissent exist. But they are barely perceptible inside the cacophonous zoo known as the Global Forum – the parallel unofficial environmental conference taking place in and around Rio's beachside Flamengo Park.

Representatives of dozens of serious environmental groups were privately complaining, after the first week of the conference, that they had been led into a political trap by Forum organizer Warren 'Chip' Lindner. They began to suspect that they had been deliberately lured into a venue designed to dilute their message. Lindner, a close associate of UNCED General Secretary Strong, had used the same sort of corporate and governmental financing to put together his $11 million budget as the Earth Summit did. And in the name of ecumenical nonpartisanship, Lindner concocted a ragtag circus that seemed to play to every media stereotype of fuzzyheaded environmentalism. In tents and stands that sprawled for acres through the park, committed environmental crusaders and activists struggling to come up with a unified response to UNCED were forced to swim among and compete with hundreds of bizarre and embarrassing exhibits not only from the Bagwan Sri Rajneesh (and dozens of other New Age cults), but also from the Summer Institute of Linguistics (whose main activity is translating and distributing bibles to Latin American indigenous tribes), purveyors of solar-powered barbecues, as well as a pavilion from the Kuwaiti Ministry of Information (which blamed world pollution not on an oil-based economy but rather on Saddam Hussein), and finally from the Brazilian State Oil Company, Petrobras, which donated $400,000 to the Global Forum (but whose dumping of toxics into Rio's bay made it impossible to swim in the ocean adjacent to the

Forum). As soon as this 'alternative' Forum opened, it was teetering on the edge of financial collapse. The influential daily *Estado do São Paulo* ran a report that Brazil's federal police were turning over to local authorities a dossier alleging that Lindner had diverted $1.7 million in Forum funding to his own environmental group – a charge Lindner denied. Caught in the middle are the sincere environmentalists who have seen their work overshadowed by brash media events starring the Beach Boys and Shirley Maclaine pitching for funds to rescue the Global Forum bureaucracy. No better metaphor for the sorry plight of the dissident environmentalists comes to mind than the visit to the Global Forum by one of America's preeminent ecologists – and a fierce critic of UNCED – David Brower. No matter that Brower led the Sierra Club for seventeen years, that he founded Friends of the Earth as well as the League of Conservation Voters, that he was twice nominated for the Nobel Prize. When his scheduled press conference at the Global Forum came around, he was surprised with a request for a $200 use charge to help keep the Forum afloat. Brower went ahead with his appearance, though there were fewer than a half-dozen, mostly alternative, press representatives there to listen.

At the same moment, across town, however, Global Forum hype of something called the Earth Parliament brought dozens of TV crews and hundreds of reporters out to hear John Denver in a Hawaiian shirt sing 'One World' and to record the inaugural words of cattle rancher and self-styled environmentalist US Senator Al Gore. Sitting there listening to Gore's nostrums on free trade – only a shade of nuance different from those pedaled by Bush – with the surgically altered face of John Denver looking on and the media glued to every word, you had to wonder what in the world any of this had to do with staving off environmental destruction.

'This is disgusting and shameful', Brazilian opposition congressman Ricardo Moraes stammered as he left the Al Gore speech. 'We come here in good faith supposedly to find a global partnership. Instead, Mr Gore talks to us like we were his voters back at home. All he can talk about is how economic freedom has finally triumphed over communism. What does that mean to us? What about capitalism? Here in Brazil, from where did we get our prostitution? Our corruption? Our poverty? Our pollution and toxic dumps? Certainly not from communism!'

Far from the platitudes of Al Gore, remote from the stultifying discourse of the UNCED, a world away from the ecogadget exhibits at the Global Forum, up on a series of rolling hilltops in southern Rio live the 300,000 people of what calls itself the biggest slum in the world – the Roçinha *favela*. It is here, deep inside this sort of tropical casbah of narrow paths and jumbled barebrick houses, where some of the more militant environmental organizations have retreated in a desperate attempt to extricate themselves from the sinking ship of the Global Forum. Greenpeace, Friends of the Earth, a coalition of Brazilian environmental organizations, the Third World Network, and groups representing *favela* dwellers as well as 'marginal populations' throughout Latin America have called some reporters together inside the steamy auditorium of the community's most cherished institution, the Samba dance 'academy'. Presenting an 'ultimatum' to UNCED, they demand a meeting with General Secretary Maurice Strong to discuss a ten-point environmental program that would radically shift the course of the Earth Summit. If the meeting is not granted in forty-eight hours – and no one expects it will be – then, warns Greenpeace, 'We intend to raise the stakes considerably. With President Bush holding the world hostage, nothing less than the future of the earth is at risk.'

No one knows what to make of the warning. Most likely it's bluster, just overheated rhetoric born from so much disappointment. But the sense of frustration with the Earth Summit is building. On last Sunday morning, a crowd of 300 Americans politely protested Bush policy on the Rio beachfront. In the afternoon, another group of about 250 young people rallied in the Global Forum, tore down and dismantled the booth of the World Bank and chased its representatives out of the park. Now there's talk of hunger strikes, of protest marches, of disruption inside the UNCED. This is hardly 'raising the stakes'. But looking down from the top of the Roçinha slum it's evident that the concepts of North and South not only separate one country from another, but also coexist inside each individual society.

The sparkling sands of the Rio beaches, the luxury beachfront highrises, the golf courses and the polo clubs of posh São Conrado are no farther from Rochina than Beverly Hills from Watts. With the collective attention of world governments still mesmerized by the serious promise of unending industrial development without serious regard for the environmental and human costs, it seems likely that for the trance to be broken there will first have to be two, three, many South Central uprisings.

ONE WEEK LATER ...

You knew the US was going to take a serious PR hit as the Earth Summit moved into its final days when you saw TV crews fighting one another to get a good shot of the American delegate that was levelled out on the floor by UN cops just because he had disagreed with George Bush. Here it was just hours before Bush's arrival (after he had already given the press some free yucks by getting tear-gassed in Panama) and here was poor Mike Dorcey, spread-eagled on his back on the patio just outside the doors of the Summit plenary; four beefy UN cops had a death grip on each of his limbs while three of Dorcey's comrades splayed themselves over his torso to keep the uniformed bulls from carting him away. At least fifty reporters, maybe a dozen TV cameras, peered on over the shoulders of a ring of nervous, pushy cops surrounding the melee. With the tape rolling, the prone Mike Dorcey kept shouting, 'I'm an American delegate. I'm an American delegate. Let me up! Let me up!'

Though the fracas lasted maybe half an hour and hundreds of shocked onlookers stood by, no other American delegate came to Dorcey's rescue. After all, the 21-year-old University of Michigan student was not only black, he was also the token environmentalist allowed on the delegation by the Bush administration's State Department. And now he had eschewed a certain reserved place in any future Republican White House and had emerged as a rather embarrassing whistle-blower. He and some ten other young people had been dragged away by police, and about twenty other of their supporters from Australia, Argentina, Brazil and Chile had been tossed from the UN grounds after they staged an 'unauthorized' open-air protest press conference during which Dorcey had called on the US to 'break the bond that it has woven with corporate transnationals and begin to seriously act on behalf of the people of our country.'

The protest erupted after the official representative of their Youth International Forum, Kenyan-born Wagaki Mwansi, was given her seven minutes to address the UN Summit plenary only to find her blistering speech suspiciously and inexplicably switched off the closed-circuit TV system that services the press. All in all, a marvelous metaphor for what has gone on here the last two weeks: in the name of the environment, the older, fatter, whiter Northern world has informed the much younger and poorer South that, earth crisis or not, it will still be Business As Usual. As the suited-up UN delegates inside the fluorescent purgatory of the RioCentro conference center nodded off, doodled, or shuffled their mountainous stacks of papers, as Ms Mwansi told them, and the handful of us from the press actually inside the plenary, that the Earth Summit had been a 'success for the all-time wielders of power. Transnational corporations, the United States, Japan, the World Bank and the IMF. Amidst elaborate cocktails, travelling and partying, few negotiators realized how critical their decisions are to our generation. By failing to address fundamental issues such as militarism . . . and regulation of transnational corporations, my generation has been damned.'

That speech may have gone over about as well as a pregnant spotted owl in an Oregon logging camp. But in just a few sentences it had, nonetheless, slashed through the twelve days of overgrown *rio-toric* that had basically endorsed the gutting of a global warming treaty, winked at the problems of hazardous waste, consigned remaining world forests as 'sinks' for First World carbon dumping, ignored economic reform, exonerated multinationals from environmental blame and scrutiny, remained silent on nuclear testing and disarmament, failed to provide significant funding for even the half-hearted remedies it proposed, and not only condoned conspicuous consumption by the North but went so far as to promote it as a recipe for global environmental salvation.

By the time George Bush stood before the world and proclaimed that 'growth is the engine of change and the friend of the environment', his words came as nothing more than a double-shot chaser to a global Polluters Anonymous-meeting-turned-prodevelopment-chug-a-lug.

Not that America's other oil-drunk allies didn't try till the last moment to bail Bush out and save some face for the world body. But try as the Japanese and the Europeans might to offer Bush some sort, *any* sort, of even purely cosmetic compromise, our Beloved Architect of Victory Over Panama and Iraq stood firm. With the rest of the G-7 countries left to twiddle their thumbs and whistle nervously, Bush knocked around and rumbled in the cellar of environmental degradation like the UN's mad Uncle Sam. Fresh from cutting US wetlands in half, sabotaging the Clean Air Act, preparing 4 million acres of Pacific Northwest forest for clear-cutting, he was now about to climb the stairs and appear before all the polite company assembled here in the world's living room.

So unseemly, so berserk a sight Bush turned out to be, that it was left to Fidel Castro to reap the greatest ovation of all from the majority of powerless Third World delegates for his four-minute simple plea to 'End this egotism, end this talk of hegemony, end this insensibility.'

Not a good sign, especially in an election year, for a sitting Republican president to get upstaged by the poster boy of the Communist Leaders Endangered Species Fund. But regardless of what political damage Bush may suffer domestically, or internationally, it should not obscure the fact that the world environmental movement took a first-class thumping at the Earth Summit.

And yet many of the largest, richest, primarily US- and European-based environmental groups seemed to be so bedazzled by their access to power that they were blinded to their demonstrated and absolute failure to influence, persuade, sway or even inform the objects of their incessant insider lobbying. The public declarations from World Wildlife Fund, or the Audobon Society, or the Sierra Club, or the Natural Resources Defense Council or the National Wildlife Federation before and after Bush's speech rarely went beyond a limp 'we're shocked, simply shocked' critique of US policy. Dry, dreary bromides expressing 'disappointment . . . sadness . . . sorrow' over the intransigent American position. All reminiscent of the days of Vietnam when, after one more wave of murderous B-52 bombing and napalm attacks, right-thinking, liberal Americans would lament what a 'tragedy' all this was – not for the incinerated Vietnamese, mind you, but for American credibility and honor.

Forget that Bush could stand up and piss on the world. All it took was a one-hour private meeting between the US President and representatives of 'leading' environmental groups so that, for example, Don Edwards of Panos International could emerge from the Rio Sheraton proclaiming that 'the president welcomed the opportunity to hear some diverse views. It was important that we did not come there and attack him. That allowed him to take notes and to be an open listener.' Pul-eeze, pass me my crystal. One official of the Environmental Defense Fund exited the huddle with Bush sounding like she had just taken up a post with the World Bank, saying that the key to getting through to governments is by working with private enterprise. 'Businesses are the people who pay people', said EDF board member Teresa Heinz. 'If we have communication and can influence business leaders, that immediately and quickly impacts in the White House.'

Where these environmental megagroups *didn't* have much impact was in taking the historic opportunity of the UN Earth Summit to organize a clearly alternative grass-roots counterconference here in Rio. In part because the North/South divide that cleaves the UN runs right through the heart of the world environmental movement. Many of the Northern environmentalists are just now getting the message that, once removed from their middle-class enclaves, ecological issues are not simply moral imperatives but rather are inextricably linked to economic and political realities. 'We don't want to be lectured as to what we should do unless it is done in a cooperative and democratic manner', Indian delegate Mani Shankar complained. 'I am not about to go to my people and tell them they must face *more* deprivation because some lady in Maine is fretting over the cutting of a tree or because some chap in San Francisco wants to drive his Volvo in better conscience. We can sit down and talk when we realize that one job in Cincinnati is not one bit more important than one job in New Dehli.'

Last week when a protest march against Bush was called, about 300 Americans and Europeans marched under ecological banners, courteously chanting 'George Bush, Eco-Wimp!' and 'We Want Leadership!' By contrast, 50,000 Brazilians marched in front of them, brought out by the national trade union federation, all loudly calling for the biological termination of both Bush and 'hangman' Brazilian President Fernando Collor. 'Those are Americans for you', one Brazilian unionist laughed. 'Crying for their Daddy Bush to please change his mind instead of them either forcing him to change it or just getting rid of him.' Brazil's largest daily, *Jornal Do Brasil*, drolly wrote of the twin marches: 'The Americans and Europeans marched to defend animals, forests and the ecology. The Brazilian march joined in protesting hunger, poverty and oppression.'

The inability of the more established environmental groups – only jokingly referred to as the 'environmental multinationals' by their Third World brethren – to clearly differentiate themselves from the failed UN conference was built right into the process leading up to the Summit. Allowed an advisory role for the first time in the two year's worth of Summit preparatory meetings, few if any of the environmental 'nongovernmental organizations' (NGOs) were willing to take their dissent to the point of rupture. And with increasingly stiff competition between environmentalist bureaucracies for the finite funding pool, individual groups were wary of going too far out on an extremist limb and thereby cutting themselves off from whatever shadow of legitimacy that association with the UN process conferred on them.

But according to a number of environmental activists involved in the lead-up meetings before the Summit, there was at least one moment in particular when it was obvious that the UN conference had irrevocably taken the road to betrayal. And, these activists say, if the various environmental groups involved in the process had at that moment made a clean break with the Summit, then the entire world environmental movement would have come to Rio much better positioned to offer a clear alternative to the UN meet. Instead, they caved in.

Last February, 139 countries voted for mandatory stabilization of greenhouse gases at 1990 levels by the year 2000, laying the groundwork for what promised to be the showcase treaty of the Earth Summit. Only the US delegation was opposing the treaty, but it was completely isolated.

'But by May something drastic had changed', says Australian-born Thomas Harding, a leader of the militant International Youth Forum. 'All of a sudden the Europeans began to waffle. Kohl made a deal with Bush. Boom. The Americans had gotten their way. All of a sudden the targets and compulsory nature of the agreement were history. It was now only empty words.'

Harding was among the environmentalists of the Climate Change Action Network (CAN) that clustered for the first week of May 1992 trying to respond to the scuttling of the global warming treaty. In one conference room, downstairs at the UN headquarters in New York, the cream of environmental movement – WWF, EDF, Sierra Club, Friends of the Earth, NWF, NRDC struggled for a unified response. 'That meeting was chaired by EDF', recounts Harding. 'One question dominated: Do we criticize the treaty, blame Bush and commit to working with the treaty to improve it? Or do we make a break and encourage governments not to sign a global warming convention that had become toilet paper? Some of us felt that we should do the latter. That if you give in, the NGOs lose their attractive role as alternatives, and you leave a monolith of consensus.'

'But that view was never able to even be fully voiced. Greenpeace of all people, who had always had the most critical, radical position, took the leadership in the meeting and accepted the compromise – to work *with* the treaty process. They were obviously very uncomfortable with their decision but they went ahead. I was sickened, really. I'm sorry now I and others weren't forceful in speaking out. What we should have done was hold a press conference saying scientists want governments to enact a sixty percent cut in carbon dioxide, and that governments must not sign any treaty that relieves them of that responsibility.'

'The problem is when activist organizations try to also become lobbyists', says Harding. 'Lobby enough and you will wind up being co-opted. Soon you are jet-set, eco-yuppies. Out of touch with the real issues and constantly scrambling for grants and funding.'

Tent 19 at the Global Forum, the sprawling unofficial environmental conclave held in one of Rio's beachfront parks, pulses and buzzes a good eighteen hours a day. On one wall, below a color TV screen, looms a huge 'Treaty Monitoring Chart' tracking the development of nearly three dozen complex agreements. Next to it is an enormous 9-foot-by-9-foot computer printout with more than 2,000 names on it – the names of those private citizens from every continent who have taken the last ten days to negotiate, write and agree upon the treaties. This tent is the command and control headquarters for the most significant positive development to come out of the Earth Summit, namely, alternative, organization-to-organization treaties to fill in the ethical, moral and environmental holes left gaping by the official UN meeting.

This so-called International NGO Forum is proof positive that many northern and southern environmentalists have been brought ever closer by the lugubrious two year build-up to and the intensive and disillusioning two-week staging of the Summit.

'There's been a gravitational pull on all the northern groups moving them toward real political concern for the needs of the poor', says Maximo Kalaw, co-coordinator of the NGO Forum and a leading Filipino environmentalist. 'A year or two ago these same groups answered with a blank stare when you asked them their position on economic issues. They are now coming to the realization their work is not just management of conservation projects, but rather facilitation of real political action.'

American environmentalists agree that their work will never be the same after Rio. 'My organization has been incredibly affected', says Barbara Bramble, International Programs Director of the National Wildlife Federation. 'For the first time I am now able to bring a full international agenda to our membership and let them see how US policy affects so many other countries. Often very negatively. I mean, we are getting these *outraged* responses from real red-blooded

Americans – and that's immensely more important than what comes out of the Earth Summit.'

Twenty-two years ago, on the occasion of the first Earth Day, iconoclastic journalist I. F. Stone deemed the affair a 'gigantic snow job'. Arguing that social protest should be concentrated on Nixon's widening of the Indochinese War, Stone looked out over the gentle gathering of environmentalists in April 1970 and wrote: 'Just as the Caesars once used bread and circuses so ours were at least learning to use rock-and-roll, idealism and non-inflammatory social issues to turn the youth off from more urgent concerns which might really threaten our power structure.'

Today that observation haunts the environmental movement. Such events as Earth Day, and its global big brother, the Earth Summit, have come full circle and now threaten to distract us from authentic ecological engagement. When every one of our environmental ills is now classified as 'global', the laying of responsibility – blame, if you will – and therefore real solutions becomes ever more remote. Certain DuPont factories may produce our ozone-eating CFCs. In a sane world we would just close down those specific plants. Instead, we convert ozone into a 'global' ill and DuPont is let off the hook as we begin to wring our hands over the future use of air conditioners and refrigerators in the Third World. The problem is no loner DuPont's. It's ours. Or as one major Brazilian newspaper headline acerbicly put it on the morrow of Bush's speech, 'Everyone Is an Environmentalist'. And if that's the case, then no one is a polluter.

The United Nations Earth Summit, far from challenging the unequal parameters of the New World Order, became part of it. 'The war against Iraq was a wake-up call as to who controls the UN, as to who controls the world', says Malaysian economist Martin Khor. 'That was a war for resources, for oil. In the future there will be similar wars. Clearly, the powerful countries of the North will be willing to simply take what they need, by force. Anything positive that might come out of the Earth Summit will be nullified by the reality of the world economic order. Southern countries now have to unite, Northern countries have to change. But elites never give up anything voluntarily. Northern activists will have to bring pressure to bear on their own governments and start solving these problems where they originate.'

That's a tall order for an American environmental movement that often can't do more than whine that Bush is an 'eco-wimp'. And for them the road forward from Rio is mined. The Bush administration, and certainly whatever political creature that emerges from the swamp of the November presidential election, will be plugging their ears and chanting the mantra of 'Jobs, jobs, jobs!' when environmental concerns are raised with any stridency. Simultaneously, the polluters and their representatives in government will be undercutting environmentalist warnings with their cynically crafted arguments of 'scientific uncertainty'. Ultimately, as others have written, public relations and not physics is the paradigm science of the modern age.

But most importantly, environmentalists in the post-Rio phase will have their own doubts and weaknesses to overcome. It's a dilemma that still bedevils eighty-year-old David Brower, the Sierra Club's first executive director and founder of both the League of Conservation Voters and Friends of the Earth. To this day he regrets a deal he made with the feds some thirty years ago. To save part of the Grand Canyon from development, Glen Canyon was offered up for a dam. Brower remembers taking a boat ride through Glen Canyon after the deal was struck and was heartbroken by the striking natural beauty that he had negotiated away.

'Every time I compromised I lost. When I held firm I won', Brower says as a light, twilight breeze blows across the terrace of the Hotel Gloria. 'The problem with too many environmentalists today is that they are trying to write the compromise instead of letting those we pay to compromise do it. They think they get power by taking people to lunch or being taken to lunch, when in reality they are just being taken.'

Two beers later it's completely dark outside. 'You've got to be bold', Brower says. 'Of thirty-eight Sierra Club presidents, thirty have been mountaineers. Seven have peaks named after them. You don't do that by sitting around. You have to go out and take risks. You have to get your balls back! You don't make a deal with the mountain. You climb it!'

Someone was paying attention. The day after George Bush's speech, under cover of darkness and defying an iron-grip military occupation of Rio de Janeiro, seven Greenpeace climbers scaled the city's landmark Sugar Loaf Mountain. Rapelling down its sheer face at the break of dawn, the eco-commandos unveiled a 14,000-square-foot banner. For the entire day, while flustered authorities scrambled for a solution, a giant picture of the earth hung before the city of 10 million. Underneath the globe a stark, one word message: 'SOLD'.

Village Voice
16/23 June 1992

16

CAUGHT IN THE HEADLIGHTS

HOUSTON: AUGUST 1992. The 4,000 people attending the Christian Coalition's God and Country Rally began their rapturous chanting a full half-hour before Dan Quayle's appearance. Taking their cue from the mammoth banner stretched from the ceiling of the cavernous Sheraton Astrodome ballroom, they sounded their refrain: 'One Nation Under God! One Nation Under God!' Then the crowd, many dressed in 'Back to Basic' T-shirts and faux Panama hats emblazoned with 'Pro-Family-Pro-Life', turned to the dozens of reporters jammed into the press bleachers and, jabbing their forefingers at us corralled newspeople, shouted in unison the same slogan popularized by El Salvador's death-squad ARENA Party: 'Tell the Truth! Tell the Truth!'

To tell the truth, this rally was the hottest ticket in town during the GOP convention week. It was also the official kickoff of the home stretch campaign, beginning with the 'rehabilitation' and 're-introduction' of Dan Quayle. The vice-president was the center of attention, of course, not only because George Bush's campaign has been hemorrhaging oil, but because long ago Quayle accepted nomination as the regime's special envoy to and interlocutor with the GOP's frothy and fanatical fundamentalist fringe. For what transpired in that Sheraton hall was a sweaty, exercised replay of pure Reaganite nostalgia, with a good deal more emphasis on Gawd than even the old Gipper himself would have been comfortable with.

Swooning, swaying, ecstatically raising their arms – palms upward – to the beat of a charismatic, supercharged version of *The Star-Spangled Banner*, this hard-core Republican Guard burst into spontaneous hymn, collectively reciting scripture by heart as 'family man' Pat Boone preached: 'We are not here to re-elect George Bush. Not yet. But here to re-elect the Living GOD as our guide and source of life!'

And no doubt a happy God, because as master of ceremonies Ralph Reed pointed out to the revelers, 'We are here to celebrate a victory for Family and America. Less than one hour ago, the Republican Party adopted *our* platform! The feminists threw everything at us. But we won and they lost!' (Another thunderous cheer.) 'And to those feminists', Reed continued, 'to the liberal media and to the radical left, we say that reports of the demise of the Christian Right have been greatly exaggerated!' Then, amid the roar, came a disembodied voice over the loudspeakers: 'Ladies and gentlemen, the Vice President of the United States!'

The walls and ground vibrated with the ovation as Dan Quayle – like a reborn Matthew Harrison Brady – took center stage, flanked by Marilyn, the kids, and the Reverend and Mrs Pat Robertson. Alas, the second coming of Dan Quayle! All set to win in '92 and then ascend even higher in '96. Let the pundits be, excuse the expression, damned. Just when millions of Americans are suspected of wanting substantial change in the body politic, Quayle has nailed himself to the cross of the Republican Party's most narrow-based Christian militants.

Vowing to slay the dragons of the 'liberal media' and the 'liberal Democrats' and relishing his 'new career as TV sitcom critic', in the wake of his attack on Murphy Brown, Quayle tightly gripped the podium and talked right through and over a bubbling of ACT-UP hecklers. 'I don't care what the media say! I don't care what my critics say! I will *never* back down!'

'The question in the campaign', Quayle told his followers, 'is which man do you trust?

Their thundering reply of 'You! You! You!' blindsided Quayle. Quayle had meant the crowd to choose between Bush and Clinton. Not between him and his boss. Visibly uncomfortable, Quayle doggedly went on. 'That man is George Bush!' And the ensuing response from the crowd was what is politely called 'polite applause'.

The crowd's lukewarm reception of the mention of George Bush's name is yet one more unmistakable sign of the growing strains in the Reagan-era coalition that had locked up the White House and dominated American politics for more than a decade. The New Right coalition, which fired the Reagan Revolution, grew out of conservative opposition to Jimmy Carter's Panama Canal Treaty. It came to consist of old-line Barry Goldwater conservatives – many of them big business, defense-oriented Republicans – along with many of the rank-and-file 'populists' who once backed George Wallace. Some of them were Christian fundamentalists.

But the coalition also included neoconservatives, some of whom were former Democratic Cold War socialists, and supply-sider, anti-tax, libertarian-

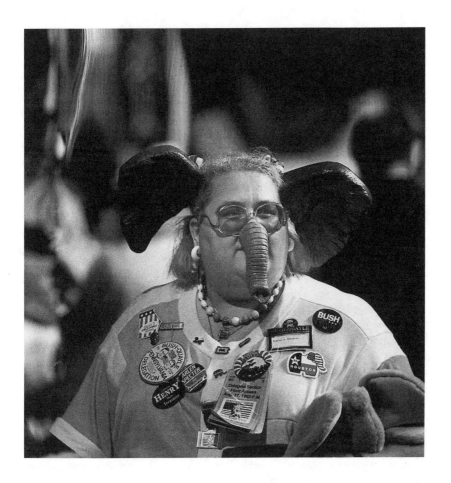

A FOOT SOLDIER IN AMERICA'S CULTURE WARS

minded Republicans of the Jack Kemp school. Moderates had little role in the New Right coalition, and its constituency has always eyed George Bush with suspicion, even hostility.

Anti-Communism held these fractious parts of the coalition together. Now, however, they have all gone to war. The Christian Right argues that family values – or cultural conservatism – is the future of the nation, that politics must reflect God's own plan on earth. The supply-side, libertarian-minded Republicans, on the other hand, insist the future lies in economics, in no new taxes – indeed, *deeper* cuts in taxes – to stimulate the economy.

But these groups dislike George Bush, the yachting patrician with his East Coast, *Fortune* 500, elitist background. And for his part, Bush seems to not know what *they* are about. This 1992 convention, with the president already dragging in the polls, mortally threatens George Bush. After having Ronald Reagan let the New Right into the establishment through the porch door in 1980, they seem – twelve years later – to have taken over the GOP living room.

Indeed, as last week's GOP convention came roaring into its final moments, as the toilet-paper confetti poured down on the First Family and a galaxy of patriotic balloons fell from the Astro-Sky, the reporter sitting next to me in the press gallery – startled by the barrage of flashing explosions above our heads and the odor of gunpowder in our nostrils – turned to me and said, 'Talk about a dramatic finale. They're ending with a bombardment of the hated media elite.'

After four nights of vitriol gushing from the Astrodome's funereal podium, after being cajoled by the Quaylie fundamentalists to 'Tell the Truth!', after some journalists were hounded and surrounded by 'Bush Brigades' of thick-necked fraternity punks, it wasn't much of a jump to confuse the bursts of 'indoor fireworks' immediately behind us as perhaps the first Buchannonade in the 'religious war . . . cultural war . . . for the soul of America.'

'Be belligerent!' was a favorite slogan of the Sandinistas who, as the Reaganites used to point out, at least had to shoot their way into power (and then held on to it while tucked into some pretty sharp uniforms). But the throbbing bellicosity that thundered forth from the convention platform came off as just a bit incongruous with a delegate pool so deep in knobby-kneed, slump-shouldered, potbellied guys in Bermuda shorts, beltless pants and big foam-rubber cowboy hats adorned with rubber elephant trunks that swung down to nip at their plastic shirt-pocket protectors.

Nevertheless, any time a Republican so much as nodded in the direction of civility, moderation or consensus, some fire-breathing werewolf was uncaged and ran amok, frightening and terrifying all in his path. The disabled vets were pushed aside by Church Lady Marilyn Quayle; Mary Fisher, who brought AIDS openly into the GOP debate, was drowned out by the Reverend Pat Robertson railing against the Democrat and homosexual 'plague'; libertarian Jack Kemp's tangled but sincere call for the empowerment of the poor was offset by the social Darwinism of a bullying Bill Bennett – and even old Babs's stage-managed embrace of all American families was paired with Dan Quayle's promise of a crackdown on 'lifestyle alternatives'. The ultimate icon of uncontested Republican enlightenment and inclusion, Betty Ford, wearing her AIDS ribbon, had to sit next to the porcine Rush Limbaugh, who has contributed the word 'feminazi' to our lexicon. And the nerve-bomb rant of Pat Buchanan – now nothing more than a lightly perfumed David Duke – made yesteryear's symbol of extremism, Ronald Reagan, seem moderate by comparison. If Barry Goldwater had materialized on the stage, he'd probably have been booed down as a special-interest advocate for the greedy elderly.

With few exceptions (notably Kemp), whether it was the smiling Major Dad or the malevolent Newt Gingrich, the message rang loud and clear: by elevating Barbara Bush as the earthly embodiment of iron-disciplined maternalism, satanizing the ambitious and dangerous Hillary Clinton, targeting welfare programs, gays and public schools, the Republicans planned to do battle and win in November under the banner of 'family values'.

Why the party had chosen such a divisive, polarizing strategy, and why it had been put forth in such a contradictory manner – now reassuring, now ominously aggressive – has given rise to much speculation. Some believe this convention was a 'mistake', that it was conceived when Ross Perot was still in the race and the Republicans needed only 34 percent of the vote to win. In that case, shore up the fanatic right and the rest of America be damned.

Others, like California-based GOP consultant Allan Hoffenblum, say what we saw this last week was 'a badly split Republican party, one with no one in charge'. With the Christian Right growing inside the party and obsessed with morality, and with the more staid 'supply-siders' focused almost obliviously on the economy, Hoffenblum says, 'The party opted to let both factions speak, because it really had no other choice. Who gets hurt is George Bush, who now seems captive of the fanatic right.' Captive, as in against his will.

But this analysis fails to tell the whole truth about the Republican Party: For all its railing at the Democrats for being a 'pre-Brezhnev' bureaucracy ideologically descended from North Korea and Cuba (as Phil Gramm claimed), it is the GOP that is mired in the Cold War. 'Moderate' Republicans can expect to fail in using their party to manage a post–Cold War world just as miserably as Gorbachev did in trying to use the faded Communist Party to run the Soviet Union. Indeed, who are Buchanan, Quayle, Robertson and, for that matter, George Bush, but America's own equivalent of still-talking statues of Lenin and Stalin? This generation of GOP leadership has been forged in and knows *only* the past half-century's politics of fear and division. With the Cold War now history (thanks to Gorbachev's self-immolation), the Republicans, prisoners of their own past, have only one card to play this election year: they will bring the Cold War home. Moderates and country-clubbers like Bush may be uncomfortable. But they know no other choice.

Cold War yes, but not in the strict McCarthyite sense, not by hunting down domestic Communists. The targets of Republican fear-mongering have never mattered as much as the political expediency of fear itself. The bonding agent in the glue of anticommunism that held the Republican coalition together was always found in the 'anti' component of the formula (the Bush-Baker entente with Deng Xiaoping's China proves that much). Few Republican planners and strategists really believed in the Domino Theory. But it sure was a handy rationale for building a national security state that for four decades always put the needs of the FBI and the Pentagon ahead of those of public hospitals and schools.

With anticommunism now a dead hand, and the Republican alliance – not to speak of the national consensus – straining at the seams, new enemies must be drummed up. Republicans, after all, are Republicans, and by definition have little to offer most of us in economic terms. All they can do is run a protection racket. With few bogeymen as convincing as the deceased Russian bear, the GOP now hopes to make up in quantity what it lacks in quality. You can only get so much mileage out of a Noriega or a Saddam, so the list swells: the media elite, the cultural elite, the Hollywood elite, pornography, drug kingpins, Murphy Brown, Woody Allen, Hillary Clinton and the whole 'radical liberal Democrat Party', gays, lesbians, welfare mothers, coddlers of criminals, criminals, urban dwellers and – in the best tradition of the Soviet generals – the very notion of change itself.

Yegor Ligachev, former leader of the resistance to Gorbachev's reforms, could have made no admonishment so alarmist as that delivered last week to the GOP faithful by Commissar Gerald Ford. 'Change', warned Ford, 'change isn't a magic word that makes everything rosy. Change may get you thirteen percent inflation. Change may get you a seventeen percent home mortgage interest rate. Change may bring risky actions abroad. . . . Change just for the sake of change may be a four-year disaster.'

What we are hearing from the Republicans, then, is not the 'low road' but the only road available, says independent political strategist Bill Zimmerman. 'The best they can do is run the most negative campaign ever. They can't stop voters from wanting change. All they can try is to scare people about the alternatives.'

Bush, in fact, recognized this in his convention speech, saying, 'There is a yearning in America. . . . Americans are uneasy today.' And much of that unease, that uncertainty which gnaws away at millions of Americans, is the very instability wrought by twelve years of Republican rule. The GOP leadership now intends to exploit and benefit from the very fear they themselves have conjured. Hence, the herding of the electorate back to the past, the appeal to the 'gentle rhythms' of country life the GIs longed for when they came home after the world war, the swaddling of rhetoric in the 'family values' of fifty years ago, grotesquely refracted through the lens of a collector's Coke bottle and half-baked in Barb's homemade chicken batter. For if some Americans yearn and pine for Beaver Cleaver's lost paradise free of blacks, gays and feminists, so many others remember the past as a time when one factory job could support a family, when a hospital stay meant something other than financial death, when government still made an effort to enrich your life. George Bush's goal is to reshape the dreams of these latter Americans into the midnight nightmare of the former.

That the Bush/Quayle strategy is anchored to a Cold War past is brought into relief by what it doesn't appeal to: 1992 is the first presidential election in history where the majority of likely voters live in suburbs and not cities – striking when you recognize that in 1950 only a quarter of the population lived in the suburbs, and only a third in 1960. A coast-to-coast sea of mostly white, home-owning voters, these suburbanites should provide clear sailing for the GOP campaign. It's an ocean that swells as the Democrat-dominated cities dry up: for example, in 1988 the Democratic vote in the city of Detroit came in at 85 percent – but the entire Detroit vote was barely 8 percent of the state total. The suburbs of Detroit went 60 percent Republican and totaled a full one-third of the Michigan tally. Michael Dukakis swept Detroit. Bush-Quayle took Michigan.

With these sorts of figures, even with the economic downturn, this election should be a demographic cakewalk for Bush. But the ossified thinking of the party leadership, so vividly demonstrated in this past week's convention, has led to a radical misreading of the suburban sector. What impassions the suburbanites is a distrust of government, a visceral hatred of taxes (if any one instrument symbolizes the suburban mentality it is California's 1978 Proposition 13, which lowered property tax to a feeble 1 percent of purchase price and today has led to a call for Los Angeles teachers to take a 17 percent pay cut).

But these millions of suburbanites who now populate the fastest-growing 'metro' areas of the United States tend to be relatively affluent, young, educated and socially engaged. Yes, they have fled the inner cities and have pulled up the drawbridges to downtown. But once ensconced behind their shrubs, fences and guarded and often walled enclaves, once they have formed their own new privatized tax base, they want to eat their granola and yogurt, maybe even recycle the trash, sleep with whomever they want, and generally think of themselves as mildly enlightened. They can afford to not be racists, they can even employ a Salvadoran maid or two and pay her above scale. They certainly have little truck with the scruffy likes of street-brawler Buchanan or the morality lessons of Marilyn Quayle. Taken as a whole, they might be a cautious, sometimes contradictory constituency – but they are definitely not the knee-jerk reactionary Silent Majority of twenty years ago, nor the Archie Bunker Reagan Democrats of a decade later.

Not to say that, with two months still to go, George Bush and the Republicans should be written off as losers. With the Democrats appealing primarily to 'the forgotten middle class', letting their blue-collar and minority urban base languish and thereby narrowing the overall electorate, they may be playing right into GOP hands. The Democrats' soundalike strategy flirts with a low voter turnout, concentrated equally among whiter, more affluent and therefore potentially more Republican voters. Electing Bill Clinton and Al Gore does nothing to effect the sort of political change necessary to begin the post–Cold War transition. But using the November election as a plebiscite to vote out the Republicans and their politics of fear is absolutely the first prerequisite for making the move.

Village Voice
25 August, 1 September 1992

17

ABNORMAL. WRONG. UNNATURAL. AND PERVERSE.

SWEET HOME, OREGON: SEPTEMBER 1992. The plume of acrid, musty smoke that crowds out the late afternoon sun reminds you of the anger that smolders here in central Oregon's 'timber country'. The 7,000 residents of Sweet Home long ago learned to ignore the pungent, nauseating fumes from the nearby wood processing mill. What turns their stomachs is that soon there may be no mills left – that soon enough the only lumberjacks left in town will be the two oddly smiling concrete statues on Main Street. So with just a month to go before a momentous national election, it's no surprise then that a spectacular turnout of some sixty people streams into the spacious Community Chapel for tonight's 7 p.m. town meeting.

The gathering has brought together young and old. A lot of timberworkers, some of them retired, some of them unemployed, some precariously hanging on. There are some homemakers. A few kids. The town doctor. And four local clergy. And though they have come tonight to discuss the 3 November election, they are not here to debate industrial policy, nor even to rail against the hated spotted owl or the despised Endangered Species Act. Tonight they won't speak of health-care relief, or family leave, or of extending their own unemployment benefits. Nor are they here to review the candidates for sheriff, Congress, the Senate or even the presidency.

Instead they are here to pledge their support for a ballot initiative that, for the first time in American history, would force a state constitution to *take rights away* from a group of people: in this case, from homosexuals.

Tonight's meeting in the boonies of Sweet Home is just a very small part of an impressively organized statewide effort to pass ballot Measure 9 supported by a five-year-old hard-right organization known as the Oregon Citizens Alliance (OCA). And for those who might have thought that Dan Quayle, Pat Robertson and Pat Buchanan were joking about their 'cultural war' – here it is in full battle dress. Measure 9 not only defines homosexuality as 'abnormal, wrong, unnatural and perverse', it also links it to sadomasochism and pedophilia. One hundred forty thousand Oregonians signed the petitions to put it on the ballot. And if passed, Measure 9 would ban the extension of civil rights protection to 'gays and lesbians' as a specific category and would require all government agencies and public schools to discourage homosexuality. Gay organizations and individuals could be denied use of public facilities such as parks and meeting rooms, state public broadcasting outlets would have to ban pro-gay programming, state licensing boards could refuse licenses to those deemed 'perverse', libraries would have to remove books with any positive references to homosexuality, school textbooks would be cleansed, AIDS treatment centers could be closed, individual employers and landlords could boot out 'abnormal' employees and tenants.

And that suits laid-off timberworker Bill Shockey just fine. 'We don't hate homosexuals', he tells me as he finds me a seat in the chapel and hands me a Dixie cup of juice and two iced oatmeal cookies. 'We just hate their behavior. Homosexual power is growing. And they are trying to get what we want to stop them from getting – protected status.' Faye Tunnel, the local OCA contact, a frail, sixtyish woman with a shock of white hair, clarifies what her neighbor has said. 'You know if you give them special status, then they get job quotas. My husband already has to face that on the job with minorities.'

These people are ripe pickings, ready to be exploited by anyone who promises to help them strike back at any enemy that can be conjured before them. Tonight the cynical magic is to be performed by John Leon, the burly, but soft-spoken full-time regional organizer of the OCA. He has set up a table of sample OCA newsletters, 'No Special Rights' bumperstickers and 'Sodomy Is Not A Special Right' buttons. His preamble is short. 'I want to show you a video. It's rather shocking. But it will teach you what happens when a city gives special rights to homosexuals. If you are offended by what you see, then just gently bow your heads. But I guarantee you this will be a life-changing evening.'

Talk about understatement. Of the fifteen or so meeting-goers I spoke to only one – a Baptist minister – said he had ever as much as met a single homosexual. But now before their eyes unfolds thirty minutes of the most raucous, raunchily edited-together excerpts from two years' worth of San Francisco Gay Pride Marches. Queer Jesuses. Bare-breasted dykes with facial war paint. 'Lesbian nuns' wiggling eighteen-inch dildos (the young woman next to me dutifully bows her head). Then a delegation of the National Bi-Sexual Network. The Bay Area S&M Community wearing black leather hoods. Guys in loincloths crawling on the ground, their 'masters' whipping them. Then the Bay Area Network of Gay and Lesbian Educators. At the chant of 'We are proud! We are gay! And we're in the PTA!' one horrified mother in our audience picks up her fixated ten-year-old and scurries to the back pews. Then the OCA's *piece de resistance*: extended footage of the North American Man/Boy Love Association. Close-up shots of little boys in the march draw audible gasps now from the Sweet Home viewers. All together a brilliant propaganda video. With practically no narration. As if any would be necessary. To the people of Sweet Home the carnival floats of the Gay Pride March might as well be SS-10 missiles rolling right out of Red Square and down past the scarlet Dairy Queen sign out on recession-ravaged Long Street.

Now comes the political hammering. 'Now you know more than 95 percent of America does about the real homosexual agenda', warns Leon. 'If sexual orientation is included in the civil rights laws that would mean special privileges and hiring quotas. Some timber workers in Corvallis said the other day, "Maybe it's good if Measure Nine loses. Then we can go over to the next town and say we are homos and they'll have to give us a job!"' An indignant rumble, more than laughter, erupts in the chapel.

'One of the main principles this country is founded on is equal rights, not special rights!', thunders Leon to the still video-shocked crowd. 'Our founding fathers would turn over in their graves to see our nation embroiled in a cultural war by people who demand special treatment because of what they do in the bedroom!'

That brings the first real applause of the evening. 'That's how simple this is', Leon continues as he goes on to praise Dan Quayle and the Republican platform and heaps scorn on Hollywood. 'Thank God for Liz Taylor', he says with a smirk. 'Saw her the other night on Whoopi Goldberg's show and she confessed what we already knew. That if it weren't for homosexuals, there would be no Hollywood!'

Now two empty and rinsed-out Kentucky Fried Chicken buckets are passed around for donations. Then membership cards are circulated, printed with a message that the OCA upholds: 'family values . . . parent's rights . . . free enterprise . . . private property . . . religious freedom . . . stiff penalties for criminals . . . less welfare spending and lower taxes . . . choice in education.'

'Now let us close our meeting with a prayer', Leon says as heads are obediently bowed. 'Father, we know we are in the situation we are in because we Christians have abdicated governmental responsibilities, of being involved in government. Oh Lord, we pray we *will* now be involved in phone trees. Father, we pray we *will* do leafleting. We *will* go door-to-door. Oh Lord, we pray we *will* support the Oregon Citizens Alliance in its battle to keep our Judeo-Christian way of life.'

Not that OCA is having any problem filling its volunteer quotas – even without the help of prayer. Some $600,000 in small donations has poured into the campaign. Some polls show the measure has the support of 40 percent or more – perhaps a majority. With the Cold War top soil of American politics blown away by the turbulent winds of the late eighties, and then followed by a veritable drought of fresh ideas on the part of the American political class, left exposed is a hardened bedrock of confused and angry populism. A growing number of Americans sense that they've been had for the last fifteen years, but don't know quite how or by whom. The end result is a politics tinged with paranoia, driven by self-interest, and fixated on a hunt for faceless and easy enemies. Five decades of conscious depoliticization, of dumbing down the American electorate, has begun to bear its deformed fruit. Why look for complicated remedies when all the answers can be found by tuning in for ten minutes to any of the 528 radio stations that carry Rush Limbaugh? And in any case, Rush's language, his invectives against 'feminazis' and 'animal terrorists' is a whole lot more forthright than, say, the 'yes, but' rhetoric of the Clinton/Gore campaign, which can't seem to find any identifiable culprits for our national decline.

Absent in this new populism is any notion of personal responsibility, any faith in collective solutions and patience for any rational analysis – at least so long as those 'rational' analyses keep sounding so fudged, oblique and remote. Consequently, even states like Oregon, and the Northwest as a region, which seem to be firmly in the Democratic column for the November election, are in no way repositories of either altruism, optimism or even tolerance. Long after the votes are counted on 3 November there's going to be a persistent, mean virus spreading through the body politic.

'Presidential politics are not majority politics', warns Jeff Malachowsky, executive director of the Portland-based Western States Center, a training and analysis center for progressive politics in eight western states. 'Whether or not we see Clinton elected, the right is growing and will continue to grow. Through the eighties, rightist strategists cleared the ways for little streams of lava. In this part of the country you had one stream of racial hatred, another of bigotry, of the family farm crisis, of white supremacy, of anti–abortion rights. Some of these hot streams burned out and turned to ash. But now in the rural west, absent a clear conservative focus, fueled by economic uncertainty, many of these little streams of them have coalesced into what is today a raging, fiery river.'

Also feeding the anger is that yawning gap between the American political system and its supposed constituents. The conscious narrowing of the electorate by *both* parties leaves more and more Americans abandoned and seething. In some places it leads to fanatical support for demagogues like Perot. Or David Duke. In Oregon, there are other forces ready to cash in. Indeed, as hateful as Measure 9 is – and it is unprecedented in its vicious intent – the people who came to the Sweet Home OCA meeting were mostly gentle, sweet and courteous. They didn't raise their voices. There is no sloganeering, no blood-cries or aggressive chanting. They applauded the presence of the *Village Voice* reporter in their midst. What they are is afraid. Terrified. 'An enormous number of people feel they have lost something, lost ground, lost jobs, community values', says Malachowsky, whose group is feverishly opposed to Measure 9. 'But that ballot initiative says, you'll lose no more. We'll stop someone, anyone from taking something. The OCA message of No Special Rights resonates with this frightened population.'

It resonates enough that a full third of the electorate in Sweet Home's Linn County signed the qualifying initiative for Measure 9. But it's not just the anti-gay message of OCA that is making headway among this embittered populace. A new national 'wise-use' movement has been recruiting rural communities to a conservative political message by blaming environmentalists for the crisis in America's extraction industries – mining and timber. Where the specter of chanting homosexual schoolteachers is used in one community to explain why Johnny doesn't listen to Mom any more, in a neighboring town timberworkers are told by the 'wise-users' they are losing their jobs because of 'pagan preservationists' who value owls over people, who worship trees and not the living Sky God. One more onslaught, they are told, of foreign values, streaming up the freeways from California, carried in the same Volvo station wagons undoubtedly driven by San Francisco faggots.

Measure 9's anti-gay campaign could win a majority in November. In 1988 the OCA led a similar campaign to overturn a gubernatorial decree protecting gay rights and though a pre-election day poll saw OCA losing 50–44, in the privacy of the voting booth, it won by a 53–47 ratio. And just last May, in the relatively liberal city of Springfield, the OCA emerged victorious when a municipal anti-gay measure won voter approval. The Springfield vote and other voter research warns the No On 9 campaign that a sizeable number of Oregonians who believe this is no time to be wasting energy on the Measure 9 debate and who are comfortable with gays – as long as they are in the closet – are inclined nevertheless to take advantage of the November balloting to make sure that gays and lesbians don't come out. They'll vote yes.

Even if Measure 9 loses, it will have struck damaging blows at its progressive opposition. 'The fact is that fighting against Measure Nine is a diversion from fighting around our own agenda for change', says liberal Democratic state legislator Tom Novick. 'All the money the gay community is pouring into this to defend itself against attack could have been much better spent on the pressing medical problems gays and lesbians face in the AIDS crisis', says one top adviser to the No On 9 Campaign,

The persistence of the Measure 9 campaign and its trial runs statewide in 1988 and in Springfield last May have also taken its toll on the Gay Rights movement itself. 'After so many attacks, the vision of what we want has imploded', says anti-9 organizer Scott Nakagawa. 'Our adversaries are forcing us to mirror what *they* say. That is, that we *do* want gay rights and not democratic civil rights. Among the younger people in our movement there's a generational amnesia about the way democracy functions. When gays and lesbians come together and we form something like a "nation", we forget what democracy is. When establishment gays are attacked by our own movement, for example, it means we feel we have so little left to fight for that we fight among ourselves. There's a notion of not trying to change the mainstream but rather just attack it as evil. I mean gays who attack people just because they wear suits! Such a narrow vision is terrifying. Twenty years of the rise of the right has helped divide us into fighting over shares, of being divided, competing communities. So when OCA attacks and says these people are out for themselves enough, we do become out for ourselves. So whether we win or lose in November, to this degree OCA has already won.'

Also fearful of OCA's unleashing of anti-gay populism is the cream of Oregon's Republican Party – a party that has two incumbent senators, Bob Packwood and Mark Hatfield, who are both social liberals. 'I've always said America could go right before left. Now I think it might go fascist', says none other than Craig Berkman, the very buttoned-down chair of the Oregon Republican Party, himself an evangelical Christian. Berkman is deeply and genuinely worried that if not the US, then at least his party could be overtaken by the radical right – as embodied locally by the OCA. Already, in 1987, pro-OCA forces won a working majority in the Oregon GOP and held it for two years. Now Berkman feels the hard right has been further encouraged by the extremist rhetoric of the Houston party convention. 'Some senior Republican officials seem to have forgotten that winning politics are always based on building pluralistic coalitions, not by encouraging theocracy, not by catering to Pat Robertson's agenda.' The reference to Robertson is pointed. While the OCA has a contentious five-year history in the state, it was only recently that it affiliated formerly with Robertson's Christian Coalition, which then reciprocated with a $20,000 contribution to the Oregon anti-gay campaign.

But Berkman's concerns go beyond the influence of Robertson. He sees a demographic trend in Oregon and the American northwest that while applauded by some Republicans sends, tingles of fear up his spine. 'There's a huge in-migration to Oregon. Thousands of new people coming in from out of state every month. And it produces what I call the politics of narcissism. These are people who have made it in America, who come here and overwhelmingly register Republican. But these are not Reagan Democrats, or even Reagan Republicans. These people don't want to share *anything* with *anybody*. They vote against their own grandkids and deny school funding. They've got theirs, figure they are going to die soon and just don't care. They may be Republicans. But on environmental issues, of course, they are no-growth. On social issues they vote with the OCA. And this goes way beyond November. And for years to come this will impact politics not only here, but in Washington, Idaho, Montana, the whole region. It scares me to death.'

From inside his offices in an industrial park just south of Portland, OCA leader Lon Mabon scoffs at Berkman. 'Sure he opposes Measure 9', Mabon says with a derisive laugh. 'I've always said guys like Berkman are more comfortable with country-club Republicans than with good-old, plain-folks Reagan Republicans.' As to the fight for the postelection Republican mantle, in Mabon's eyes, the battle is already joined. 'If Bush wins it will only slow down not stop the country's degradation', he tells me. 'The real fight's going to be in 1996. There is a vast number of people out there who want to actively take back lost ground.'

In this battle, Mabon, who looks like a shorter, younger clone of California Congressman Bob 'B-1' Dornan, fancies himself as the loyal follower of the National Republican Party, posited against the heretical 'liberal' Oregon GOP. 'I was so pleased with the GOP convention, it could have been scripted by the OCA. Both Bush and Quayle spoke to our Christian Coalition Road To Victory meeting last week. [HUD Secretary Jack] Kemp, [Senator Phil] Gramm, [Former Drug Czar Bill] Bennet, [Senator John] McCain, all these guys are speaking our language.' None of which has kept the entirety of the State GOP party from opposing Measure 9, with Chairman Berkman publicly branding the OCA as Nazis. But Mabon couldn't care less. His detailed office war maps show vast networks of genuine grassroots organization – a fact even his enemies acknowledge. By breaking the state down into ten-precinct quadrants and cultivating area and block captains, OCA now wields not only a formidable network, but also controls about half of the Republican Party's precinct committee positions.

To drive through Oregon's big city of Portland today, you'd think that Measure 9 is absolutely doomed. Seemingly every third car has a No On 9 bumpersticker. Pink-triangled No On 9 buttons are seen by the hundreds, even the thousands. Dozens of restaurants have signed up for a Dine Against Nine program, donating a percentage of their profits to oppose the measure. But the No On 9 campaign's top organizers are not so sanguine. Last week Billy Graham's Crusade came rolling into Portland and an awesome 300,000 people came to his five days of rallies. The state's leading daily, *The Oregonian,* shocked Portland liberals by publishing a Special Supplement promoting Graham – paid for not by Graham, but by display advertising. The local ABC affiliate's perky news anchor, Julie Emrey, was a featured speaker at the Crusade, a fact that didn't bar her from also 'reporting' on the event. All in all, a religious revival of the sort seen nowadays in Warsaw or Moscow. 'Not only does Oregon have a history of white supremacy, but there's nowhere where the national religious movement is growing faster. This state has the highest percentage of "unchurched". That's fertile territory for the OCA, a soft entry point for the right to recruit through Christianity. And OCA organizers are particularly good and committed, passionate and zealous', says No On 9's Scott Nakagawa.

What troubles the No On 9 forces is that even if OCA fails in November, it will have in any case galvanized under its radical right umbrella a third or more of the electorate – a sobering force to be contended with in the years to come. And if you factor in the weight of the anti-environmental 'wise-use' movement – only a partial overlap with OCA – it means there's going to be an ongoing conservative, populist pull on state and regional politics long past November. 'It means a paralysis, a fear of angering these new activist constituencies', says one Portland lawmaker.

'We are not dealing with rational states of consciousness', says No On 9 campaign director Peggy Norman. 'It's more like a feeling state. So many people out there are feeling pinched and want to blame it on someone. They don't want to say goddamn it, it was my vote for Reagan and then another one for Bush that helped get us into this mess. They'd rather blame it on someone else.'

Which means that the right's ability to exploit the bubbling populist anger in places like Oregon is due, in part, to abdication by more liberal forces. Whether it's well-meaning but out-of-touch environmentalists who lobby for changes that overturn the lives of people they never talk to, or Democratic Party candidates who pander to suburban 'Reagan Democrats', the end result is an increasingly alienated middle ground. No more striking example of how the populist vote is ceded to the right is Bill Clinton's campaign visit to Portland a week ago. 'It was truly fascinating to see the Clinton people at work here', says No On 9 director Norman. 'Here he was with the whole West Coast locked up in his favor, campaigning in what is probably politically the safest city in America for him. And he still wouldn't put on a No on 9 button when everybody else in Portland has got one.' Nor did Clinton publicly mention Measure 9, though it is the most hotly debated political issue in recent state history. 'I could only think, what a serious strategic mistake Clinton was making', says Norman. 'People want real leadership, especially from presidential candidates.'

Some disgruntled Democrats remember back to 1988 when Jesse Jackson campaigned for the presidency and won about 40 percent of Oregon's vote – much of it in rural areas, almost all of it white, much of it among the same people today who will vote Yes on 9. What they say is that Jackson's success proved the populist vote is up for grabs. That it *can* be taken by progressive Democrats – even black ones who had embraced Yasser Arafat, so long as the language of real people and their real pain is spoken.

White working-class people, rural white people, are feeling the squeeze. Certainly anyone with a progressive agenda who is still half sane cannot dream of building a political consensus in this country by writing off white people (or is it just heterosexual white males to be discarded?). Clinton has understood this, but he has preferred to shave off just enough of the white vote to get elected by pandering to their fears of welfare and crime, by promising boot camps and national police corps, at times sounding as stern a disciplinarian as John Leon of the OCA did in his Sweet Home meeting.

But progressives need a better politics. One that can discourse with the people of Sweet Home, with college professors and feminists and also laid-off timberworkers. But discourse with them not to mollify their biases, but rather to move them forward. If we don't want them blaming gays, lesbians and environmentalists for their woes, then we better give them some real enemies to go after. And not mince words about it in the yes, but fashion of the Clinton/Gore campaign. 'That's what worked when Jackson campaigned through here in 1988', says Jeff Malachowsky. 'But his populism was a progressive one. He also said there should be no more taking. No more *corporate* taking.'

In another church, this time in Portland's 'transitional' northeastern sector, another crowd has gathered around Measure 9. This time to oppose it. The featured speaker is Reverend Jesse Jackson. He's come to Portland again to do the dirty work that Clinton won't. More than a thousand people have overflowed the church, its balcony, its basement. The unseasonably warm Portland evening has brought hundreds of paper hand-fans into blossom. And it's more than this visual image that harks back to Martin Luther King's 'beloved community' that filled the churches of Montgomery almost forty years ago. For almost an hour and a half, Jesse Jackson, sweating and straining, sparing no effort, spins a highly emotional sermon about love and tolerance and pain.

The audience falls into an awe-struck hush as Jackson reads from scripture. And then saying that 'love casts out fear' Jackson goes on to speak of the 'tremendous pain' of 10 million unemployed, of one in ten Americans on food stamps, of 40 million without health insurance, of closing plants, of the poor who work at the Burger Kings, of those who change the bedpans in hospitals they cannot afford to use themselves, of schools that are forced to close, of 'hungry babies who cry not because they are white or brown but because they are in pain', of a society willing to 'pay $37,000 to keep a young man in jail when it only costs $18,000 to send him to Yale', of an administration more concerned with granting favors to corporate backers than to remedying the conditions that led to the immolation of more than a score of workers in a chicken processing plant. Truly an astounding oratory tour de force. But that's not all.

After the ovations end, and in spite of having just put in an eighteen-hour day in three different states, Jackson remains at the dais. Clearly exhausted, now almost hoarse, he spends another full half-hour meticulously but humorously squeezing out two dozen people from the audience that are yet unregistered to vote. Coaxing, exhorting, hounding and haranguing, he plucks them out of their shame and reticence – one by one – and brings them forward, as if in a Baptist revival, down the aisle and to the altar where they are matched to volunteer registrars. In an election year where even the Democrats seem to blithely write off whole strata of the electorate, to see a work-weary politician at this late hour of the night still take so much time and trouble to value the involvement of each individual potential voter is simply staggering.

The whole marvelous spectacle says a lot about Jesse Jackson. But even more about the American people. Because all Jackson has done is make it possible, against all odds, to see that Americans are still capable of compassion and love. Because here in that steamy church, 1,000 of them have been sitting or standing for more than two hours, almost all moved to tears, all believing in this message of anguished humanity, all convinced that their votes can and will make a difference, all impressed that 'we' too can have our populists, all singing 'We Shall Overcome' not for nostalgia's sake but because they believe in it. And all of us wondering, why isn't *this* man, or someone like him, running for president?

Village Voice
13 October 1992

NOTE: Though Measure 9 was defeated in the November 1992 election, it did gather nearly 45 percent of the Oregon vote. A similar anti-gay measure did pass in Colorado. The Oregon OCA is currently preparing a new version of Measure 9 for the November 1994 elections. The Oregon Republican Party is now under the control of the Christian right.

18

TUBIN' DAN QUAYLE

STUDIO CITY, CALIFORNIA: OCTOBER 1992. In a state where unemployment runs almost as high as Bill Clinton's double-digit lead, and where even Republican strategists concede their party may be cratering, it was no easy task to find venues secure enough to host Dan Quayle's eleventh-hour Golden State tour. After making the mistake of openly walking San Francisco's Chinatown – where Quayle was met with flipped fingers, chants of 'Bush and Quayle Belong in Jail!' and placards reading 'Go Back to Houston You Republican Scumbag!' – the Los Angeles portion of the veep's junket was conducted under more controlled circumstances: a photo-op at a suburban hospital, a speech before Northrop defense workers safely sated with a new F-18 contract, and a fundraiser breakfast with 700 Republican contributors.

Though this breakfast meeting was held in a San Fernando Valley neighborhood only a stone's throw from the sound stages of the feared *Murphy Brown*, the fact that it was held indoors and under a stifling security blanket kept several dozen protestors exiled to the parking lot, where they were left to jeer at the caravan of arriving BMWs. Inside the waspy Sportsman's Lodge, Quayle triumphantly took the stage flanked by a Perma-Tanned Pat Boone, County Sheriff Sherman Block and three clergymen who opened the proceedings with a triple-header invocation that was followed by a seven-minute version of *The Star-Spangled Banner*.

Though last April's rioting came within a few miles of the breakfast site, Quayle made no reference to urban policy in his fifteen-minute speech. California now spends 20 percent less than the national average on public school children and teachers have taken to wearing black armbands, but the vice-president had nothing to say on education, either. Instead, he sounded a 'wake-up call' warning of the 'scary thought' it is to imagine Bill Clinton in the White House:

'A tax-and-spend-liberal with a runaway Congress ... 21 percent interest rates ... 13 percent inflation ... a wasteland of unemployment because of defense cuts'. The audience was custom-made for this nightmare vision of America Held Hostage to Democrats. Here in the Empire Ballroom were the last tenacious defenders of Los Angeles as-it-used-to-be: not the creamy downtown elite, but the car dealers, insurance agents and real estate brokers of the sun-drenched suburbs, as horrified by the hordes of encroaching Latinos and welfare moms as any Afrikaaner was by Nelson Mandela's release from Robbins Island. No need here for any Republican pretense at inclusion or fairness. Quayle's message was simple: vote for us or else – or else the Democrats will increase your taxes to pay for the public schooling of illegal aliens.

Strikingly absent, then, from Quayle's oratory was any reference to 'family values' or any jibes at Hollywood's 'cultural elite'. But frankly, without Quayle aggressively bashing TV and film, his discourse is stiff, disjointed, boring. Without Hollywood to kick around you have to ask yourself, what's a Dan Quayle left to do?

Fortuitous it was that Quayle muted his attack on the popular culture. And not only as a sop to local sensibilities, given that Hollywood is about the only industry left standing in California after twelve years of Reagan/Bush/Quayle. But also because no better metaphor exists for the Republican failure to understand American society this election year than the party's earlier onslaught against the entertainment industry – America's only sacrosanct institution. In these final days of the campaign, Republican fire is concentrated on dismantling Bill Clinton. But, if trends hold, and when the autopsy of Campaign '92 is conducted, political pathologists are likely to ascribe as a contributing cause of the GOP's demise so many anti-Hollywood toxins still found in the congealed party bloodstream.

And who should have known better to take on television than Dan Quayle, the mention of whose very name evokes *no* association with previous thinkers, legislators or statesmen, but *only* with TV images: part Michael J. Fox, part Doogie Howser, a little Dobie Gillis and a whole lot of Gilligan. Dan Quayle was chosen vice-president precisely, almost exclusively, for his youth-alluring telegenic similarity to Robert Redford's 1972 John McKay – *The Candidate*.

More chilling to Republican chances than any voter preference poll was, on the eve of Quayle's Los Angeles appearance, the congressional override of President Bush's veto of the cable TV regulation bill. A veto on family leave? On more welfare benefits? On scaling back the Pentagon? Or on thirty-two other bills in the last four years – who cares? But let George Bush void a measure that would cap cable TV fees and even Republican senators are ready to switch channels.

IT'S NOT JFK

They had no doubt read the same poll figures in last week's *TV Guide* that found that The Tube, with or without Murphy Brown or Dan Rather, was infinitely more popular than George Bush, Dan Quayle, Bill Clinton or any combination thereof. Thirty-six percent of Americans said they leave the TV on as 'background noise' while conducting the rest of their lives, 29 percent fall asleep regularly with the tube, 46 percent said they wouldn't give up TV for less than $1 million and a full 25 percent wouldn't surrender the clicker even for that amount. And all demagogy about 'family values' aside, only 27 percent thought there was 'too much sex' on TV (ever mindful of their own 'family' readership, the editors of *TV Guide* didn't ask how many thought there wasn't *enough* sex on the tube).

Republicans know very well, or at least used to know, that the real message of TV, beyond any ideological gloss, is simply and only: Watch More TV! Indeed, the ethic of television culture is wholly supportive and conducive to Republican rule. Television as the command center of American Culture, as New York University's Neil Postman calls it, erases literacy, reduces the level of public discourse, atomizes all sense of a cohesive society responsible for its history or future, rewards emotion over thought, substitutes spectacle for analysis and symbols for ideas, celebrates the market as a proxy for democracy and ultimately and inexorably downgrades citizens into mere consumers. In short, TV Culture *is* the New World Order. Note that the *TV Guide* poll revealed that only 7 percent of Americans said there were 'too many commercials' on television. The repeated image of Spuds Mackenzie or Ronald McDonald becomes as reassuring and comforting in a turbulent world as does the video likeness of an avuncular president, first introduced to us as a B-Actor, and now soothing us with a voice as mellifluous as honey-laced Lipton Tea.

Certainly, Quayle's own current campaign is based wholly on entertainment values. His speeches are tightly scripted and no meatier than a sitcom sketch. Like all other candidates, his live crowds are nothing but props for network cameras as political 'constituencies' are replaced by 'target audiences'. At Quayle's fundraiser breakfast in Los Angeles, the emcee was 'Dallas' actress Susan Howard. The warm-up 'speech' was a stand-up monologue. Even Quayle's introduction wasn't performed by a human, but rather by a huge TV monitor screening the same golden-tones video version of Dan and Marilyn's own *Wonder Years* aired during the Republican convention. And why not? Quayle's audience is no different than that of any other American politician's. *All* audiences today, all campaigns, our entire political process, even our national ideology is directly informed by network television.

'For reasons that have partly to do with television's capacity to reach everyone, partly to do with the accessibility of its symbolic form, and partly to do with its commercial base', Postman wrote in his *Disappearance of Childhood*, 'Television promotes as desirable many of the attitudes that we associate with childishness – for example, an obsessive need for immediate gratification *[read: the Gulf War]*, a lack of concern for consequences *[read: deficit spending]*, an almost promiscuous preoccupation with consumption *[read: mushrooming personal debt]*.'

Quayle's campaign invectives against certain targeted shows and films fades to absurdity against this backdrop. (Though Quayle joins company with many liberals who also believe that the editorial content of television has any significant political relevance). This mythos of television applies equally to *Major Dad* and the *Rush Limbaugh Show* as it does to *Murphy Brown* and *The Simpsons*. Let it be noted that Diane English, the creator of *Murphy Brown*, who used the Emmy ceremonies to denounce Quayle and to encourage single-mothers 'not to give in', runs a production company that is non-union and offers no health care benefits to most of its employees (and herself has no children).

Our popular culture has demonstrated a phenomenal capacity to identify and then absorb the tensions and conflicts that cleave our society, and then repackage them and safely sell them back to us as sort of an ever-changing menu of personal and/or political identity. From Malcolm X the man, to T-shirts and caps with an X to a Spike Lee movie. Can a marketing tie-in with Burger King be far off? You don't like Dan Quayle? You demonstrate not by, say, demonstrating, but by sitting on a couch at a *Murphy Brown* party and cheering lustily and smugly for your favorite fictional character. Hollywood, as a community in itself, does speak out on political issues, either on-screen or off, but only when enough consensus has been reached to not ruffle the ratings.

Which sit-com of the eighties excoriated Reagan's dismantling of the safety net? Which weekly drama condemned the intervention in Central America? Which soap opera legitimized gay life-styles? 'The real litmus test was the Gulf War', one actor/activist says. 'We were talking deafening silence on that issue. And I mean off-screen. It was really an eye-opener for me. When people's lives were immediately on the line, Hollywood was running for cover as if it were under the bombs.'

Instead, celebrities have attached themselves to causes that, while at times controversial, also have much popular appeal. TV and film stars, swimming all day in rivers of sleaze, wish to show their 'commitment' by dabbling in politics. Likewise, politicians, scorned by the public, have learned that in this society, association with celebrity is ultimately more important than employing the right policy wonks. It's a lesson the Republicans and Dan Quayle in particular have tried to ignore. As the Reagan/Bush administrations polarized American society, and in the process solidified the Democratic grip on the entertainment industry, the least that GOP leaders should have done was to keep hands off – to not pick a fight with an industry whose popularity dwarfs all three branches of government.

For all his public hostility towards the 'cultural elite', Dan Quayle in his quiet moments must resent, must downright envy the hell out of a politician like California senatorial candidate Barbara Boxer who, by rooting her campaign in the fertile soil of the entertainment industry, has racked up a 20 percent lead over opponent Bruce Herschenson, himself a TV commentator. 'There's a great ripple effect in working with celebrities', Boxer gushes to me in an interview. 'Each one of these celebrities is identified in the public mind with certain issues that I also support. So when Jill Eikenberry says she's with me it's important because she's identified with work on breast cancer. Jerry Moss at A & M records works on dolphins. Joanne Woodward and Paul Newman on arms issues and drug-addicted babies. Katherine Hepburn on choice. If voters see Ted Danson they recognize him not only from *Cheers* but also know he's done more for the oceans than anybody. So, if they see him with me, that can only help me. That alone gets me into the news. And people see [the celebrities] and say "these are busy, private people" and if they are out donating time to me, it must mean that I too am to be taken seriously.'

Unless you count the first vice-president of the local Farm Bureau, there were no celebrities on the stage when Dan Quayle made his final appearance in California, addressing a campaign crowd in the city of Fresno, capital of the state's agriculturally rich Central Valley. There weren't many people in front of the stage either; though campaign organizers had cheerfully predicted a turn-out of 1,500 or more, barely 250 showed up. For nearly an hour before Quayle actually spoke, a string of farmers and ranchers harangued their neighbors that the *only* issue for them this year was water, water, water – cheap, heavily subsidized federal water, the supply of which is being threatened by several Democrat-sponsored reform bills.

When Quayle finally came to the mike to speak, his shirt-sleeves rolled up, his collar open, he looked immediately uncomfortable and awkward. There was no Teleprompter, no podium, no place to lean, to rest his hands on or to hold the notes that he nervously gripped and fumbled with. After the greeting of applause he tried to look down at his notes but that just wouldn't work.

The result was disastrous. As bad as any prime-time taping without rehearsal. He verbally grabbed at snatches of his stump speech, first repeating part of the previous day's scenario of America Under Clinton, then disjointedly segueing to a promise to lowering taxes and 'getting government off your backs' (presumably a different government than the one that pays their water bills), then jumping to a wisecrack about Clinton visiting Moscow, which somehow led to him saying he'd rather have Americans 'write the future of America' than have Hollywood do it and then back again to where he had started raising the specter of runaway inflation and taxes under a Clinton administration. Listening to Dan Quayle, deprived of script or notes, so bumpily and torturously come back full circle was uncannily like making the rounds of a TV tuner with a nervous kid in control of the zapper. Finally, it occurred to the vice-president that he should end his speech saying something about water policy. The closest he came was to deride Al Gore for his environmentalism and, convinced he had now found his applause line, jabbed his fist in the air and cautioned the farmers that if they voted Clinton/Gore it would mean 'Goodbye to water . . . to food . . . and good-bye to your job.'

The extremism of that remark left even his followers perplexed. They were able to muster only a polite ovation. Probably like that of a studio executive who has just viewed the last segment of his favorite prime-time series but knows in his heart that cancellation time has finally come.

As the small crowd readied to leave, the invited band – 'Next Exit' – struck up some travelling music. As the lead singer crooned, 'Oh you may think I'm foolish, with the foolish things I do.' Vice-President Quayle reached into a Santa-sized sack on stage and began tossing foam rubber California oranges and blue Bush/Quayle frizbees into and at the departing crowd.

Village Voice
20 October 1992

19

RACE TO OBLIVION

LOS ANGELES: MARCH 1993. If no one else was willing to rebuild Los Angeles a year after last Spring's disturbances, the good people at Universal Studios were. And with no federal funds or tax increases, either. The studio's parent company – MCA – sank $100 million – about five times the aid given L.A. by the Bush administration after the riots – into its new CityWalk venture. And when it opens in a few weeks, Los Angeles will be reborn. But this time around with no messy Mexican settlers poking around some God-forsaken Plaza like they did two hundred years ago. Oh no. This is the nineties – the 1990s. And this new, improved L.A. sits like a fortress on a Hollywood Hills summit, buffered on one side by Universal Studios Tours and on the other by Universal's gargantuan Cineplex, accessible to the rotting sprawl below only by a steep company-built roadway.

But once ascended, for four blocks, along some 200,000 commercial square feet, CityWalk will unfold before you as an idealized Los Angeles street, a living museum of everything the city used to be and everything it never quite became. Not a Chinatown, nor a Little Italy, nor a Little Tokyo. Not a Swiss Village. Not a harborside Ports o' Call. But rather a self-contained, albeit downsized, replica of Los Angeles itself. A 'people place', a collection of restaurants, stores, public spaces, entertainment venues, a 'real working business street', says PR guy Kim Reed, one built from scratch just like the 'real earthquake' ride next door on the Studio Tour. Like an assembly of ghosts, each building along the walk fronts its own unique L.A. architectural style – Spanish colonial, Art Deco, 'Fifties Googie', modern, futuristic – a reminder of the city's once-rich, eclectic heritage, now all but paved over by metastasizing galerias, strip malls and minimalls. For those who remember the pristine days of the city's fabled shorelines, now polluted and usually under police curfew, Gladstone's restaurant has installed an

artificial beach surrounded by palm trees specially selected for their bent pos-
ture, 'making it look like the wind is blowing', Mr Reed says. For CityWalk's
dining clientele, at least those who prefer 'beachside' tables, atmosphere will be
heightened by regularly staged volleyball games and wet T-shirt contests. At the
other end of the Walk, a wave machine in an imitation ocean will stir memories
of Annette and Frankie dancing to the rhythms of an endless summer. As icing
on the ersatz, the Museum of Neon Art is donating thirty-five vintage neon
streetsigns taken from the city's streets over the decades. For those who dreamed
of attending UCLA before its freshman class became majority minority, before
tuition spiked upward, before neighboring Westwood succumbed to gangbanging, the school will now maintain fourteen Extension classrooms on CityWalk,
all built above the Bruin Spirit store, which will sell only UCLA memorabilia.
For $100 or so, now you can get a class *and* a sweatshirt, and dinner and cap-
pucino without moving parking places.

But don't think this is just some whitebread paradise, there's plenty of mul-
ticulti correctness. A 'real working rain forest' inside the Nature Company store.
A Mexican 'cantina', a sop to whose land this is all built on. Even some real
lived-in-like inner-city grit. 'We're leaving some ugliness, like a real city', says
Reed, 'there'll be some pipes and drains visible, rough edges'. There are plans for
billboards too, maybe even some acceptable graffiti.

CityWalk, then, debuts as the highest expression of Los Angeles's most secret desire: urban life without the urbans. The perfect antidote to dystopic civilization. A city traditionally phobic about crowds comes up with the final
solution: a miniature city only for the upscale, and sans the homeless, the foreign-born, the panhandlers and the . . . the . . . um . . . you know who. For City-
Walk, I'm told, has no intention of skimming from the out-of-town, polyester
drag-ass crowds coming to Universal Studios, who are left penniless in any case
by the time the Tour is over. No. CityWalk fancies capturing a more sophisticated local trade. 'The surveys we've done with local homeowner groups', says
Reed, 'show they want a place for shopping and dining. L.A. is not a strolling
city where you can feel safe. But CityWalk is a pretty secure area – about as safe
as you can get.'

Indeed. Because unlike the real city, CityWalk will have real cops – L.A.
County sheriff's deputies – walking the beat. And while down below in the
smog layer, 911 response time can stretch to half an hour, up here on the hill
these four blocks will have their own exclusive, sheriff's substation, making City-
Walk about the best-policed neighborhood in a fifty-mile radius.

Yes, Reed says, security is a concern, a top concern, given that the Cineplex
next door attracts, in his words, a 'certain gang element'. But CityWalk is prepared. You bet it is. 'Just to get up here', my guide says, 'you have got to go

A YEAR AFTER THE RIOTS: THE LAPD STRUTS ITS
'UNUSUAL OCCURRENCE TRAINING' FOR THE WORLD PRESS

through a toll booth, you've got to have money in your pocket.' Regular parking will cost $5.50. 'And of course, valet parking will cost more for those who can afford it, like at any restaurant', Reed adds. 'CityWalk is open to the public, but we have the capacity to control access, we can sort of keep an eye on who wants to come in. I wouldn't say it will be sanitized – just controlled.'

If there was ever a moment when you could sell a 'controlled' version of Los Angeles back to its own people, this is it. If Los Angeles itself seemed beaten into confusion by the fifty-seven televised blows struck night after night against Rodney King, then a year after one of the greatest civil disturbances in modern American history, the city appears now as only blinded by the fires, permanently brain-damaged from excessive smoke inhalation. That the city has learned nothing from its recent travails is symbolized not so much by CityWalk itself – which has been on the boards for a decade – but by the revealing detail that of the 100 or so construction workers I saw on the site last week, not one was black.

Above the cacophony of police and fire sirens, of sniper and police gunfire that drenched the city last April, one slogan rose: 'No Justice! No Peace!' And in the eleven months since, there has been neither. But although the city faces its first truly competitive mayor's contest in twenty years, the competing campaigns – so detatched from the city's real needs – seems like nothing more than a race to oblivion.

The balance sheet a year after the riots:

Police Chief Daryl Gates, perhaps the man most responsible for leading the city into the abyss, finally resigned last year, only to be awarded first with a best-selling memoir and now with a 50,000-watt drivetime talk radio show.

The appointment of Willie Williams as new LAPD chief has, prematurely, stifled all public criticism of the force. Even though 1992 marked a ten-year high of LAPD-involved civilian shootings. For the fifth straight year, gang killings broke records, topping out at more than 800, part of nearly 1,100 total murders in the city. In the last few months, for the first time in history, a city school became the site of a gunshot killing. And then a few weeks later, again. Then the city was transfixed by the spectacle of a 'disgruntled patient' shooting down a couple of doctors inside the county hospital emergency room.

The triple whammy of the recession, defense cuts and the 1978 tax-cutting Proposition 13 coming home to roost have levelled the California economy, Los Angeles the epicenter of devastation with an 11.2 percent unemployment rate. The city faces today a 25 percent – $500 million – budget shortfall.

Hopes for local economic recovery in the short term are grim, contributing to the city's funeral atmosphere. Twenty-seven percent of all jobs lost nation-wide in the recession were lost in the Los Angeles area. Economists predict the disappearance of 50,000 more local aerospace jobs through 1994.

Can it be a surprise, then, that 43 percent of Angelenos say they are staying here only because they haven't the money to leave? Or that the L.A. Times recently profiled Salvadoran war refugees who say they are going back home because L.A. is too poor and too dangerous? Or when some city pols recently suggested we might try out a local version of an I Love New York campaign, only to be told by critics that a more realistic theme would be a sister city campaign with Sarajevo?

Against this apocalyptic backdrop, the pious promises made while the embers still glowed have been blown to the wind like so many heaps of ashes. 'The politics of riot control', says local social historian Mike Davis, 'have replaced the politics of reform.' Indeed. In these tense weeks leading up to the first anniversary of the 29 April riot, local television and newspapers have over-flowed with pictures and stories promising that this time around, if necessary, the forces of law and order will be ready. It's a rather bellicose laundry list:

County sheriff's deputies showing off new rubber bullets, the Simi Valley police introducing a new pepper gas, dozens of US marshals grunting and jabbing their nightsticks vowing to protect government buildings, National Guard troops rehearsing contingency plans to put 7,000 soldiers on the streets in 'Operation Angel Guard', and last but not least the 'new' LAPD treating whole divisions of image-hungry reporters to weekly 'unusual occurrence' training sessions in the stark and sterile parking lots of Dodger Stadium, screeching around in patrol cars, swarming out with gas masks fixed, viciously 'power-stroking' their aluminum batons, rehearsing their 'Crossbow, Pulsate and Bump' riot-control techniques. Every night's newscast, every morning's paper brings a new scoop on stepped-up preparedness inducing a collective psychosis, a siege mentality.

Over this past year Mayor Tom Bradley, who had often been seen as little more than a rumor, has as much as vanished from the public eye, not bothering to face a city he helped cede to disaster. His fabled multiracial citywide coalition has exploded, fragmenting like a cluster bomb, each divided neighborhood of the city hunkering down and bunkering in. Currently, the city has before it 147 separate neighborhood requests that their public streets be gated off or barricaded.

Bradley's political heirs have all gone their separate ways, like so many warlords, each competing to succeed him. Twenty-four mayoral candidates, ten in the top tier, taken together appear on the stage as a stumbling troupe of political and moral midgets. With the city facing potential self-immolation, the candidates have, in the best cases, armed themselves with programmatic squirt guns. In the worst cases, with gas cans and matches. The candidates chatter round the clock about Rebuilding Los Angeles, while the schools are systematically dismantled, the trauma care centers closed, the parks and libraries shut down, the promised jobs nonexistent. Here's one set of 'liberals', white liberals, feverishly promising to break up the school system and do away even with the myth of equal access to public institutions. There's another liberal, a former Jerry Brown cabinet official, a former deputy mayor to Bradley, embarked on a desperate nativist crusade calling for the summary deportation of illegal alien gang members. Over there is the African American city councilman, also a mayoral candidate, calling for immediate enforcement of the city's archaic curfew law permanently confining minors to their homes after 10 p.m.

Other candidates want to sell off different city airports to pay not teachers but, of course, police. Anything but raise property taxes. And all together, the pack of candidates, hands linked, eyes tightly shut against reality, as if transported in a bizarre ritual dance, pretending they can exorcise the demons that haunt our city, hearing only themselves, madly chanting a common mantra:

More Cops, Higher Walls – More Cops, Higher Walls. And yet, the city, disoriented and confused, perilously perched on the sort of suicidal, demented episode played out on the screen by Michael Douglas in *Falling Down,* pays little attention to the mayoral election. Los Angeles, for the most part, doesn't care who gets elected mayor because Los Angeles, as we have come to know it, Los Angeles, as a coherent city with its own identity, has ripped itself apart.

On a recent weekday night, a crowd of 250 adults overflows the seats of Dixie Canyon Elementary School auditorium. The three mayoral candidates most likely to produce the two winners of next month's primary – Mike Woo, Richard Katz and Richard Riordan – are on hand for a debate. But the crowd, called together by the Sherman Oaks Homeowners Association (SOHA) has more urgent things than the mayoral race on its mind. For more than an hour, the three candidates sit facing the virtually all-white, mostly middle-aged audience with frozen, nervous smiles, fidgeting with their fingers and their papers, as the Association's regular business meeting clanks on. Truth is, if necessary, the candidates would sit obediently for two more hours, stand on their heads even and maybe spit blue nickels too, because few gatherings in Los Angeles are so potentially politically rich as this one.

Situated in and along the rear side of the Hollywood Hills, Sherman Oaks is one of the wealthiest portions of the San Fernando Valley, the northwestern quadrant of greater L.A. Fixer-upper homes run $300,000 in these neighborhoods, populated by older professionals as well as scads of younger entertainment industry types. Some overachieving couples move to Sherman Oaks just to allow their kids to attend this one public elementary school, which has been 'adopted' by local parents, lavishing luxury on it that other public schools can't dream of. In a city where as few as 20 percent or less of the registered voters are likely to participate in a mayoral primary, where as little as 15 percent of *those* votes can boost you into the general election, then Sherman Oaks looms as a strategic prize.

Voter turnout in the Valley is disproportionately high, even higher in this educated, middle-class bastion, and downright astronomical among homeowner clubs like this, who are often the sole active constituencies of city politicians. Voter turnout in this district is, in absolute terms, six times greater than it is in the more populated, poorest district of Los Angeles. Latinos make up 40 percent, maybe more, of Los Angeles's population, but barely 10 percent of the actual voters. So a few hundred votes more or less in a neighborhood like this fifteen miles from downtown can easily determine who will rule a city of 3.5 million.

So the candidates wait patiently. And no doubt struggle to fully grasp the significance of the spectacle before them. As I do. Because it's hard to figure if, given the recent history of the city, I have just dropped down from Mars or has the Sherman Oaks Homeowners Association? The Association tonight is mighty worked up, but not over jobs, or police brutality, or this or that trial. Riot? Which riot? Rather, the Association is irked that a 'marginal and inappropriate' business, the chain-operated Jiffy Lube car service center, has been given permission to open on their hallowed Ventura Boulevard, alongside such more 'appropriate' enterprises as lingerie boutiques, Thai restaurants and McDonald's. 'We need a higher level of business for our community', says a riled Association official, already stressed out by falling real estate prices in what was once the country's most preposterously overheated housing market. SOHA has already brought pressure, so far unsuccessfully, to shut down another local business, the nonalcoholic, pseudo-boho Insomnia Cafe, which has outraged neighborhood sensibilities by keeping its doors open well past midnight. The thought of hordes of caffeine-crazed teenagers stumbling to their cars parked on the residential side streets has chilled the neighborhood.

Herein lies the key to understanding the emotional undergrid of L.A. politics. We have no Bensonhurts here, not at least in Sherman Oaks. These dapper couples in chinos and cords, Florsheims and Nikes are neither cracker racists nor trailer trash rednecks, nor are they buttoned-down Republicans or Country Club conservatives. These precincts went overwhelmingly for Clinton and for any other pro-choice candidate on the ballot as evidenced by the plethora of Volvos and Saabs that prowl nearby.

These folks don't believe that blacks are inferior or that Mexicans are lazy. What they do believe in is property values – and property values *über alles*. And in that sense they *hate* equally anyone and everyone who threatens devaluation – rioters, gangs, taggers, noisy teenagers, Jiffy Lubes and, tonight, even a group of senior citizens. For the second order of business tonight concerns a zoning variance, again for Ventura Boulevard, permitting the construction of a handful of housing units for 'low-income' elderly. 'On such an expensive piece of property', fumes one enraged SOHA member. Another homeowner rails that $7.5 million in *federal* funds, that is, *our* tax dollars, has been poured into such a pointless cause. Discussion of this project seems to elicit a general consensus among these petty gentry that they have, indeed, been 'forgotten' and betrayed by every level of government, from the zoning commission, to the city council, to the United States Congress.

Into this atmosphere steps the first of the candidates to speak, Hollywood-area City Councilman Mike Woo. With about a 20 percent plurality, Woo leads the current citywide polling. Sounding very much like Bill Clinton in his programmatic discourse, with the greatest name recognition of all the candidates, and with his Asian background appealing to a city that today is less than one-third Anglo, Woo has a virtual lock on one of the two ballot places in the June run-off election. He seems headed for victory in the city's nonwhite primary.

But tonight among the white folks he quickly becomes their fodder. Woo opposes breaking up the school system, whose current design allows South Central blacks to be bussed, albeit in small numbers, into Valley schools. But worse, Woo commits the tremendous faux pas of reminding these white homeowners that he alone on the City Council, on the heels of the Rodney King beating two years ago, called for Daryl Gates to resign. The auditorium bursts into jeers and boos. Doubtful that any of these people would have invited Gates over for dinner, but they sure did like the old chief's ass plunked down on the lid containing the rest of the town.

Rival Richard Katz moves in for the kill. Katz may be the state legislator most highly rated by the Sierra Club, his campaign's strategic advisor is none other than Bill Clinton's campaign general James Carville, but in this Los Angeles election Katz comes off a lot more like Hangin' Judge Roy Bean than he does like Maya Angelou. 'Let me tell you how I differ from this downtown crowd here', he says, pointing to Councilman Woo and avoiding the fact that as a State Assemblyman he's a card-carrying member of the even more-discredited Sacramento crowd. 'I'll tell you how, I'm for the death penalty! And what's Mike Woo's stand on that? It's time we got serious on crime.' A staccato eruption of applause shakes the auditorium, a due warning to those Jiffy Lube mechanics and low-income old farts that they'd damn well better toe the line. But Katz isn't finished. Now he attacks Woo for having suggested there be a one-seat quota on the city's Police Commission for, gasp! – a gay or lesbian representative. More ecstatic squeals from the crowd. As to Katz's plan for fixing L.A. – well, 'It's more police, stupid.' The assemblyman vows to sell off the city's Ontario Airport 'and with just the interest from the $350 million we'll get we can staff one-half million hours a year more of police service.' Talk all you want about more jobs, Katz argues, there won't be any until the city is made safe again. And as to the asphyxiated city schools? First priority: citywide metal detectors. And then, in what is no doubt his cheapest shot, Katz says that while he does not go along with the school district break-up per se, he does support 'giving the pink slip' to the entire district administration.

The third candidate, multimillionaire Richard Riordan, is the only credible Republican running in what is formally a nonpartisan race. A 62-year-old cross between Eddie Albert and Ted Knight, Riordan campaigns on the slogan, 'Tough Enough To Turn L.A. Around'. Posing as the local incarnation of Ross Perot, financing his run with $1 million withdrawals from his personal accounts and preaching law and order, free enterprise and deregulation, Riordan's got a good shot at scooping up the white vote and making it all the way to City Hall. He genuflects to issues raised by the riots, emphasizing educational funding and reform. But one can imagine the visions in his head of educating and taming all those black kids so they'll be fit to work happily in one of his factories for five bucks an hour. Riordan makes it clear that his well-known yen for philanthropy should not be confused for some soft-on-the-underclass compassion. 'The best way to deal with the homeless', thunders Riordan, 'is a major PR campaign to tell the people of Los Angeles to stop giving them handouts.'

At the end of the evening, a battered and wounded Mike Woo attempts some damage control, trying to win points for sincerity. Facing his audience, his voice trembling with anxiety and indignation he makes a final plea for support saying, 'I don't believe in pandering. I know you support the break-up of the schools and I can stand here and say I don't. And yes, I do oppose the death penalty. And in any case, the mayor of L.A. has nothing to do with the death penalty.'

In the vast room, one person applauds.

The L.A. uprising of 1992, some thought, might have been an effective, if necessarily rude, way for the black community to reassert itself in the political arena: the 'wake-up call' theory. In retrospect, the riots might now better be viewed as the community's political death rattle. 'The black middle class, the black political class, fights today mostly to protect what it had won in this city', says Joe Hicks, the combative executive director of Los Angeles's Southern Christian Leadership Conference. 'But all that has added up to is great access to the mayor. For twenty years you could pick up the phone and get Tom Bradley on the phone. But now this black elite feels threatened by Bradley going, by the explosion of Latino and Asian populations. And this black political class had hardly shown much political vision.'

Striking evidence of the political enfeeblement of L.A.'s black community is amply on display a week after the Sherman Oaks forum when a similar mayoral debate is held at South Central's most important church, the First A.M.E. A thousand people, only half of them black, the rest Latino and Asian, many of them elderly, neatly and quietly line up in front of the church annex to receive their monthly dole of two shopping bags worth of donated food staples. But these are not the same people inside the church at the mayoral forum. In fact, the A.M.E. leadership did virtually no publicizing of the forum, though the top ten candidates all promised to be present.

And once the candidates' debate begins at the A.M.E., it becomes clear that much of the middle-class black audience present is composed of small cheerleader groups of eight or a dozen people brought in by each competing candidate to create the illusion that he has significant support among African

Americans – a patent untruth across the board. Even real independents are effectively reduced to being black props for a candidates' pack that no longer feels it needs much African American support, because community's vote has shrunk down to 8 percent or less of the ballots to be cast.

Even more disheartening, after twenty straight years of rule by Tom Bradley, after blacks have finally won a respectable number of seats on the city council, Los Angeles's African American community has little to show for it. It has no unified political movement, not even one credible candidate for mayor, a rather astounding thought given that this campaign began just a handful of months after the eruption.

Tom Bradley was originally elected mayor by a coalition of inner-city blacks and white liberals. The whites have since deserted the coalition, forging new alliances with emerging Latinos. 'And our boys just fell asleep', says one black political aide. 'It's twenty years later and we awake to a nightmare. We have failed at every level, and I mean from way before the uprising. The African American leadership failed to take risks in identifying areas of collective and individual responsibility, including not incidentally Tom Bradley. I hold him personally responsible for much of what you see now. I mean we're talking about a five-time incumbent. Someone who possessed enormous political capital he chose not to expend on his own community. And no one said "boo".'

The decline of African American political fortunes in Los Angeles neatly parallels the ever-mounting isolation and impoverishment of the South-Central heart of the city. The result is an increasingly ugly, and sometimes violent, scramble between two minority communities for the meager resources left behind. And in Los Angeles, employer preference is unquestionably pro-Latino. Los Angeles, says James Johnson, head of UCLA's Center on Urban Poverty, 'is a labor surplus environment where employers can act on their prejudices. Blacks are caught between a rock and a hard place. Our political leaders have often failed to see the wedges planted among us by a white power structure who has not sat idly by passively watching huge demographic shifts. The wind is blowing in the wrong way for us, the numbers are not on our side. Blacks have to understand our only hope is to ally electorally with others. Latinos. Asians.'

But too many black activists are just too pessimistic. The SCLC's Joe Hicks cringes at the growing race-based politics sprouting in all of L.A.'s communities: the surfacing of a militant, anti-black group in the Chicano sphere, the drowning out of the progressive minority among Korean-Americans, the mean-spirited mood of the white suburbanites and the mushrooming afrocentrism in his own community, which he feels is fed by the traditional black leadership turning ever inward. 'There is a frightening dimension of growing nihilism out there, a glorification of the lumpen, of gang members.' And that symptom, says Hicks, is most visible in the political activity surrounding the so-called 'L.A. Four plus' – the seven young black men accused of beating white trucker Reginald Denny at the onset of last year's disturbances. 'Not a lot of courage in our community to stand up at a meeting and say, "L.A. Four Committee? That's bullshit!" It's not like defending Huey [Newton] or Angela [Davis]. It says something politically about our community being at a low point. No moral component to the struggle, nobody willing to speak out for everyone in this city.'

Hicks doesn't discount the egregious elements of injustice in the case, but says they are not the point. 'Hey, we know the D.A. is trying to fuck those guys', he says. 'We know all about the dual standard of American justice – yeah. But that's a different issue. The people defending the L.A. Four are saying something else. They want to cut those kids loose. And I admit there's a *lot* of sympathy for that position. Because there's no movement out there, no center of gravity that will take issue and say, "Look, forty people on that corner of Florence and Normandie were brutalized on the basis of their color alone. And that's not what Malcolm X was talking about." But no, people are saying they kicked that white boy's ass and good for them, because *we* get our ass kicked *all* the time.'

The central defining truth of Los Angeles resides in reading the pyramid of social hierarchy in the city: at the pinnacle an aging, Anglo *rentier* class that retains the levers of control, below it an Asian business and scientific strata, just below it a black professional elite hanging on to footholds in the city government and service bureaucracy and at the base of the pyramid, supporting the whole structure on its back, a mass of faceless Latino laborers.

The great under-reported fact of the L.A. disturbances was that most of the 12,000 people arrested were Latinos, not blacks – 45 percent as compared to 41 percent. Most of the city's poor are Latinos. And soon most of the city itself will be Latino: they already represent 73 percent of children in public kindergarten. Two-thirds of the births in the county hospital system are children of undocumented Latinos. For these new immigrant groups, upon whom *all* of the growth industries of Los Angeles increasingly depend for cheap, available and non-union labor, last year's riots were their own fiery Boston Tea Party. Blood, sweat and taxation without representation lead to violent confrontation.

During his twenty-year tenure, Mayor Bradley mesmerized the media and the commercial class, spinning out a glittering fantasy that had something to do with Los Angeles becoming a world-class jewel in the crown of something called the Pacific Rim. Well, he turned out to be half right. The Japanese did buy up most of the downtown skyscrapers. But the globalization of the local economy has much more to do with L.A. drifting south than merging with the East. With or without the North American Free Trade Agreement, Los Angeles is quickly being reclaimed by the Latinos driven out by Manifest Destiny. The process is accelerated by local businesses only more than happy to reduce working conditions and wages to those of southern Mexico.

Indeed, the signposts of L.A.'s global economy point toward a model not of Tokyo or even Hong Kong, but rather Mexico City or Rio de Janeiro. Any morning of the week, including Sundays, on literally scores, probably hundreds of street corners, from downtown to Woodland Hills thirty miles away, knots of ten and crowds of fifty Latino men, almost all in jeans and caps, stand and wait to be 'hired' – by construction foremen, contractors, painters, restaurant managers, by young couples with rent-a-trucks looking for 'movers', even by homeowners needing someone to lift some patio furniture for an hour or two. On the same street corners, these laborers' wives and sisters pile into busses and ride across town for as much as two hours serving in the city's brigade of nannies, babysitters and maids. Prevailing wage for any of the above: five dollars an hour. And no one even dreams of social security. And those who have steady jobs find little different, except maybe another dollar an hour. Though the city's Latino newspaper, La Opinion, runs classified ads daily, written in abominable Spanish by white families, offering live-in maids room, board and $50 a week – actually a little bit less than the Mexico City bourgeoisie is willing to pay. Ninety percent of L.A. restaurants are non-union, mostly Latino-staffed. A full 90 percent of the luxury hotels along the corridor coming out of L.A.'s international airport pay no health care benefits for their heavily Latino service staffs.

Overcrowded housing in Los Angeles, which afflicts primarily Latinos, has doubled just since 1980, now affecting almost a quarter of the city's population. In the Pico-Union district, which encompasses 'Little Central America', live an average of 147 people per acre, four times the density of New York City. More than 40 percent of renters in Los Angeles pay more than 35 percent of their income for housing alone.

On weekends, this army of Spanish-speaking workers and their families leaves their cramped quarters and fully occupies the streets of the historic downtown civic center where *all* business is now conducted in Spanish. Along the main thoroughfares branching west, Pico and Olympic Boulevards, the last year has seen the opening up of the same, out-of-code and therefore illegal informal street markets – called by their Aztec name of *tianguis* – that provide subsistence for the unemployed millions in Mexico City. Local gangs have moved in with their protection rackets, charging the near-indigent barterers $10 or $15 a day for the right to occupy a few feet of city sidewalk in relative peace.

'Nothing, nothing at all has been learned from the riots', says María Elena Durazo, leader of the mostly Latino Hotel and Restaurant Employees Local 11. 'It's not just that the promised jobs didn't materialize. It's that talking just about jobs in the first place is already a mistake. Our people *have* jobs. What Los Angeles needs are good-paying jobs. And even that doesn't mean creating a few hundred high-tech jobs. It means raising the wages of all jobs in this city, raising people's living standards, and nobody wants to hear about that.'

'When the business community says this is not a business-friendly city', Durazo continues, 'what it means is that they want to squeeze even more out of a vulnerable work force. Don't they see they are creating more of the very same conditions that led to the riots?'

Perhaps they do. Perhaps it doesn't matter. Maybe Los Angeles is just one more illusion America has to shed. Ten years ago, a white, middle-class engineer never dreamed that *after* his retirement, the corporation he worked twenty-five years for would betray its promise to continue health coverage – as is the case today for hundreds of thousands of Americans. So why assume any longer that L.A. has to get fixed, or else. Or else what? It's not going to disappear. It will just go on. Again, no need to look any farther than Mexico City to see that a world capital of 20 million people has learned to get along just fine with *no* functioning public school system, with a *totally* corrupt and aggressively abusive police force, with a city government *no one* takes seriously, with *millions* living in substandard housing, with *twice* the unemployment rate of Los Angeles, with razor wire and armed guards protecting the monied enclaves, and even with a level of street violence that, while not as intense as the L.A. riots, is certainly more sustained – a permanent 'quiet riot'.

But even as the Latino population swells there are harbingers of some very ugly nativist days to come, as a hobbled state and city finds no one left to blame its woes on other than 'illegals' – that is, Latinos. Governor Wilson has increasingly used the immigration card in calling for welfare cutbacks. And Los Angeles–area Congressman Tony Bielensen, a long-time liberal mainstay of the Southern California congressional delegation, is promoting legislation that would deny citizenship to the American-born children of illegal aliens.

Disturbing as these trends are, I believe it's doubtful they will mature into an organized anti-immigrant onslaught. The xenophobia campaign offers, for sure, an allure to the victims of the white-collar recession, to the poorly educated, to the besieged elderly survivors of increasingly violent neighborhoods.

But in the long run, ethnic purity collapsed even in South Africa, where the architects of Grand Apartheid drafted plans to physically banish all blacks to remote 'homelands'. The newer generation of industrialists, however, while no friends of civil rights, looked around and said, if you do that, well, who's gonna do the dishes and dig the gold mines? Likewise in Los Angeles. Most of those demanding summary deportation are retired blue-collar workers who have always seen darker-skinned people not as their servants, but as their rivals.

ROLL OVER, CHE GUEVARA

Not so in more upscale Sherman Oaks, to which I returned last Sunday
morning. At the local car wash – 'All Hand Wash – No Brushes' to protect the
clientele's custom paint jobs – there was no hint of a city in tension, no suggestion of past or future riots. Negotiated multiracial conviviality had been
achieved. Under a warm pre-spring sun, the Lexuses, the Jags, Cherokees and
Volvos lined up for service. On the other end of the wash tunnel, the easy-going
customers, laid-back as we say in Los Angeles, about a dozen at a time and
always white, sat in comfortable beach chairs under a sole palm tree, all facing a
huge concrete lot full of cars being dried off. Prototypical Southern Californians
in short pants, tank tops and sweats. Sunglasses covering their eyes, they sat
reptilian-like, not talking to each other, many fidgeting with the cellular antennas they removed before handing over their cars, a few reading, others gazing
into the Big Nowhere around them, but most of them staring at the fifteen or so
Mexicans and Salvadorans in blue aprons drying off the cars, polishing the rims,
shining up the mirrors. When a car was finished, the worker would honk its
horn and wave his rag and, opening the door for its owner, would be handed a
tip – usually a dollar. Five other Latinos, surplus workers, squatted behind a
shed on the lot, drinking Coke and playing cards. As customer volume built, but
only as it built, the white crew foreman would walk out to them and 'employ'
the next man: handing him an apron, two rags, and noting the startup time on
his clipboard. By 11 a.m. the fifth and last man was about to go on line, guaranteed maybe two hours of work before the afternoon drop-off. As the foreman
handed him over his towels he reminded his new employee, 'Remember, when
the customer comes, smile.' Seeing he had not been understood, the foreman
said, more forcefully, 'Smile! Smile!' And then taking his right thumb and fore-
finger he stretched the corners of his mouth open, baring his glinting teeth.

Village Voice,
23 March 1993

256

FEAR AND LAVA: BYE-BYE BUGSY

No, this is not a good town for psychedelic
drugs. Reality itself is too twisted.
Dr Hunter S. Thompson, in Fear and Loathing in Las Vegas, *1971*

LAS VEGAS: NOVEMBER 1993. Heeding the good Doctor Gonzo's advice, I did not repeat his mistake of twenty-two years ago by carting across the Clark County line two bags of grass, seventy-five pellets of mescaline, five sheets of blotter acid, a salt shaker of coke, or even a galaxy of uppers, downers, screamers and laughers. But just as Thompson had brought his Fat Samoan Attorney in tow to the Vegas strip, I thought it a prudent idea to invite along my corpulent Neapolitan literary agent, The Big Vig, for our follow-up visit. The Big Vig is along strictly for moral support. As a semi-compulsive gambler, who better to have sitting next to me at the twenty-one table, approving each more reckless maneuver with a knowing nod, than one more irretrievable card and dice junkie?

And so far my strategy is working. No sooner do we dump our bags in our Tropicana Hotel 'garden suites' (both with a commanding view of the neatly furrowed rows of cars in the hotel parking lot) than we sit down at the blackjack table and within no time at all are experiencing financial free-fall. 'Better double up or even triple your bets now if you wanna win back what you're down', The Big Vig wisely advises as he rummages in his Bugle Boys for yet one more crumpled C-note.

Not that we are at this table on a fully voluntary basis. Actually, we're more like indentured servants. Checking into the Tropicana nowadays, or into just about any other Strip hotel, is like signing up for a stint in debtors prison. The balding gnomes that run these outfits – infinitely more sinister than their mob predecessors – have come up with a fantastically evil device to keep you glued to your casino seats. No, not the fabled free drinks in the casino. Nor the blasts of arctic air and rushes of pure oxygen pumped through the gaming rooms in quantities sufficient to raise an army of Haitian zombies and burnish them with a baby-pink glow. Not the absence of clocks so you forget to check in with your babysitter, or the dearth of pay phones just in case you do remember.

No. Instead it is a devilishly simple ATM-like card, handed to us at check-in, already embossed in gold letters with our names, making us members of the Island Winners Club. And, we were told, our $85-a-night room charge would be waived – for two nights – if we simply played the quarter slots or $5 blackjack tables for only four hours over the next two days. Hey, just like the Big Rollers, we were going to get a 'comp'. You just hand the card over to the dealer when you sit down or stick it into the bar code reader now attached to every one-armed bandit. Computers will clock our gaming.

'How in the hell can fourteen minutes pass so slowly?' The Big Vig asks, a hint of alarm spreading over his broad visage, his Manhattan pallor turning a southwestern rust color under the effects of the casino air management system. He has just run his Winners Club card through one of the few – very few – electronic meters in the casino that read back your time logged at the tables. Here we are three hours and forty-six minutes of gambling away from free rooms, if not freedom itself, and so far we are down $300. At this rate, they'll have to give us the whole fucking Garden Wing and parking lot by the time we finish our four hours. Sitting back at the twenty-one table, and being dealt, during my fifteenth and sixteenth minute, a series of stiff hands – thirteens and fourteens – with the dealer showing jacks, queens and tens, it seems evermore that calling us members of the Island Winners Club is a little like dubbing the guys in Cell Block B participants in the Indoor Chess and Weight Lifting Society.

Things take a disorienting turn for the worse when the Ohio schoolteacher next to me splits a pair of tens against the dealer's seven and then *wins* both hands even though the dealer draws to nineteen. Her move makes about as much sense as people voting for Republicans because they want 'a change'. But she wins. I, playing by the book, lose, choking out with an eighteen. 'Harv, we better go now', the schoolteacher says to her husband, scooping up her green and orange chips, and checking her watch. 'The volcano goes off in eight minutes.'

In fact, the volcano in front of the Mirage Hotel just down Las Vegas Boulevard goes off every fifteen minutes until 11 p.m. and being that it is eight minutes to eleven its final belching session for the evening is a perfect excuse for The Big Vig and I to take a gaming hiatus. We zoom up the Strip, the oven-dry night lit with an atomic glow from the 100 megatons of neon around us, and soon find the Volcano. Difficult to miss. For crowding on the sidewalk in front of it, packed behind a protective railing, are hundreds, perhaps as many as 1,000 people, obediently waiting for the scheduled volcanic blow-out.

This is Ground Zero of the New Las Vegas. The traditional sleaze and cheeze that had always made this place a great weekend refuge from the monotony of an ordered and decorous life is being swept away by a lava flow of Respectability and Family Values. Anxiously gathered at the foot of the Mirage Volcano are these herds of beefy middle Americans, and regardless of the hour, almost all dressed in short pants, shirts and baseball caps, enough of them wearing those pastel-colored fanny packs around their waists so it looks like the city is immersed in a continuing convention of colostomy patients. If Bugsy Siegel were to walk by now, half of these lookie-loos would call the Feds. If so much as one old-time Vegas showgirl were to shimmy by in boas and pasties, this assembled Decency League would stone her to death.

Now as the Volcano begins to rumble – that is to say as the sound effects cassette begins to play through the weatherproof loudspeakers hidden among the faux rocks of the volcanic lagoon – the awe-struck crowd, heretofore to be known as the fanny-packers, first goes into a reverent hush, and then itself erupts in its own way as whole batteries of hand-held movie cams begin to whiz and clatter and whir.

Note that we know this structure in front of us is a volcano only because that's what management at the Mirage calls it. Otherwise it looks more like what it is: a rather squat, mostly symmetrical, triple-tiered, 54-foot-high concrete, pump-driven fountain cum waterfall that empties into an oversized pool with a lot of pumice stone Krazy-glued to its sides.

Its scheduled eruption consists of the aforementioned sound track, accompanied by dozens of red floodlights nestled under its cascades flashing on and off. As the drama builds, a piped vent just clearing the top surface of the volcano begins to blow out puffs of steam. Then a gas jet next to the steampipe ignites and a large flame politely reaches toward the sky, soon setting off five or six rows of similar gas burners running down the slope of the slab and into the pool making the whole thing look like a slightly damaged kitchen stove on steroids. The flames burn a gassy bluish-yellow for about a minute and then – suddenly – the show is over. But the onlookers all agree that this is cool, marvelous, worth the wait, worth seeing again, worth filling an 8-mm tape with, worth having lost title to their home and boat to have come to Vegas to witness.

And this is where, customarily in an article like this, The Writer is supposed to come up with some pithy, penetrating observation. Something like this scene in front of the phony Volcano reveals some new insight into the national zeitgeist, that it symbolizes something about a culture where people prefer simulation over the real thing, or that in a country where everything is screwed up and nothing works anymore (or as Vegas philosopher George Carlin has noted – 'where we can't even build a VCR worth a fuck'), Americans find their only solace in the worship of technology, even technology at this infantile level, solely because it *works*.

Or, perhaps, the Writer should be compelled to expound on how a TV-dominated culture has erased the line between adulthood and childhood, that kids and grown-ups spend all their time watching the same TV shows and therefore it should be no surprise that young and old both now eat food with their hands, that they all dress like Beavis and Butthead and that therefore this mechanical Volcano brings equal glee to the gathered ten-year-olds *and* their parents. Anything like that might be said here. But it is The Big Vig who, gazing out at the gas flames and burping steam puts it best. 'It makes me nostalgic for my childhood', he says, remembering lazy summers spent collecting industrial artifacts in the shadow of chemical refineries and cracking plants. 'It looks just like Elizabeth, New Jersey.'

Vegas may seem like old times to The Big Vig, but to the rest of America it has become the last chance at a future. It laughs at the thought of recession, this last boom town in America. Make that boom city. For Las Vegas is the fastest growing metropolitan area in America. As New Jersey, New Hampshire, Texas, California and about forty-five or so other states went down the toilet in the eighties, Las Vegas saw its population double from 465,000 in 1980 to 925,000 today.

Las Vegas is also quickly becoming America's favorite tourist stop – doing slightly better than, say, Mount Vernon, logging some 22 million person-visits per year, the city's casinos piling up about $3.5 billion in annual revenues, a chit less than the total US sales of movie tickets.

But there's a glitch in this rosy scenario. Las Vegas has never before had so much competition. As everyday economic life in America has become a breathtaking risk, when its an all-out crapshoot to know whether you'll still have a job next month, or an even bet if your insurance will really pay off your medical claims or as much as a roulette spin as to whether you can make the next mortgage payment, who needs to travel to Vegas for gambling thrills? The recession-ravaged infrastructure of America is being retooled nationwide for gambling. There's not only Atlantic City, but new riverboat gambling in the heartland and oceanfront betting in the south. Mining-town gambling in the Rockies. Cruise boat gambling in the Pacific and the Caribbean. Indian reservation gambling in the Southwest and, of course, multimillion dollar lottos and lower-stake lottery tickets in just about every supermarket and corner convenience store coast to coast.

Fifty percent of Americans have now been inside a casino, up a dramatic 4 percentage points just in 1991. But less than a third of that group has been to Las Vegas. Now Las Vegas wants to lure the 85 percent of Americans who have yet to set foot in this desert paradise. To do so a couple of Vegas casino kings are remaking the face of the city, pouring in $2 billion of capital.

But their story can wait till later. I couldn't care less about *their* capital. Now, after the volcanic parentheses and a midnight nosh, it's 1:40 a.m. and The Big Vig and I are trying to win back *our* capital, engaged in hand-to-hand combat on the slippery slopes of the so-called Island of Las Vegas – the Tropicana casino. Some fanny-packer moron next to me at the blackjack table insists on hitting thirteens and fourteens while yelling out 'Come on eight! . . Come on seven!' But the dealer keeps busting her out, wickedly snapping down one face-card after another. As my pile of chips atrophies I ask The Big Vig just how much he figures we can lose during the required four hours of gambling. But I've lost him. Down about $400, The Vig just stares at his cards, absolutely intent on climbing back out of the hole.

I do the math myself. Betting $5 or $10 a hand you can easily blow $100 in five minutes – maybe $500 an hour, $2,000 or more in the required four hours. I've got about an hour and a half logged on my debit card and I'm $375 in the hole.

But then the cards turn. Sarge, who's been dealing twenty-two years, starts busting. I win three hands in a row. Then I get a blackjack on a $20 bet. I let the $30 in winnings ride. I get two deuces, the dealer showing a six. I split the deuces into two separate hands, and now have $100 on the table on two $50 bets. My first card is a queen, so I stay on that hand, a limp twelve. My next draw is nine. I put down another $50 to double-down on one card. A red king! A perfect twenty-one. The dealer flips over his hole card. A nine, giving him fifteen and forcing an obligatory hit. Another nine and he's out. My $20 bet of two minutes ago had morphed into $300.

Some seesawing up and down but I'm on the upswing. The Vig is also win-ning now and tells me he's about even on the day. And suddenly I'm reborn. The lump is gone in my throat, the tightness in my chest has eased, time is passing much more quickly, I'm drinking Wild Turkey with a bit more abandon, and though I'm freely tipping Sarge, by about 2:30 a.m. I'm actually ahead $75. The Vig, who is up $100, packs off to bed and advises I do the same. I tell him I'll be up in five minutes. Which turn into ten, then fifteen and soon I'm losing again. Disgusted with myself, I take a bathroom break and pull $400 in cash out of my pocket and stuff it into my shoe, leaving me $300 or so to play with.

Resuming play, I might as well have stepped back into a draining whirlpool.

Now down within minutes to one ten-stack of $5 chips, I know sure as shit that I'm going to lose everything. Sarge bravely countenances my world-weary chatter, my increasingly feigned nonchalance and keenly eyes my evaporating stash, knowing full well that he's seen the last of his tips from me for the evening. And then, about 4:00 a.m., with the casino A/C still keeping us last survivors breathing, it is, nevertheless, all over. My last chip is lost and only my bone-deep fatigue keeps me from dipping into my shoe-covered reserve.

But there's a certain existential epiphany, a veritable frisson, that I always feel at these moments of the last, lost chip being swept away. All the previous hours of chit-chat, of know-it-all exchanges between the ice-cool dealer and the jaded writer from the big city, the kibitzing with the T-shirted rubes and the pony-tailed sharpies around me, the false promises of the casino, the little stories you tell yourself while you're sitting at the table – all of this comes to an abrupt, crashing halt because when you're last chip is gone, so are you. No seats for the onlookers. And the other players at the table, the dealer and the pit boss, who a moment before were your asshole buddies, could no longer give a fuck whether you live or die. And that's when I feel that perverse thrill. Because it's one of the only few fully honest interludes you have in modern America. All the pretense and sentimentality, all the euphemisms and fairy tales are out the window. You are out of money? OK – get lost.

I had, however, fulfilled my four-hour obligation. My $85 room would be free for two nights. And it had only cost me $310 in gambling.

Now about that $2 billion capital investment. Alan Feldman, the vice-president in charge of public relations for the Mirage Resorts and Casinos, looks at my business card from the *Village Voice* and then up at me across the desk from him and asks, 'Hey, you're not going to write one of those cynical stories about Vegas, are you?'

Cynical? I think, before answering. *Moi?* Cynical about a place that suckers you into its casinos with $4 prime rib dinners, $3 lunch buffets and 93¢ shrimp cocktails? Cynical about a town that puts slot machines in the 7-11's, the gas stations and gas station bathrooms? Cynical about this being the only place in the world where pawn shops are open twenty-four hours a day, including the Dantesque automobile pawn shops? Cynical about casinos that bus in old people from 300 miles away, give them a book full of two-for-one scrip, force them to amble from gambling hall to gambling hall for eight hours after a five-hour bus ride and then turn around and bus them back home through the middle of the desert night sans their Social Security checks?

'Cynical?' I answer. 'No way. I'm here to write about the New Las Vegas.'

Of course, what Feldman has in mind when he says cynical is something

very specific. His company is just about to open a place next door called Treasure Island, 'an adventure resort' that will feature not an erupting volcano, but a
once-an-hour, nine-minute battle royale between a ninety-foot pirate ship and a
full-scale British frigate, replete with cannon blasts, sword fights and three dozen
real, live actors. T.I., as this new $300 million property is called, is one of three
new-wave resort hotels opening this fall, the $2 billion investment I mentioned,
that is turning Las Vegas into one sprawling Disneyland.

Also just open for business is the $400 million Luxor, owned by the Circus
Circus company, and boasting a thirty-story, 2,500-room glass pyramid hotel, a
ten-story sphinx, a piercing mega laser lightbeam that can be seen by planes 250
miles away over Los Angeles, a winding Nile river, barges that float you to your
elevator, a seven-story movie screen that exhibits three virtual reality movies, an
18,000-square-foot video arcade, a replica of King Tut's tomb and a lobby atrium
that claims to be big enough to hold nine 747s stacked on top of each other
(perhaps all those unfortunate jetliners downed by the hotel's blinding laser
beam).

Across the street from the Luxor looms Kirk Kerkorian's new $1 billion
MGM Grand. A mammoth collection of aqua and black glass blocks, like a re-
pository of every leftover office building in Dallas, the Grand debuts as the 'biggest hotel in the world', with 5,005 rooms, thirty-three acres of adjoining theme
park, the 'biggest casino in the galaxy', measuring in at 171,000 square feet, an
88-foot-high MGM lion whose mouth you suggestively walk through to enter
the complex, and lobby and room decor based on MGM's *Wizard of Oz,* including emerald green carpets, a yellow brick road through the casino and into the
amusement park and paintings of Dorothy, Toto, the Tin Man, the Lion, the
Scarecrow and the Wicked Witch of the West on the walls of the guest suites,
thereby confirming to dazed but awakening gamblers that they are, indeed, no
longer in Kansas.

Taken together, these three hotels mark the conversion of Las Vegas into
what is now called a 'multidimensional resort destination where entertainment
resorts are the rule, rather than the exception', to quote the marketeers who
kicked off this new phase when they opened the Mirage in late 1989.

So when Feldman worries about me being 'cynical', he worries that with so
many Egyptian mummies, swash-buckling pirates and dancing munchkins now
taking up residence on the Vegas Strip I might get the same wrong impression
that other reporters have recently come away with, that this new adolescent-
minded Vegas is up to something *really* dirty like hooking a new generation of
gamblers by getting them into the hotels while still in diapers – you know, the
Joe Camel strategy.

'The fallacy about what's really going on here is the concept of the Family.

Family is the "F" word here. A casino is no place for kids', Feldman swears. 'Las Vegas is not going after kids. But we have to find a new public for Las Vegas, and the biggest untapped pool are those people who won't travel without their kids. So we're giving a little something for the kids to do too. What we are really after is what Disney said. He's not after the kids, but rather, the kids inside all of us. We are building adult theme parks.'

I tell Feldman not to lay it on too thick, because he had me convinced before I walked into his office. He needn't bother to explain how Vegas is simply catering to an increasingly adolescent national culture. Coming to Las Vegas as I have since toddler age in the mid fifties, I have seen the rapid transformation of the town from mobster and starlet hideaway, to haven of sin and vice, to low-roller heaven. The latter phase began in 1974 when Circus Circus opened featuring rooms for under $20, 24-hour circus acts and a mezzanine full of carnival games for the kiddies. The family revolution took a quantitative leap when the 3,000-room Mirage opened in 1989 as a full-service resort and quickly became the most successful hotel in Vegas history.

Mirage boss Steve Wynn, a kid who grew up in the gaming business as a slot and bingo manager, beat the odds by raking in the estimated $1 million a day the naysayers predicted he would need to amortize his $670 million investment. ('The volcano has been key to that success', notes Feldman. 'It brings by thousands of people every day.')

Today the 51-year-old Wynn, the highest paid executive in the nation ($34 million a year, says *Fortune* magazine) also stands as the most powerful force in the Vegas desert. It's his vision that drives the current ranking of the city, and now he's poised to enter state politics. He personally led a drive to register 97 percent of his employees and now boasts that his work force accounts for a crucial 10 percent of the people who vote in Clark County.

But most of all Wynn, more than any other corporate power in Las Vegas, has best understood the gestalt of entertainment and diversion in modern America. Give 'em spectacle, spectacle and then a little more spectacle. Age, class and educational differences wither under the wow'em neon and the knock-out theatrics. The ultimate populist, he seems to be able to geometrically reduce the lowest common denominator on a daily basis. His concept of Las Vegas is to Bugsy Siegel's what MTV is to *Playhouse 90*.

A concept that works to the nth degree. Sure, Vegas *is* trying to hook the kiddies. But, as Feldman argues, that's not the real point. Nor is the signal truth here that in American grown-ups have kids lurking inside them. Simply, it's just that America's adults have *become* kids. As I walk out of Feldman's office and drift through the Mirage, the actual number of children I see is minimal. But the public spaces of the hotel teem with adult street foot traffic, undoubtedly drawn by the volcano.

What a scene. Veritable mobs of fanny-packers pointing to, photographing and posing in front of the 20,000-gallon saltwater aquarium that takes up the whole wall behind Reception (God help the clerks when the next 7.8 shaker hits!). More fanny-packers flocked around the Mirage's ten-foot-long glass enclosed mock-up of Treasure Island, all jostling for room to take the best video shots. (Now there's a mind-bending study for the McCluanites: when these videos are played back the audiences will be watching the graphic representation of a scale model representation of a full-scale representation of a pirate lagoon that never existed.) Hundreds more fanny-packers ooing at a pair of exotic (and very real) royal white tigers forever imprisoned in what the Mirage calls 'spacious accommodations'. Nearby is the ecologically correct (at least in name) dolphin habitat, where more videocams record the captured bottleneck mammals on millions of feet of silver nitrate–covered film. (I can just hear George Raft or Meyer Lansky hacking to death while reading the Mirage propaganda that waxes on about how the dolphin tank offers a 'multisensory approach' to learning about 'marine mammal protection issues'. Well, why not? I suppose you can also learn about micro-economic budgeting principles at the crap tables.) Then toward the front exit is the ninety-foot-high atrium and tropical rainforest, which offers the passerby one more late-century aberration, this time the fanny-packers videocaming the plastic and rubber flowers for later family viewing in living rooms from Peoria to Podunk.

As I leave the air-conditioned paradise of the Mirage foyer and open the doors onto the parched concrete of Las Vegas Boulevard I think of Alan Feldman's parting line: 'What we do for entertainments tells us who we are.' Walking out toward the Strip I shut my eyes tight, not only as protection against the snickering sun, but also to blot out that gawdawful Volcano starting to vibrate again in front of me.

By the time I get back to the Garden Wing of the Tropicana, The Big Vig is fairly frustrated, reduced to watching Monster truck races on ESPN. Boris Yeltsin, he has heard, is doing something dramatic to save Russian democracy, like firing tank shells at his Congress, but The Vig could get no confirmation. Like most Vegas hotels, the Tropicana refuses to carry CNN, lest continuing coverage of some trivial event out in The World, like Hawaii sinking into the sea or the US Air Force punching holes into someone else's country, might distract you from your unfinished business downstairs in the casino.

The Big Vig, however, completed his four-hour sentence at the Trop, while I was plodding through the Mirage rainforest and, unlike me, has come out with his free rooms *and* $80. Which means . . we are free at last! Free from the Tropicana, white and over twenty-one, we can now choose among dozens of other round-the-clock casinos.

After a ceremonial burning of our Island Winners Club Cards, which create enough of a toxic cloud to set off the smoke alarm but, fortunately, not enough to trigger the in-room sprinklers, we debate where to best satisfy our swelling urge to play. Maybe the last outpost of elegance, the Desert Inn. Maybe the hangout of the open-shirted high-rollers, Ceasars Palace. How about the Stardust? The Hacienda? The Sands? Nah. We *know* where we are going. And if visiting any of those places is like searching for a date with Lady Luck, then what we are about to do is equivalent to a back alley encounter with anything but a lady. The decision is in. We are going as low as humanly possible, on a beeline up the Strip to Bob Stupak's Vegas World, which, unlike the Volcano, looks just like it sounds. Or at least almost. If not exactly Vegas World, then, with its NASA decor, perhaps Vegas on the Moon. Or more precisely, like an RV colony on the Moon. There's lots of black light, thousands of miles worth of strings of all-clear bulbed Xmas flashers, hundreds of tons of green jelly of indeterminate origin bubbling in giant floor lamps, a couple of life-size Apollo capsules suspended over performance stages and astro-mannequins hanging from the rafters. About the only touch missing here is Bill Murray singing 'Fly Me to the Moon' in the Space Lounge.

Vegas World is the creation of self-styled 'Polish Maverick' Bob Stupak, whose public rep in Vegas registers two ticks lower than Charles Keating's among Sun City pensioners. But Stupak could give a fuck what the locals think. For Vegas World is perhaps the world's only direct-mail casino. Every month, Stupak mails out tens of thousands of invitations to lunch pail Joes and makes them an offer that even Don Vito Corleone couldn't top: for only $400 a couple Stupak offers two nights' lodging, $200 back in cash and an armful of worthless freebies (mostly two-for-one gimmicks that require additional spending), which essentially means that any bozo who answers is forking out $100 bucks a night for a room that can be had anywhere else in the city for $24.95.

But then again, Stupak goes one step beyond the mechanical reproductions of the Mirage and T.I. He even beats the King Tut simulation at Luxor. Stupak actually takes celebrities who you swore were dead (or at least hoped were so) and brings them breathing, kicking and crooning on to stage. His brochure tantalizes: 'See stars like Allen & Rossi, Zsa Zsa Gabor, Frank Gorshin, Jerry Lee Lewis, Helen Reddy, Mickey Rooney and Donald O'Connor.'

And don't think Stupak isn't in step with Steve Wynn and the New Vegas. At the cost of $50 million, the Polish Maverick is going twenty feet higher than the Eiffel Tower and completing his 1,012 foot Stratosphere Tower . . . that's right, 'the tallest tower in America', which will feature $6 elevator rides and four revolving wedding chapels at its summit.

Stupak reels me and The Big Vig in with a different come-on: a blackjack variant called Double Exposure 21. Played just like normal twenty-one, with one twist: *both* of the dealer's cards are dealt face up. How's that for levelling the playing table? But old Bob had it all figured out. What he gives with one hand he takes away with another. In this case, the dealer hands me a Double Exposure rules card that is only a bit denser than the Government Printing Office's new two-volume set of NAFTA regulations. All I know is that somehow or other I am dealt three twenty-ones in a row and never win one chip. The Vig gets pissed off as well when the dealer keeps winning on ties (a no-no in pure twenty-one), wanders off and develops a passion for $1 video poker.

I stick it out at Double Exposure, striking up a table friendship with a palsy-ridden San Franciscan named Lennie who, on this final night of his two-night package deal, is about $750 and a quart of Jack Daniels into it. 'Hey, you take care of me, I take care of you', Lennie slurrs, nodding toward the dealer, pushing him a fiver chip. But down Lennie goes. Another hundred, then another. 'This is all I got left, man, not even anything for a taxi when I get home', he says, showing me six or seven $5 chips. 'What should I do?' Before I can shout, GETHEFUCKTOBEDLENNIE!, he goes on: 'My plane outta here isn't till noon tomorrow, man. I gotta play, but maybe I'll take a food break.' Lennie motions to the nearest pit boss, who even at Vegas World all look like Chazz Palmintieri's cousins. Dino or Vinny or whatever his name is keeps slowly chewing his gum as Lennie explains he has been playing fifteen hours straight, is a grand in the hole, has $30 left and wants the casino to 'comp' him a breakfast so he can recharge his batteries. Any other place in town that would be no problem. What's a a $3 meal against keeping this john playing for another six hours? But this is Bob Stupak's Vegas World, and Dino/Vinny hangs tough and shakes his head. 'If I comp you, big guy, gotta comp everyone else', Dino/Vinny manages to articulate. 'No can do.'

I think Lennie is going to pass out. But taking a deep breath, and quivering on the verge of tears, he puts his last $30 on the betting line and somehow gets a hand that the Double Exposure rules let him win. Now with a $60 stake, Lennie forgets about food, cuts his bet down to the $3 minimum and has enough capital for another half-hour or so. He tosses the dealer a silver dollar and, revived now, says: 'Take care of me, and I'll take care of you.'

That about takes care of it for me, however. I do some quick figuring in my head and estimate I am down $250 total since I hit town. The Vig is still ahead $100 and suggests we head downtown to the even lower-end casinos.

The Big Vig calls his Vegas cousin Bobby, who's been a cabbie here for fourteen years. After some bearhugs and how-are-yas, Bobby, who brings along his buddy (aptly named Slim Ken), offers to drive us to the infamous Chicken Ranch, one of Nevada's legal bordellos an hour up the road. 'Sorry it's so far away, guys', Bobby says. 'But ever since that bastard Steve Wynn took over with this family values crap they drove all the hookers off the Strip.'

We decline, explaining how we are getting all the screwing we can handle inside the casinos. 'Know what you mean', says Slim Ken, before he explodes into a lung-splitting Chesterfield cough. 'Ever since the hotel strike a few years ago, these bastards have got the slots and videos locked down tighter than a nun's snatch', says Ken, explaining the payoff frequency the casino managers can program into their gambling machines. And if anyone should know payoff frequencies it's Slim Ken. Along with his other retired buddies – Long Beach Bob, Big Dave, Trotsky Tom and Dice Larsen – Slim Ken usually loses the bulk of his Social Security check by the sixth or seventh day of each month and spends the next three weeks scrounging to survive playing 5¢ Video Poker, where a Royal Flush can get you a $40 payoff – enough to stake a few throws on the crap table.

And these guys would die before setting foot inside one of the glitz palaces on the Strip, choosing to play only Downtown, only at Binion's Horseshoe Casino, where there's still 25¢ craps and $1 blackjack. Downtown, separated by a three-mile stretch of motels that all seem inspired by the Jetsons, flanked by round-the-clock wedding chapels (ring, flowers, marriage video and motel room all included for one price, credit cards accepted), is Fremont Street, the original Glitter Gulch presided over by that beckoning neon cowboy, and, except for the one where Heidi Fleiss lives, the most photographed street in the world.

Bobby and Slim Ken disappear into Binion's, but The Big Vig is ecstatic. Catercorner from the Horseshoe and Steve Wynn's yuppified Golden Nugget is the real bottomfeeder of all Vegas casinos – Sassy Sally's. Where Vegas World is real sleaze, Sally's can be accused only of a totally innocent kitsch. The brocaded floor carpets are worn to the padding, held together by strips of gaffer's tape. There are no tables here, only slot machines; and they have been presided over by neon lamps shaped as prairie dogs, cacti and covered wagons since long before anyone heard of Ssouthwestern decor. On the rear wall is a huge digital clock counting down the minutes before 'Double Jackpot Time'. Every fifteen minutes a bell rings, and for the next sixty seconds any slot jackpot pays double, provided you've been playing the machine for at least four minutes, as operations manager J.J., a spitting image of Matt Dillon's friend Kitty, explains.

It's five minutes to the next double-up period and The Big Vig and I are ripping through two rolls of quarters. Then the bell rings, a siren wails, a red and blue bubble-gum lamp begins to twirl and a scratchy tape sounding eerily like The Chipmunks begins singing: 'Its dubba, dubba, dubba, dubba, dubba, dubba, Double Jackpot Time! . . . Dubba, dubba, dubba, dubba, dubba, dubba

Jackpot Time!' And The Vig and I are singing along at full volume, still pumping in the quarters.

We win *bubkas* of course. But it is the best minute so far in Vegas.

Walking outside for air, we run into Mister Ed. That's what he calls himself. And appropriately so, because Ed's job in the New World Order is to stand in front of Sally's from the early afternoon till midnight and pass out two-for-one scrip while wearing a three-foot-in-diameter, yellow, foam-rubber ten-gallon hat, and a matching apparatus around his waist that makes it look like he's a riding a yellow foam-rubber horse. 'Best goddamn town on earth!' Mister Ed assures us. And to break the monotony he tells us his life story: 'Came here a year and a half ago after a big bust up with the old lady. We were livin' in New Mexico and I owed the IRS, so I just sold my truck. A real beauty. A '57 Apache, 3100 Series with the big block. I got two grand for it and came out here and I love it. Love it. I work seven days a week and nine hours a day, but I got my apartment and my bills paid and who doesn't love this 24-hour-a-day lifestyle. It's a happening place, brother. No place like it in the world.'

'You can say that again', says The Big Vig

So Mister Ed says it again: 'No place like it in the world.'

Every month 2,300 more people become Las Vegas residents after landing, for the most part, jobs like Mister Ed's – which in our America of the nineties is not only more than what most people ask for, it's all they dream of. Unemployment in Las Vegas is at 6 percent – a figure that twenty years ago would have been considered catastrophic, but today sounds like full employment.

Consequently, 41 percent of all new Clark County drivers licenses this past year were transfers from recession-scorched California. Twenty-five percent of new homeowners are also from the Golden State. And with 18,000 new jobs coming with the opening of the Luxor, T.I. and the MGM Grand, you'd expect incoming traffic to backed up to the Santa Monica Freeway. Which it is. So far an estimated 100,000 people have applied for those jobs.

The Treasure Island Employment Center takes up three floors of office space, its eighty-seat application room almost always full. As a propaganda video on an endless loop insists on how 'fun' it is, how 'adventurous' you must be to work at T.I. ('Pirates Plunder! Cannons Thunder!'), the applicant must fill out a long form and indicate which jobs he or she prefers to be considered for.

Reading the list of 'employment positions' you see – by omission – all the things America no longer does. This must be what Dylan meant when he said 'twenty years of schoolin' and they put you on the day shift':

ARCADE ATTENDANTS
BUS RUNNERS
BUS PERSONS
COIN VAULT ATTENDANTS
FOOD SERVICES
COUTNER SERVERS
GUEST ROOM ATTENDANTS
HUMAN RESOURCE CLERKS
MIDWAY ATTENDANTS
RECORDS CLERKS
SATELLITE BANK CASHIERS
SOFT COUNT ATTENDANTS

Apparently the only creative job left in Vegas is the copywriter who thought up all the above euphemisms for gopher, waitress, maid, dishwasher and coin-counter. And how much do these jobs pay? Who knows? 'You don't find out what the salary is until the second or third interview', says one aspiring Guest Room Attendant from Arizona. And when you do find out, there's still the obligatory drug test to verify that you are moral enough to work in Las Vegas.

Las Vegas is, after all, a great place to live, even a better place to raise your children, according to the dozen or so recently arrived hotel and casino employees I speak with. That means two things: housing is still cheap. And that Las Vegas is still one of the most segregated cities in America. In this sense also Vegas is an appealing model for America's future: a whole desert full of low-paying service jobs for a displaced white working class. In return for their allegiance to the new, downsized order, these white workers are offered a city free from the ills of urban America. Taxes are kept low, schools are kept functional, and people with different skin colors are kept on the other side of the Maginot line – in this case, literally, on the other side of the railroad tracks that border the Vegas Strip.

Dear, departed Bugsy Siegel helped set the racial tone here back in 1948 when he hired Lena Horne to sing at the Flamingo but banned her from walking into the casino, and then ordered her room linen burned after she used it. The casinos were desegregated by a 1960 bench decree, but blacks still lag far behind in city employment. The current economic boom has leapfrogged right over the city's blighted Westside, where there isn't a single supermarket, fast-food outlet or even a casino.

When Los Angeles erupted during the April 1992 riots, Las Vegas had its own $6 million disturbance. In the aftermath, which took one life, and after

Mayor Jan Laverty Jones appealed to the casinos to dampen tensions, the city's major hotel and gambling concerns all agreed to hire a grand total three blacks each.

Taking a suggestion from Mister Ed, The Big Vig and I evacuate the Tropicana and move across the street and through time to the medieval-themed Excalibur – a whipped-cream white monstrosity topped by massive gingerbread towers. 'Best place in town', Mister Ed has assured us.

'All they need is straw on the floor to make this place a total barn', The Vig affectionately notes as we stand in line, just to check-in. Another line snakes behind the counter where the fanny-packers buy tickets to the 'twice Knightly' dinner-jousting show. Yet another triple file lugubriously filters into one of the eateries that offers Lance-A-Lotta Pizza. More lines in front of the casino cashier windows, purposely scarce to deter you from cashing in your chips. There is even a human traffic jam in front of the room elevators, because Hotel Security demands a valid room key before allowing passage. The Excalibur, it seems, is what Camelot would have been like if the East German Interior Ministry had seized it.

Comrade Walter Ulbricht's men have certainly designed the Excal's guest rooms, definitely Dungeon Lite. Dizzying brocades on the rugs and drapes, hot pink wallpaper imprinted to look like . . . well . . . the brick walls of a dungeon. Ceilings so low that at five-foot-three, I can actually spring up and touch them. And bellboys and maids in nauseating blue and purple and red and gold costumes, reminding you that humanity has indeed progressed – at least in wardrobe tastes – over these past 500 years.

'Let's get out of here, let's hit the casino', I say to The Vig as soon as we put our bags down.

But The Big Vig has gotten religion. The oversized oaf is up $160 since we arrived and is now so self-satisfied, so self-righteous, so goddamn cheap, that he is about to become a fanny-packer before my very eyes. 'You know', he says to me in a professorial tone, 'Las Vegas has other things to do beside gamble.'

A pregnant pause . . . as we *both* wonder what he'll say next.

'You know they have wonderful museums here', and he pulls me out the door.

Wonderful to The Big Vig means the triple-complex of museums cleverly hidden inside the same strip mall as the Fatburger. I have to say I am a lot less impressed than The Vig is by the combination Elvis/Antique Doll/and Boxing museum that Chicago George runs, paying only $21,000 a month in rent. ('I'm 100 feet from the MGM Grand', he explains). As french-fry fumes and the odor of charred beef float in from the burger joint next door, and as The Big Vig snaps up a Mike Tyson Is Innocent T-shirt and an Elvis clock whose legs tick as a pendulum, my thoughts begin to drift back to the twenty-one tables that are still holding $500 of mine. In fact, I can think of nothing else until Chicago George speaks up.

'When you boys are done here, go over and see my wife Bunny', he says. 'She works over at the Liberace Museum.'

Did he say Liberace *Museum*? Hell, blackjack can wait another hour or two. A ten-minute jaunt down Tropicana Road and the one-story Spanish colonial–style building, humanity's monument to a great pianist, holds down the corner of yet one more shopping mall, looking functional and glum like a Pierce Bros. Mortuary. But the Liberace Museum is the third Most Popular Tourist Attraction in Nevada (meaning there must be a BIG drop off after number two, but still pulling a respectable 150,000 visits per year). For just $6.50 you get to tour the three buildings of the museum, all oddly separated by other mall shops including a religious bookstore and an Armenian deli, and ponder the accumulated memorabilia of a Great Artistic Life as the maestro's recording of 'Bewitched, Bothered and Bewildered' tinkles demurely through the sound system. Far be it from me to rob the reader of the joy of discovering the contents of this temple on his or her own, but let me advise that when you make the pilgrimage, don't forget your sunglasses. The glare, even with indoor lighting, is vicious: here's the rhinestone-covered Baldwin grand piano, the coordinated rhinestone-covered Rolls Royce (if you have trouble finding it, just look for the Rolls painted like an American flag next to it), the rhinestone-covered Excalibur motorcar (no relation to the hotel), the rhinestone *and* coral-pink convertible VW with a Rolls grille, Liberace's collection of rhinestone-studded velvet capes, yet one more rhinestone-covered grand piano and the rhinestone frame around the picture of Liberace with Tony Orlando.

In the third and final room of the museum, just beyond the Liberace Library, which has no books but lots of Czech Mozer crystal, and right past the Liberace death chamber – the re-creation of his private bedroom complete with a chinchilla bedspread – that is to say, inside the Liberace Gift Shop (where we found the Liberace snowstorms to be the best buy), we finally find Chicago George's wife, Bunny, furiously puffing away on a brownish More while she gift wraps a piano-shaped ashtray.

'Say', The Big Vig asks her. 'I didn't see any explanation of how Liberace died. Do you know how?'

'He was old, he just died', Bunny says through a nicotine cloud.

'Oh', The Big Vig says. 'Funny, I thought, it was AIDS.'

'His heart went', Bunny says diplomatically. 'What killed him was the heart attack, honey.'

We would like to further discuss these necro-nuances with Bunny, but are pushed aside by streams of bubbly fanny-packers just arriving on two busses, part of an organized tour from Arkansas. Americans, even these elderly women with blue rinses and men whose paunches hang over the conch buckles of their wide leather belts, are quite forgiving to celebrity and wealth. Liberace is still an untarnished hero in many of those same parishes that today are embarked on campaigns to outlaw gay rights.

Soon we are back at the Mirage, where we have come to pick up a couple of comp tickets that Alan Feldman got us for the Siegfried and Roy show, the longest running spectacle in Vegas. After so much high culture this morning, I am ready to relax at the twenty-one table when I remember that The Vig has gone cold turkey.

'Can you hang on just ten minutes?' I ask him, as I sit down at the third base seat at a $10 table. Before he can answer, The Vig takes up his position at first and announces to me in a voice so dispassionate that it chills my soul: 'I'm going to play, too.' I don't know what has come over him, what has suddenly led him astray from his new found path of thrifty rectitude, but whatever it is, he soon regrets it. As I do.

Never have I seen such a stretch of pure, rotten, stinking bad luck. With every hand we play things get worse. Double down on eleven and I draw an ace. Split aces and I draw two sixes. Stand on twenty and watch the dealer take a stiff fourteen, draw a deuce, then a five. Worse, The Vig and I are mesmerized. Our table is one of the select few equipped with Steve Wynn's patented $6,500, continuous action, automatic eight-deck shuffling machines, which means that the game progresses like a brush fire through Malibu. And the deeper in we get, the harder it becomes to stand up and leave. Too much is invested. Somewhere, midway through the massacre, I have to go to the bank of ATM machines in the casino corner and pull cash for the both of us from my bank account *and* American Express. When that wad is shot, we have no choice but to retreat. Between the two of us we drop $1,100. In maybe forty-five minutes.

I stagger out the door and, sick to my stomach, I hand the car keys to The Vig. I get into the rented Mercury, put the seat back, and close my eyes. I have not really slept in three days, but now I do. I awake only when The Vig slams on the brakes and I see us face to face with a barbed wire, concrete anti-tank barrier.

'Just what the doctor ordered', The Big Vig says, regaining some of his composure.

Drawing on the experience of previous debacles in Vegas, The Vig has brought me to the most therapeutic place in town – the Survival Store. We aren't here to buy the Ross Perot newsletters displayed on the counter, nor the

Green Beret Survival Guide, nor the 'Fight Crime – Shoot Back' T-shirts nor the 'I Didn't Vote For Bill Clinton' bumper stickers, nor the boxed collection of 'Video Guides to Nevada Brothels'.

'We are here to rent some Uzis', The Big Vig proclaims to the guy behind the counter, who makes up for his nerdishness by wearing a .357 Magnum on his hip with two auxiliary fastloaders of ammo.

'Will that be semi-automatic or automatic, sir?' asks the nerd.

'Fully automatic, please', The Vig answers, knowing that Nevada is one of thirty-eight states where machine guns are legal. And for $25 (a mere forty seconds' worth of casino play) plus the cost of ammo, the Survival Store will rent you a fully automatic Uzi and let you shoot it off at their indoor firing range. I let The Vig take the one available Uzi, while I opt for the more politically correct .50 caliber semi-automatic Desert Eagle handgun, the ultimate gangsta piece, the same gun Sir Mix-A-Lot calls the 'Ferrari' of handguns, that is SO big it makes that puny .44 that Clint Eastwood was waving around in that movie a few years back look like a turtle weenie. 'Nevada's a great place', The Vig says as I heft the Eagle over the counter.

'A lot better than there', the Nerd says, motioning his head toward a hammer-and-sickle-emblazoned bumper sticker reading 'The People's Republic of California'. At that I decide to let The Vig put the charges against his New York ID instead of mine from the Sacramento DMV.

As we blast and fire away I look at the holes being ripped in the paper targets and try to imagine the heads of Steve Wynn, Bob Stupak and every bleached-blonde and Grecian-formulaed dealer I have sat against over the last three days superimposed over the target.

But when the smoke clears and we are turning the guns back in I tell The Vig that this really hasn't made me feel much better. Overhearing me, the Nerd has a brainstorm. 'If that didn't do it for you, sir, I've got a World War Two .50 cal machine gun off a B-17. Wanna try it?'

I tell him thanks. Not right now. I have a headache.

No more than five minutes into the Siegfried and Roy Show I could have used that machine gun. I am hoping for floods, earthquakes and firestorms. I am hoping those royal white tigers I saw penned up in the lobby and who are now on stage would shake off what appeared to be their PCP-induced stupor and put us all out of our misery by simply chowing down on the two Austrian Nazis at the center of this pageant. The Big Vig just sits next to me and moans.

This is a sound and light version of *Marat/Sade* meets *The Wizard of Oz* with a soundtrack by the jet motor engineers at Boeing. A butch S & M fantasy, repackaged and remarketed as a magic show for the Des Moines Rotary Club.

The first hour is about five minutes of mediocre magic and fifty-five minutes of explosions, dry-ice smoke, computerized dragons spitting out more gas fires, a cast of dozens strapped into brass suits and trundling off to a death march against thunderous timpani, Siegfried – or maybe it was Roy – flying out over the audience on a cable like Peter Pan, oodles of chains, bushels of whips, a few torture boxes and even a good old-fashioned rack. Come back, Liberace, all is forgiven. Come back Buddy Hackett, for that matter.

At half time, the gotterdammerung recedes as the two boys – both in shiny, knee-high black boots – come out in front of the curtain to chat with the adoring audience. Arte Johnson has nothing on their accents as Siggy waxes serious and says how much he and Roy, really how all of us, need to 'preserve nature in all its *vohn-der*'.

To thunderous applause, the room blacks out and a giant screen drops down over the stage. A pumped-up home video of Siegfried and Roy romping around their 'jungle palace in the desert' with a pack of domesticated white tiger cubs elicits gushes of squealing approval from this crowd, who probably just voted down the last school bond measure but somehow are not offended at the thought of just having plunked down $150 per couple to watch TV in a big room.

The video plays before us like bad pornography. I really am not having fun anymore, yet I have to keep watching to see what outrage will come next: Siggy rolling on the ground with a couple of creamy cubs. Roy, dressed only in a bikini bottom, riding on the back of a full-grown tiger across the mansion backyard. But when the film cuts to the 'natural wonder' of Siegfried and Roy frolicking in their frigging swimming pool with a pair of 600-pound tigers and when the audience around us begins to ahhh as if they are looking at one of those paintings of big-eyed waifs, The Big Vig and I head for the exit.

Now used to tallying multiple digits in our heads, we come up with these numbers: Siggy and Roy perform six nights a week, two shows a night, about 300 performances a year. Every show is a near sell-out, drawing an average of maybe 1,500 people. That's about 450,000 viewers per year, at $75 a pop, adding up to a gross of about $30 million a year. 'I must be a real *putz*', The Big Vig says, turning deadly serious, a sure tip-off of a profound existential crisis. 'Here I've been struggling eleven years as a literary agent, busting my ass so that a *good* book might bring in 50,000 readers and gross a million. Where did I go wrong?'

We have plenty of time to contemplate the answer to that one. In our Excalibur room, sleep is elusive. More than the stunning loss at the Mirage, more than the debasing spectacle of the tiger trainers plague us. For, the wholly malevolent designers of this hotel have placed piercing blue-wash lights at the bottom of the exterior walls and set them at such an angle as to guarantee that sleep-rattling light will pour in around the margins of the black-out window shades, driving the guests back into the casinos, if not into insanity itself.

Having fallen asleep at dawn, which was darker than the floodlight-illuminated night, I sleep till noon. The Big Vig has left me a note, saying that the tiger show left him suicidal and he thought it best that he take the 10 a.m. flight home. At least I think that's what the note says. My left eye is swollen almost shut and hurts like hell.

An ophthalmologist on Paradise Road who outfits me with a grotesque eye patch says I have probably broken a blood vessel out of stress or fatigue. Or both. Even in the doctor's office, the nurse sees me off not with a 'Good-bye' but with a 'Good luck!'

Is it that obvious? Even to strangers? That the only thing I have on my mind, even while the doctor was patching me, is to get back to the tables? True, I am in a panic. The traditional Last Day Panic. I fac the music and total it up. Eight-hundred fifty dollars is the damage so far. I have to be home tonight and that means only a handful of hours are available to win it all back. Like Truman beat Dewey, I'll pull it out at the last moment.

I choose Bugsy's old place, the Flamingo – now owned by Hilton – to make my last stand. But the Last Day Panic means you do everything wrong because you know you have so little time. You hit fifteens. You split nines. On the way from one twenty-one table to another you put $5 down on your wife's birthday on the roulette wheel. You lose, and then you try your birthday, your weight, your IQ (which is now down to double zero). You buy $10 worth of Keno cards every ten minutes and play your social security number, your address, your body measurements.

Or you take the big plunge and try a whole new game. I find Caribbean Stud Poker. An absolutely brilliant game – for the casino. This one is designed by computer. Every card game in the world punishes the player when the dealer has a good hand. As does this game. Fair enough. But Caribbean Stud Poker also punishes you when the dealer has a *bad* hand. That's to say your good hand doesn't really count if the dealer doesn't have a minimum or so-called 'qualifying hand'. Which means you lose on both ends of the spectrum. Truly fantastic.

So why do people, why do I, sit down to play it anyway? Because the game is nifty. It's played on a table that looks like twenty-one, but here there is no tension among the players because everyone plays only against the dealer. Unlike blackjack, you can't screw up someone else's hand by making a bad move. There's also a perfect balance of technology and humanity: an automatic shuffling machine and little slots that suck your ante down off the table and right into some casino accounting room.

The dealer has plenty of space to ham it up. My dealer, Kevin, is terrific. He didn't even make a joke about my eye patch (perhaps mistaking me for a pirate on leave from T.I.) Like a carnival barker he entertains us as he cleans us out. Showing a King? 'A cowboy!' says Kevin, 'You know those cowboys don't ride alone!' A trey? 'Treacherous threes!' warns Kevin. A queen becomes 'twin sisters', or 'little girls'. A jack, we are told, hints at a full-scale 'jack attack!' Not just plain sevens, but 'easy sevens'.

This game, I would say objectively, is impossible to win at. But it's addictive, the most fetching I've ever seen. It's genius is that it is s-l-o-w. You lose, all right, but it takes a long time. And that's what it cost me near a thousand dollars to learn. I could have read it for free in a study on gambling by Harrah's casino that I picked up after I left town. The study says the number one reason why Americans gamble, more important than a chance at winning, is the ability to 'socialize' – with both 'the dealers and the other patrons of the casino'.

I haven't yet read this report as I play Caribbean Stud, but I can see this truth right there at the table. Gambling, much more than the Volcano, or King Tut, or Buccaneer Bay, is the ultimate fantasy in America. Because in a society in which the only currency is currency, and where most of us are absolutely irrelevant and powerless economic entities who attain significant value only when we are bought and sold in massive numbers, to sit down at any Vegas table creates at least the illusion of empowerment. As long as our money holds out, we are real players – if not outside the casino doors, at least at this table, for this moment. And while there we can talk the talk and sit in close proximity to the only person *we* know whose blood pressure registers no variation as he handles hundreds of thousands of dollars each day: the dealer. And while there no one will ask how much money we really have or don't have, what we do for a living, what we feel or want or yearn for. While at the table, it's enough to know you are just one of those powerful enough to throw money down the sewer. In your heart you know you will lose. But, God, let it be slow. Let it be as long as possible before I'm returned to civilian status, to become one more sorry-assed fannypacker relegated to my sofa, watching Oprah and Ivana and Robin Leach flaunt it in front of me.

My last hundred lasts a magnificent three hours at Caribbean Stud. When I bust out I feel the same depraved tingle I had two nights before when I bombed at the Tropicana. Kevin, the dealer, asks me politely to buy more chips or get up as there is a line of people waiting for my place. I have no choice but to leave.

I start up the Mercury and head west toward L.A. on I-15. My head is light from no sleep, my one good eye is starting to cloud. I haven't showered or eaten a real meal in two days and a pit burns in my stomach. And not just from hunger. My newly purchased insight into why we gamble does little to salve either my pain or my guilt. But then I remember I am only forty miles away from Stateline, Nevada – home to two supercasinos joined by a monorail running over the highway, the final legal gambling oasis before re-entering California.

In this America, in this land of endless opportunity, I was being offered one last shot at redemption.

Village Voice
30 November 1993

POSTSCRIPT

WAR OF THE WORLDS

SAN CRISTOBAL DE LAS CASAS, CHIAPAS: JANUARY 1994. When some 800 mostly Mayan Tzetal soldiers of the Zapatista Army of National Liberation (EZLN) occupied the local city hall on 1 January 1994, declaring war against the Mexican government on behalf of the 'miserable and dispossessed', they scored a victory heretofore unattainable by any other hemispheric insurgent movement. They took over and held a First World city.

I say city because this is no banana backwater – almost 100,000 people live here (the Salvadoran guerrillas at their height never controlled a town of more than a few thousand). And I say First World because San Cristóbal's narrow streets are not only clogged with too many cars and belching busses, but also because they are lined with shops selling most – if not all – the imported paraphernalia of modernity: BMX bikes, Nintendo and Sega video games, dish antennas, Mont Blanc and Pelikan pens, cappucinos, organic and vegetarian lunches and even study seminars in Karma and Reincarnation hawked by some ex-pat gringos and aimed at those very First World, hairy-legged ecotourists who feel so much better about themselves for coming here to gawk at Indians instead of ogling the bikinis and buns in Acapulco.

Not that this place, 700 miles southeast of Mexico City, is a metropolis. Indeed, compared with any First World capital, this colonial outpost with its graceful porticos, balconies and shaded plazas, is no more than postcard quaint. But nevertheless, as waves of crass Yankee consumerism washed ever southward over the years, it seems that the global marketplace reached its highwater mark right here. Step out of town either to the east or south and you are unremittingly marooned in the Third World (in fact, so quickly does the consumerist tide end that just a few miles away in a place called San Juan Chamula, some entrepreneurs have figured out a way to make Pepsi so exotic that local Indians have been persuaded to purchase the soda for their daily religious rituals).

So when the 800 Zapatistas poured into the municipal offices here, opened the police and property archives and set them on fire, and when another 1,000 – maybe 2,000 – of their comrades simultaneously seized five other nearby towns, opening the food warehouses to the poor, chasing out and in some cases killing the local police, dismantling one town hall stone by stone with sledgehammers, and another with axes and saws, and then fought the Mexican army to a stand-still for more than a week, they were not acting out some pathetic revolutionary *retablo* left over from the Central American cataclysms of the eighties. No. Precisely because the EZLN chose San Cristóbal as its major theater of operations, because the timing of the uprising coincided with the implementation of NAFTA and certainly because of the complex nature of the EZLN and what it is fighting for, this Chiapas rebellion is much much more than an Indian Uprising, far more significant than a recycled Marxist guerrilla movement. The shots fired in Chiapas this past month – even though nudged from our front pages already by the L.A. Big One and the earthshaking news about Tonya Harding – signal the End of the End of History. Rather than the final rattle of the snake of revolution, Chiapas is the first armed battle *against* the Global Market and simultaneously – in a way Americans cannot grasp – *for* Democracy.

The twelve-year-old project of the current and previous Mexican administrations to bring this country into the First World – in the words of Carlos Fuentes – as instantly as brewing a cup of Nescafé has crashed on the hard beach of political reality. Hundreds of millions of foreign investment dollars, a red-hot stock market, the dismemberment of the social welfare state, the nurturing of a new class of Mexican yuppies – yuppies, hell: a new class of Mexican *billionaires* – and all crowned a few months ago by NAFTA as much as went up in smoke along with the San Cristóbal town records. 'Just when were telling the world and ourselves that we were looking like the US, we turn out to be Guatemala', says one Mexican friend, a writer.

Mexican President Carlos Salinas de Gortari, a Harvard-educated technocrat, attempted to modernize the country that his Institutional Revolutionary Party (PRI) has ruled in one-party fashion for more than six decades using the reverse formula employed by Gorbachev. 'It was the Chinese way', says long-time political activist Luis Hernandez. 'Economic modernization without real democracy. Perestroika without glasnost. Now that plan is in pieces. And without there ever being even any real perestroika.'

Now it seems that Salinas, whose term is up next year, might be joining Gorbachev for dinner in that great garbage dump of history. For NAFTA, which many Mexicans argue was mostly intended as a US-provided political prop for Salinas and the PRI, might now ironically turn out to be the detonator that

SUBCOMANDANTE MARCOS IN THE CENTRAL PLAZA
OF SAN CRISTOBAL DE LAS CASAS, NEW YEAR'S DAY, 1994

blows him and his party out of power. Just when it seemed that the PRI would easily ride the trade agreement to sure victory in presidential elections this August, the most unthinkable of all Mexican taboos, the unseating of PRI, is now on the lips and minds of millions of Mexicans – all thanks to the powerful political shockwaves unleashed by the Zapatistas in Chiapas.

To say that the timing of the EZLN attack was dazzling is an understatement. If the Zapatistas had struck before the signing of NAFTA, 'it would have made passage very problematic in Congress', as one US Embassy official said. But the way would have been clear for the Mexican state to retaliate massively, frying the EZLN and probably tens of thousands of civilians in a scorched-earth campaign. But by waiting until January and the kicking in of NAFTA to launch its offensive, the EZLN put the Mexican establishment in a political pickle. With Big Trading Brother's eyes cast southward, the Mexican army would have to restrain itself.

But more brilliant than the EZLN's timing is its political strategy. Mostly unreported in the American press is that the EZLN has nothing in common with the guerrilla vanguards of the last thirty years. The Zapatistas' mortal threat to Salinas, the PRI and NAFTA is that instead of proposing what they could never achieve and what would turn all of Mexico against them – seizure of power and the installation of a revolutionary dictatorship – the Zapatistas call for the two things most Mexicans support, which are, not coincidentally, the only two things the PRI is unwilling and unable to provide: truly free elections and the real democratization of Mexico.

Election fraud is a longtime PRI tradition in a country where no real opposition has been allowed to prosper. But when the PRI was faced for the first time with a viable opponent, Salinas won the presidential sash in 1988, awarding itself barely 50.7 percent of the vote. PRI officials vehemently claimed that any vote fixing was a thing of the past, that Salinas had won fair and square. But millions of Mexicans loudly protested that Salinas had stolen the election from center-left opposition leader Cuauhtémoc Cárdenas (who still refuses to accept Salinas as the 'duly-elected' president) and the country teetered in uncertainty for months.

Again in 1991, opposition partisans occupied dozens of rural city halls, and crisscrossed the nation with militant marches, once again claiming PRI fraud in state elections. In these last five years, almost 300 Cardenista supporters have been killed in political violence, and each national election seems prelude to full-scale confrontation. NAFTA, in many ways, was designed to provide the PRI with the cloak of legitimacy and stability necessary to deflate the opposition and its protests.

But now the eruption of the Zapatistas on to the political stage has turned Mexican politics upside down. Overnight the national political debate has shifted from a focus on markets and monetarism to one of aiding the poor and the indigenous, increased reform and more social spending. All in all, a golden opportunity for once-again opposition candidate Cuauhtémoc Cárdenas, whose very name and chiseled facial features invoke an image of indefatigable Indian resistance to conquest, and whose father, Lazaro, is remembered by the poor as the boldest of Mexican reformist presidents. In short, the PRI has less than 200 days to figure out a way not to lose the elections. Or it could try to jimmy them. But this time around, fraud, even the suggestion of fraud, could be suicidal. Mix in the resulting widespread protests with an already simmering Zapatista insurgency and you have the recipe for full-scale civil war and insurrection.

Certainly, the Mexican government's initial response to the uprising revealed anything but the sort of democratic vocation that George Bush and Bill Clinton swore to be the ethos of a new, reformed PRI. Foreigners and 'catechists' blamed as 'professional manipulators' of the poor were singled out as the cause of the tumult. Government spokespersons refused to let the words EZLN or Zapatista sully their discourses, referring to the rebels in an Orwellian way as only 'transgressors of the law'. During that first week, as bombs and rockets rained down on hillside villages, tanks rolled into town squares, Mexican army troops began door-to-door searches for subversives.

But as mounting reports of journalists being rocketed and cadavers showing up with their hands tied behind their backs brought in caravans of national and foreign human rights workers, as the world's newspapers dedicated whole pages to the 'forgotten' poor of Chiapas and the heartrending indigenous face of the 'other Mexico', as hundreds of public declarations from unions, universities and neighborhood groups across Mexico poured forth condemning the violent tactics of the EZLN but nevertheless endorsing the rebels' call for reform, a cold panic set in at President Salinas's official Los Pinos residence.

Mexican policy toward the outside world has always been a game of images, and the image now roaring out of Chiapas on the wings of Air Force bombers was the wrong one. With an opposition call for a truce and negotiations building like a political snowball, President Salinas moved to preempt and co-opt. For the first time in modern Mexican history a local political event – the Chiapas rebellion – had near immediate repercussions in the presidential cabinet. On the eleventh day of the conflict, Salinas fired a number of hard-line and key ministers and replaced them with a group of respected, and fairly independent, liberals.

The former mayor of Mexico City, and then Foreign Minister, Manuel Camacho Solís, a *Prista* with a rep for being open to talking to the opposition, was named as a special, non-governmental, non-salaried peace commissioner and was handed the mandate to hammer out an agreement with the EZLN. In rapid-fire succession, Camacho Solís as much as recognized the EZLN, asked a leading bishop – who only days before had been accused of leading the EZLN – to be his chief aide, called on the Zapatistas to begin a no conditions dialogue with him, and arranged for Salinas to institute a unilateral cease-fire with and general amnesty for the rebels.

'No less than a full 180 degree turnaround overnight', says Mexican novelist Paco Ignacio Taibo II. 'The Zapatistas had won more in eleven days than the Salvadoran guerrillas got in eleven years. No PRI government had ever been forced to make so many spectacular capitulations.' So dramatic had been Salinas's turnaround that some political commentators argued that, in effect, Salinas had met the EZLN demand for a 'transitional government' to take Mexico into the August elections.

I catch a full blast of the new national political line as I sit in a Chiapas hotel room and, along with a reporter from the *McNeil-Lehrer News Hour*, interview 'Peace Commissioner' Camacho's top adviser, Juan Enriquez. Like his boss Camacho, like the president, the 35-year-old fair-skinned Enriquez is a product of Harvard Business School, and even here on the outskirts of the southern Mexico jungle he wears his tasseled loafers, beige chinos and a Brooks Brothers chambray blue shirt under his navy lambswool pullover. But in truly flawless English, Enriquez tonight sounds more like an anthropology professor than an MBA. Faintly ridiculous, fairly unnerving of it is to watch this very model of Mexican elitism sit here and spin like a top about 'poverty', 'government mistakes', 'indigenous rights', 'solving the root causes of the conflict', and the 'need for more education, more health, more jobs, more balanced rural development.'

Just who other than his own party does he think's been running this country for the last sixty-five years? Wasn't it just three days ago that he was chief of staff to the Foreign Minister when Camacho held that post? 'We're now going to have to be a lot more careful in modernizing Mexico', Enriquez says, now that the *News Hour* cameras have been turned off. 'Until now there's been a lot of arrogance in that process. That will have to change.' And change very soon, he agrees. And then even he admits that Great Unthinkable Thought. 'The government has to be seen making real changes before the August elections', he says. 'Either that, or none of this thing is going to work.'

Two compelling sets of circumstances lead one to believe that 'this thing' – a negotiated return to Mexican business as usual – is, indeed, not going to work: the military strength and strategy of the Zapatistas, on the one hand; the lack of real political will for reform by the government, on the other.

The Mexican government may be in a hurry to settle this dispute, but not the Zapatistas. 'The Zapatistas operate on the time schedule of the Gods', says one organizer who knows them well. 'Their tactic now will be to flirt with Camacho and maybe even sit down at the table with him. But, in the end, they will stick to their demand for a transitional government and free elections. Either the government gives in to that, which is hard to imagine, or on the eve of the elections, the Zapatistas walk and then strike again if the PRI wins. Only this time God knows how many peasants from Michoacan and Oaxaca will join them.'

In the meantime, the EZLN conserves its military strength. In none of the six towns it held earlier this month was the rebel army dislodged, it simply withdrew. 'The army will never find them in their home bases', says one activist who spent years organizing peasant unions in Chiapas. 'The jungle is so thick the sun doesn't hit the ground. You can make sure that the Zapatistas didn't organize for ten years to fight for only ten days and then disappear.'

Ten years is actually an understatement. Though the Mexican government claims the EZLN presence as a surprise, its organizing roots go back at least to a celebrated Indian Congress in Chiapas in 1974. A plethora of radical and revolutionary organizing projects were spawned and dozens of peasant and Indian unions mingled with veteran leftist activists of the generation of 1968.

'The presence of radical groups in the jungle was something we and everyone else knew about for years', says the union activist. 'The state incubated them, the collusion between landlords and the police, fomenting conflicts between peasant groups. By whatever name, we knew of the Zapatistas as they worked for years in our area. First they were very discreet, working within already existing institutions, at least until two years ago. Then it became clear they had their own agenda and strategy, and I have to say they have grown very quickly.'

By May 1993 several Mexican press reports told of increasing guerrilla activity in the Chiapas region. Several sources confirm that this past September a number of Indian and rural communities voted to not plant the fields, thereby consciously deciding to go to war. That same month, say Mexican government sources, military intelligence had compiled detailed videos on the Zapatista presence. But, apparently, a political decision was made by the Mexican government to not imperil then-pending NAFTA approval by launching a noisy counterinsurgent campaign. The Zapatistas, it argued, could be contained with social welfare programs.

But that decision backfired, in part because of a gross underestimation of Zapatista strength. Mexican political scientist Jorge Castañeda, an expert on the Latin American left, says that unlike the Salvadoran or Guatemalan guerrillas who set themselves up as a vanguard in search of a social base, the Zapatistas carefully built up their mass support for years and only *then* drew an army from their ranks. 'This is a guerrilla movement destined only to grow as long as it doesn't commit mistakes – which till now it hasn't, as long as it has money and logistical networks – who knows but it seems probable, as long as it doesn't lose its ranks – and the number of casualties it suffered or the prisoners it gave up indicate the contrary, as long as it does not alienate its supporters – and the gains won so far constitute the best argument in many years in favor of armed struggle in all of Latin America. Under these circumstances, time works in favor of the Zapatistas. They certainly can't be in any hurry to negotiate in a serious way.'

Nor is it that clear there's much to negotiate. To travel from San Cristóbal into the highland heart of Chiapas is to marvel not only at the rocky pine forests and the bursts of banana trees, eucalyptus, and yellow-and-orchid-colored vines and wildflowers exploding alongside the rutted highway, but also to descend into a world of base-level poverty that seems to have hardly changed at all since the collapse of the Mayan empire a thousand years ago. Fractured into more than twenty language groups, and still wearing magenta, aquamarine, hot pink, orange and crimson costumes, still walking down jagged hills on bare feet in search of water, the Mayan Tzetales, Tzotziles, Choles, Tojolobals, Zoques and Mames make up about a third of Chiapas's 3 million inhabitants.

Three-fourths of the indigenous are illiterate. Twenty percent of Chiapan adults have no employment. Sixty percent who do make no more than the minimum wage of $4 a day. Fifty-five percent of the country's hydroelectric power is produced here, yet 30 percent of the homes have no electricity, twice as many have only dirt floors.

The most productive land is held by large *caciques* – all-powerful landowners with the police and private militias at their beck and call – turning Chiapas into one of the most consistent violators of human rights in all of Mexico. Reduced to scratching out subsistence crops of corn and beans from tiny and exhausted parcels of land, the average impoverished farmer fights a daily battle with hunger. Whatever product is left over he sells on the national market. At least until now. Under NAFTA there is legitimate fear that cheap food imports from the United States will wipe out whatever small margin currently exists for the small producers. Bad news for the 90 percent of Chiapas communities already classified as economically 'marginal'.

And yet, it is here in Chiapas where the Mexican government has spent much of its so-called Solidarity money, its social welfare program. Which underlines this central truth: the problem in Chiapas isn't economic. Rather, it's the archaic, mummified and authoritarian political structure, a *ménage à trois* of the

PRI, the landlords and the security forces that cements in place such brutal exploitation. And to ask the PRI to solve this problem, to negotiate it away, is to ask the PRI to sever its own decades-old political base. Hence, the simple brilliance of the Zapatistas demanding political reform, not revolution.

Pulling into the town of Ocosingo – 'gateway to the Lancondan jungle' – a two-hour ride east from San Cristóbal through a series of army checkpoints, the intact political monopoly of the PRI is immediately evident. The night before, in Juan Enriquez's hotel room, cultured talk of a new peace movement sounded soothing. Here in Ocosingo, one of the six towns the Zapatistas held for a few days, there is a more aggressive interpretation. Though the army has declared a truce, hundreds of its troops occupy the town. Townswomen navigate long lines in search of government food relief, only to find that at the last moment soldiers deny them food unless they can prove who and where their husbands are, lest they be Zapatistas. At last count, soldiers took away 139 locals accused of being subversives.

The PRI mayor in the meantime has lined up some 200 peasants in a 'peace' march and leads them on a parade around the town square, chanting for the army to please stay on. As the parade passes by the Catholic parish, the mayor's men shout insults at Padre Pablo, who they imply is a guerrilla supporter. Later on inside Pablo's courtyard, a number of demonstrators stand around taking shade and sipping water. They tell me they participated only because the mayor was keeping an eye on them. They laugh at the thought that Padre Pablo is a guerrilla. And even they admit to a certain sympathy for the Zapatistas. 'When they came into town one of them started talking to me', says a sixty-year-old subsistence farmer. 'They came from the jungle, he said. And then he said, "Why are some men rich when some are so poor? Why do we have to pay for water when God made the water for all of us? Why do some men have so much land and others don't when God made the earth for all of us? We are all Mexican *campesinos*", he said. "We both need to eat the same." I agreed with him.'

On the outskirts of town, at the local cemetery, a gravedigger shows me the mass grave the army asked him to make earlier in the month. Eleven people are buried in an unmarked plot, in a corner of the graveyard, next to a three-foot-square hole in the concrete wall facing the street. Eight of the bodies are supposedly Zapatistas killed in fighting. Three others, says the gravedigger, are civilians killed by soldiers for violating curfew. The bodies had been piled up outside the cemetery wall, twenty-five yards from the main gate. 'Instead of carrying the bodies through the gate', says the gravedigger, 'they opened up that hole in the wall, dragged the bodies a few feet into the cemetery and buried them right there. They didn't want to bother to bring them through the front gate.'

Halfway back to San Cristóbal sits the dusty village of Oxchuc, another

Zapatista target, one more town that would make even Sergio Leone squirm. If God ever made one little acre to encapsulate every ill that besets Mexico it is Oxchuc. It's market day and shoppers jostle to pick up the half-pound gutted rats for sale as stew stock – 75 cents each. Vendors warn me that the town is 'divided' and that I shouldn't ask too many questions.

Within a few minutes the political fault lines emerge. In the town square, the PRI mayor has gathered up his loyal men for another blood rally like the one in Ocosingo. But here there's no lip service to peace. The *Pristas* claim that a local opposition group, the 2,000-member Civic Association, is really the Zapatistas. 'When the subversives came to town, I saw the guys from the Civic Association join them and start tearing down all the municipal buildings', says one of the mayor's followers.

What no one can explain to me is how it is possible that if there are so many Zapatistas living in town, why did the PRI get not 90 percent, not 99 percent, but exactly 100 percent of the 11,300 votes cast here in the 1991 election? One possible answer emerges from searching through the rubble of the local PRI office trashed by the guerrillas. There, scattered over the floor, are boxes of official election ballots – from the 1985 vote – ballots that should be only in possession of election officials, not party workers. Oh well.

A half mile from the mayor's rally, the Three Knots Civic Association has called together an emergency meeting of its own. As 200 delegates stand in a school room for one hour to hear their leader's report, I can understand nothing. The meeting is in Tzetal and only a dozen or so words come out in Spanish: 'bombardment . . . arrests . . . human rights . . . individual rights . . . they told us to fuck off. . . .'

As the meeting broke up, organizer Francisco Gomez tells me in Spanish that his group is worried that today the mayor will have the homes of the leadership of the Civic Association bulldozed. In the past, six militants have met such a fate. Three others have been killed in political shootings. For the last five years, Gomez says, the mayor's office has refused the Association members birth records, draft certificates and other vital papers. 'They hate us, they hate what we stand for, but we are peaceful.'

What about the rumors that the Association is part of the EZLN, I ask.

'The Zapatistas did pass through here', Gomez answers. 'And some people went off with them. Some because they were forced to, and others because after five years of frustration they see no other way out. I find that what the Zapatistas ask for is just. We don't have land and there are people here who eat once every three days.'

Going back to the town square I conclude that as tense as things are nothing is going to give. But I'm wrong. The next day as many as 1,000 army troops arrive in two dozen trucks and armored personnel carriers, supported by combat aircraft. The mayor climbs into a jeep with two army officers and begins patrolling this fiefdom, pointing out alleged subversives. Within a few hours, at least sixteen people have been detained. The leadership of the Civic Association, with whom I spoke the day before, has gone underground. Things are back to normal in Oxchuc.

But perhaps only temporarily. For all of Mexico is in frenetic ferment. An atmosphere like that of the Prague Spring has prevailed since the first of the year. In Chiapas, 140 peasant and Indian organizations, after an unprecedented day-long unity meeting, have issued a call for total social and political reform. Similar rumblings are heard from the states of Tabasco, Hidalgo, Oaxaca and Guerrero.

In the capital of Mexico City some 80,000 police have heightened security in the wake of a half-dozen bombings. But even in the bourgeois capital there's much more a mood of giddy, upbeat expectancy of real change than there is of fear. By 10 a.m. every morning the opposition daily *La Jornada*, which has committed as much as twenty-five pages a day to the political crisis sparked by Chiapas, is sold out while stacks of progovernment papers linger into the evening.

The PRI's official presidential candidate – Luis Donaldo Colosio – has become the Invisible Man, overshadowed by Peace Commissioner Camacho. And in a land where PRI candidates expect and unfailingly, until now, receive about as much attention as, say, an Egyptian Pharaoh, this unprecedented fact alone brings glee to millions of Mexicans. The best measure of President Salinas and the PRI's predicament is to understand that Camacho is the arch-rival of Candidate Colosio. And Camacho was the odds-on favorite to be named as Salinas's successor until the president opted for the more loyal and docile Colosio.

When Salinas had to turn to Camacho as peace negotiator it was an astounding recognition of weakness. Camacho was, in effect, the last living, ranking *Prista* with enough public integrity to pull off his mission. And therein lies the government's conundrum. If Camacho fails to negotiate a lasting peace, the PRI goes into the election with a guerrilla war at its back. On the other hand, to the degree that Camacho is successful, the PRI candidate Colosio is diminished.

The precipitous fall in the PRI's fortunes after NAFTA can be compared only to George Bush's slide after scaling the popularity heights of the Gulf War. Facing the August elections, says Mexico's top political columnist Carlos Ramirez, the PRI may have run out of options. 'The EZLN can extend the armed conflict at low intensity until August and then sign a peace agreement if the elections are clean or launch a big offensive in different parts of the republic to protest fraud', says Ramirez. 'Perhaps [President] Salinas fears the defeat of

Colosio and wishes to repeat the electoral unpleasantness of 1988. In that case, the only real guarantor of the elections will be not the Federal Electoral Institute, but the Zapatista army.'

Whatever the outcome of the elections, many Mexicans are not waiting around for change. Two weeks ago, before Salinas declared a government cease-fire, opposition leader Cárdenas called for a massive nighttime Mexico City street demonstration calling for a truce. In classic PRI style, Salinas chose the morning of the planned march to announce his unilateral cease-fire. As I prepared to go to the march with a group of friends, many speculated it would be a small affair, rendered redundant by Salinas's maneuver.

But as we got to the downtown Monument to the Revolution at 5 p.m., a sea of humanity roiled before us. Contingents of university students, health workers, Indian groups, the homeless, smartly dressed bureaucrats and office employees, architects, writers and journalists, neighborhood organizers and professional political agitators converged in the most joyous, euphoric and infectiously optimistic march I can remember since the sixties. I joined the contingent led by the masked wrestler Superbarrio, who in his red and gold lamé outfit has become a folk hero and symbol of resistance to greedy landlords and repressive authorities.

As high as our spirits were, they soared further as we saw the crowds multiply exponentially as we thundered along the city's main boulevards toward the colonial-era National Palace, the Zocalo. Who could not be moved by the thousands of carefully hand-lettered cardboard signs that blossomed along the route expressing the thoughts of so many ordinary people who could still understand how their own personal destiny was linked to that of others. 'We want solutions for our brothers in Chiapas', read one sign. 'Enough hunger and misery. We want respect', read so many others.

Moving through the cement and glass gullies of the most populous city in the world, our ranks continuing to swell, vendors did brisk business with stenciled T-shirts proclaiming 'I am a Zapatista!' and 'All of Mexico is Chiapas!'

No one said it so bluntly, but what fueled our cheer was the knowledge that the hypnotic, one-way-only trance-mantra of the last fifteen years of Global This and Global That had been beautifully snapped. That the eerie light provided by the muzzle flashes of 2,000 Tzetal fighters had captured in a freeze frame – for the whole world to see and recognize – the total absurdity of opening Price Clubs and Domino's Pizzas and Taco Bells in Mexico and calling that progress, the imbecility of grown men with advanced degrees quoting the economic theories of an orange-haired and narcoleptic Ronald Reagan, the inanity of starting to believe that less really is more especially if it is for the more needy. With this notion in their hearts, 150,000, maybe 250,000, Mexicans – in any case more people than anyone can remember in any demonstration since 1968 – streamed for two and a half hours into the nation's town square, intent on stretching this into something lasting, committed to rolling back those who have rolled over them and thought they would continue doing so forever, and facing toward what I thought was the north, danced and laughed and shouted at the top of their lungs 'First World! Ha! Ha ! Ha!'

Village Voice
1 February 1994

NOTE: In March 1994, PRI presidential candidate Luis Donaldo Colosio was gunned down in Tijuana. In June the indigenous communites of Chiapas voted down the government's peace offer. Peace Commissioner Manuel Camacho Solís resigned his post and withdrew from political activity. As we go to press on the eve of presidential elections, Mexico faces its greatest moment of uncertainty in recent history.